"A FACT-PACED ACCOUNT OF THE LARGEST AND MOST INTERESTING ACQUISITION TRANSACTION OF ALL TIME. It is a business story that reads like a novel. Hope Lampert is one of our best business reporters and *True Greed* is her best."
—Martin Lipton, Senior Partner,
Wachtell, Lipton, Rosen & Katz

"Shows the biggest deal ever for what it was: a mad scramble to be king of the hill by men who had huge amounts of money to throw around and little apparent concern for the fundamentals of business."—*Los Angeles Times Book Review*

"WILL BE IN SOLID DEMAND . . . effective description of corporate greed that motivated key players in the takeover scenario . . . Lampert is concerned with the nuts-and-bolts financial events, as well as how the results will affect current monetary trends, practices, and expectations."—*Booklist*

"IT IS INDEED A GREAT STORY."—*St. Louis Post Dispatch*

HOPE LAMPERT is the author of *Till Death Do Us Part: Bendix vs. Martin Marietta* and *Behind Closed Doors: Wheeling and Dealing in the Banking World.* She has written numerous business articles in such magazines as *Newsweek, Manhattan, Inc., The New York Times Magazine,* and *Los Angeles Times Magazine.* Her reporting has won her both the Washington Dateline Award and the New York Deadline Club Award. Miss Lampert lives in New York City.

TRUE GREED

WHAT REALLY HAPPENED IN THE BATTLE FOR RJR NABISCO

HOPE LAMPERT

A PLUME BOOK

Published by the Penguin Group
Penguin Books USA Inc., 375 Hudson Street,
New York, New York 10014, U.S.A.
Penguin Books Ltd, 27 Wrights Lane,
London W8 5TZ, England
Penguin Books Australia Ltd, Ringwood,
Victoria, Australia
Penguin Books Canada Ltd, 2801 John Street,
Markham, Ontario, Canada L3R 1B4
Penguin Books (N.Z.) Ltd, 182–190 Wairau Road,
Auckland 10, New Zealand

Penguin Books Ltd, Registered Offices:
Harmondsworth, Middlesex, England

Published by Plume, an imprint of New American Library, a division of Penguin
Books USA Inc. This was previously published in an NAL Books edition published
by New American Library, a division of Penguin Books USA Inc.

First Plume Printing, December, 1990
10 9 8 7 6 5 4 3 2 1

 REGISTERED TRADEMARK—MARCA REGISTRADA

Library of Congress Cataloging-in-Publication Data
Lampert, Hope.
    True greed : what really happened in the battle for RJR Nabisco /
Hope Lampert.
      p.   cm.
    ISBN 0-452-26530-4
    1. RJR Nabisco (Firm)   2. Leveraged buyouts—United States—Case
studies.   3. Consolidation and merger of corporations—United
States—Case studies.   4. Conglomerate corporations—United States—
Case studies.   I. Title.
[HD2796.R57L36   1990b]   90-47702
338.8'3664'00973—dc20   CIP

Printed in the United States of America
Original hardcover design by Leonard Telesca

In memory of my grandfather

Henry Vining Seton Ogden
1905–1989

who always had so many ideas for what I could write.

Contents

Cast of Characters ix

PROLOGUE
A Champion Never Loses in a Draw 1

CHAPTER 1
The "Non-Company" Man 5

CHAPTER 2
A Modern "Medi-chichi" 23

CHAPTER 3
Oh, to Be a Merchant Banker 44

CHAPTER 4
It Happened So Quick 59

CHAPTER 5
Protecting the Franchise 74

CHAPTER 6
The Once and Future(?) King 87

CHAPTER 7
White Hat? 97

CHAPTER 8
Cigar Smoke, Jesse Helms, and Sideline Cheers 110

CHAPTER 9
Kangaroo Court 120

C H A P T E R 10
Mad Enough to Punch the Wall 125

C H A P T E R 11
Waiting for Shearson and Godot 139

C H A P T E R 12
High Stakes, High Fashion 148

C H A P T E R 13
Gone About As Far As We Can Go 158

C H A P T E R 14
Jumping Up and Down on a Stick 169

C H A P T E R 15
Refereeing from Moscow 186

C H A P T E R 16
The Chicago Missile 190

C H A P T E R 17
The Fix Was In? 208

C H A P T E R 18
Thanksgiving Maneuvers 218

C H A P T E R 19
Negotiating in the Middle of the Night 232

E P I L O G U E
Greed Really Turns Me Off 251

Cast of Characters

RJR Nabisco (management group)

F. Ross Johnson, chief executive officer
Edward A. Horrigan, vice-chairman and tobacco chief
James O. Welch, vice-chairman and Nabisco chief
Andrew G. C. Sage, director and former Lehman Brothers
  president
Frank A. Benevento II, investment banking consultant
Steven Goldstone, lawyer at Davis Polk & Wardwell
James D. Robinson III, American Express chairman and informal
  adviser
Linda Robinson, public relations consultant

RJR Nabisco (board of directors)

Charles Hugel, chairman of RJR Nabisco and the RJR special
  committee; chief executive of Combustion Engineering
Dolph von Arx, U.S. tobacco chief
John Greeniaus, president of Nabisco Brands
William Anderson, Special Committee member and former chair-
  man of NCR
Albert Butler, Special Committee member and chairman of
  Arvista
Martin Davis, Special Committee member and chairman of Gulf
  + Western

John Macomber, Special Committee member and former chairman of Celanese Corporation

John Clendenin, director, chairman of BellSouth Corp.

Ronald Grierson, director, vice-chairman of General Electric plc

Vernon Jordan, director, partner at Aiken, Gump, Strauss, Hauer & Feld

Juanita Kreps, director, former U.S. Secretary of Commerce

John Medlin, director, chairman of First Wachovia Corp.

Robert Schaeherle, director, former chairman of Nabisco Brands

Peter Atkins, lawyer from Skadden, Arps, Slate, Meagher & Flom

Felix Rohatyn, investment banker from Lazard Frères

J. Ira Harris, investment banker from Lazard Frères

Luis Rinaldini, investment banker from Lazard Frères

Franklin "Fritz" Hobbs, investment banker from Dillon, Read & Co.

John Mullin, investment banker from Dillon, Read & Co.

Shearson Lehman Hutton

Peter Cohen, chairman

Jeffrey Lane, president

George Scheinberg, vice-chairman

J. Tomilson Hill, M&A chief

James Stern, junk bond chief

Jack Nusbaum, lawyer at Willkie Farr & Gallagher

Salomon Brothers

John Gutfreund, chairman

Thomas W. Strauss, president

Jay Higgins, investment banking chief

Chas Phillips, junk bond expert

Michael Zimmerman, merchant banking chief

Peter Darrow, lawyer at Cleary, Gottlieb, Steen & Hamilton

Kohlberg Kravis Roberts & Co.

Henry Kravis, partner

George Roberts, partner

Ted Ammon, associate

Richard Beattie, lawyer from Simpson Thatcher & Bartlett
Casey Cogut, lawyer from Simpson Thatcher & Bartlett
Stephen Waters, investment banker from Morgan Stanley
Eric Gleacher, investment banker from Morgan Stanley
Jeffrey Beck, investment banker from Drexel Burnham Lambert
Peter Ackerman, investment banker from Drexel Burnham
    Lambert
Bruce Wasserstein, investment banker from Wasserstein, Perella
Paul Sticht, consultant and former RJR chairman

Forstmann Little & Co.

Theodore Forstmann, partner
Brian Little, partner
Nicholas Forstmann, partner
Steve Fraidin, lawyer from Fried, Frank, Harris, Shriver &
    Jacobson
Geoffrey Boisi, investment banker from Goldman, Sachs & Co.

First Boston Corp.

James Maher, investment banking co-head
Brian Finn, managing director
Jay Pritzker, Pritzker family head
Jerry Seslowe, partner at Resource Holdings
Melvyn Klein, partner at Klein, Gray & Associates
J. Tylee Wilson, consultant and former RJR chairman

Journalists

Bryan Burrough, *Wall Street Journal*
James Sterngold, *The New York Times*

P R O L O G U E

A Champion Never Loses in a Draw

October 19, 1988

If there was one thing that RJR Nabisco chief executive F. Ross Johnson had learned in his thirteen years at the top of corporate America, it was the importance of preparing your board. With the directors behind you anything was possible: from unseating your boss to closing the century-old headquarters to initiating a leveraged buyout. Johnson was a winner; he had no intention of plunging his company—and his career—into uncharted waters without first making sure that he had the support to succeed.

Which was what this evening, October 19, 1988, was all about. Johnson had made a habit of inviting the outside directors to dinner at the Waverly Hotel across the street from RJR's Atlanta headquarters the night before the monthly board meeting; now, after the meal, Johnson and a handful of senior RJR managers were sitting around the coffee table in tobacco chief Ed Horrigan's suite talking over what Johnson had said.

The dinner discussion had gone well. Johnson had explained how frustrated he was with RJR's persistently sagging stock price; he had reminded the directors that he had "done everything but walk on my hands" to get the price up, improving earnings, raising the dividend, cleaning up the balance sheet, buying back stock. Nothing had worked, and Johnson had finally concluded that it couldn't be done: The stigma of being a cigarette maker was too great. A leveraged buyout was the best, possibly the only, alternative.

The directors had seemed enthusiastic. Only Juanita Kreps, the former Commerce Secretary, had had doubts. "Isn't it a shame to break the company apart?" she had asked.

If the others agreed, they didn't say so. Vernon Jordan, the civil rights leader and Washington-based partner at Aiken, Gump, Strauss, Hauer & Feld, the politically connected law firm, had been more concerned about the possibility that Johnson would lose. "Won't that put the company in play?" he asked.

"That's the point," said Johnson.

"Do you have a proposal?" asked another director.

"No," said Johnson. "I wanted to talk to you first. If you want to go along with this, we will make a proposal quickly. If you don't, press the button and we'll look at something else."

Johnson and the other would-be members of the buyout group had left the dining room after that, and as they waited to be called back they talked about what a "yes" from the directors would mean. A buyout of RJR would be the largest transaction in corporate history; at $75 a share, the price Johnson had been using in his preliminary calculations, it would total $17 billion, dwarfing the largest previous takeover, Chevron's $13 billion acquisition of Gulf Oil in 1984, and three times as big as the then-record buyout, the $6 billion Beatrice deal. The buyout would touch every American; RJR's product line included such grocery mainstays as Oreo cookies, Ritz crackers, Blue Bonnet margarine, and A1 Steak Sauce, as well as Camel, Winston, and Salem cigarettes. The proposal was also unprecedented in that it flatly contradicted the traditional wisdom. Just two days earlier, on October 17, Philip Morris, the world's largest cigarette company—RJ Reynolds Tobacco unit was number two—had bid $11.5 billion for Kraft, the Chicago-based cheese and grocery products company, confirming that Philip Morris believed that the way around the tobacco stigma was diversification, not going private.

Johnson and the other managers in Horrigan's suite agreed that the RJR board would make no decisions that night, nor likely the next day. It seemed clear that before taking so momentous a step as endorsing a buyout, the board would want to consider alternatives for at least a month, giving Johnson ample time to personally discuss the matter with each of the twelve directors before they committed themselves.

Thus it was something of a surprise when, after only forty-five minutes, Charlie Hugel, RJR's chairman and the chairman and chief executive officer of Combustion Engineering, called Johnson back down to the dining room. Johnson and Hugel were long-time friends and Johnson expected that Hugel would support him on the buyout even if RJR's more traditional directors were less gung ho. "We need to be sure that the number you were thinking about is not frivolous," said Hugel.

"Define frivolous," said Johnson.

"Higher than the highest that the stock has ever traded," said Hugel.

That was $71 a share. "I can do that," said Johnson.

By now it was 11:40 P.M., but there was one more item: Hugel wanted to put out a press release first thing the next morning saying that Johnson planned to make a bid. Hugel's draft statement didn't include a blank space for the price, but his question about being frivolous had implied that he wanted one, so Johnson caucused with his investment banker, J. Tomilson Hill, the head of mergers and acquisitions at Shearson Lehman Hutton, who was standing by in a separate conference room.

"What's the best we can do?" asked Johnson.

"Seventy-two a share," said Hill, a dollar above Hugel's minimum.

"Can we finance $75?" Johnson asked. That would cost an extra $750 million given RJR's 228 million shares outstanding, but Johnson thought it would be worth it; bidding one dollar over Hugel's minimum looked cheap. Seventy-five dollars a share, however, seemed like a generous price. It was 40 percent higher than the $53.50 that RJR had paid in the stock buy-back in March that had been substantially oversubscribed.

Hill thought he could get the money.

Johnson penciled in the $75-a-share number and handed the release back to Hugel.

"Suppose it goes to $82 or $84?" asked Vernon Jordan.

"So be it," said Johnson, although it seemed inconceivable that anyone could raise the $19 billion that that implied. "It proves what I've been saying all along."

* * *

Johnson left the Waverly that night confident that his deal was all but done. Certainly he did not guess that the dinner marked the end of a brilliant career. Until he made his buyout proposal, Johnson had been considered one of the most talented executives in America, the very embodiment of the new non-company man who focused on the bottom line without a sentimental attachment to people, products, or places. Six weeks after the October 19th dinner, his marketing achievements had been forgotten. Johnson was pictured on the cover of *Time* magazine as the personification of True Greed, a man who, as *Time* put it, "initiated a raid on his own company" on terms that "would enrich him beyond the dream of Midas."

But although Johnson became a lightning rod for criticism, his greed paled beside that of the financiers who quickly muscled in: Peter Cohen, chairman of Shearson Lehman Hutton; Henry Kravis, founding partner of Kohlberg Kravis Roberts; John Gutfreund, chairman of Salomon Brothers. In their hands, cold-blooded economics gave way to paper money and passion. Jealousy, distrust, and towering egos turned what had started as a business-like auction into the most unseemly corporate brawl since Bendix had tried to buy Martin Marietta Corp. in August 1982.

When the bidding finally closed at the end of November, it was Kravis who had won, although his bid was "substantially equivalent" to Johnson's, according to Hugel's official statement. "There's a saying in boxing," said a long-time Johnson friend and Hugel's adviser. " 'A champion never loses in a draw.' "

Johnson, surely a champion, surely lost.

To this day he doesn't understand why.

CHAPTER 1

The "Non-Company" Man

To September 1987

Before he became infamous as a takeover artist, what Ross Johnson was known for was golf. An enthusiastic fan and fine player, Johnson, fifty-six, liked to bum around with the pros and he had even arranged for RJR Nabisco to sponsor several events on the Professional Tour. But although he loved to play, he didn't love country club society, so instead of making the rounds at ten in the morning as one of a stuffy foursome, Johnson slept in, showing up on the greens only late in the afternoon when he and his young, blonde, second wife Laurie could play their eighteen holes in two hours. While certainly a sensible way to golf, that did not always go down well with fellow clubbers. Miffed members of Morris County Golf Club, one of the dozens to which Johnson belonged, observed testily that sitting alone in a golf cart at twilight was a clear sign that Johnson had social problems. "No one had done that since Don Regan [then Ronald Reagan's chief of staff and formerly chairman of Merrill Lynch]," recalls one, "and it was regarded as odd then."

Johnson never did things simply because that was the way it was done, be it playing golf with country club members or running his company by the book. Although he was certainly not averse to chauffeured cars and fancy restaurants, he horrified some watchers by driving around Winston-Salem in a jeep and brown-

5

bagging a peanut butter and lettuce sandwich for lunch. Planning sessions, interoffice memos, video presentations, the typical stock-in-trade of managers, were anathema to Johnson. He ran his company by gut and wits, and he made sure that his subordinates did too. Convinced that executives work better when they aren't complacent about their jobs, he was forever moving them around; once he ordered employees in two very different-sized buildings to switch locations, just to make sure that no one got too comfortable.

For most of his career, being unconventional won Johnson effusive praise. Months before the buyout attempt, *Fortune* magazine labeled him "America's Toughest Marketing Man" in a glowing cover story, while the *Wall Street Journal*, in an equally admiring Page One article, called him the ultimate "non-company" man. Later, disrespect for tradition would be termed Johnson's greatest fault.

Johnson had golf on the brain. A ten-handicap player, he did business over golf, he relaxed over golf, he spent his spare time watching golf. He had played every major golf course in the country—and belonged to most—and even oriented himself by the local putting green. "Where did you live in relation to the golf course?" he once asked a reporter when she told him she had grown up in San Francisco. He also suffered what one observer calls, that "corporate royalty complex." Johnson, who earned more than $2.7 million in 1987, "had trouble remembering what was his and what was the company's." When it came to the chief executive's needs, no expense was spared, be it a fleet of corporate planes, a suite in Palm Springs, or a staff of advance men. Most of Johnson's golf memberships were paid by the company, and the corporate hangar was equipped with golf club racks and carriers, since the chairman couldn't be expected to tote his own.

For all his love of wine, women, and sports, Johnson was refreshingly unpretentious; "he wouldn't know Chassagne-Montrachet if you gave him a bottle," laughs a friend, "he'd think it was just good wine." Johnson had nicknames for everyone: he called Michael Masterpool, his public relations chief, "Numero Uno," because "he is the only one who has an unlimited budget and exceeds it every year." Johnson put a plaque reading "Ronald Grierson's Office" on the door of one of the telephone cubicles in the executive suite because Grierson, the vice-chairman of British General Electric and an RJR director, was always on the telephone. When he found out that one of his investment bankers, Jeffrey Beck of Drexel Burnham Lambert, had been known as "Mad Dog" in his army days, Johnson showed up at their next meeting with a box of Milk Bones, a Nabisco product. He had a flip, self-deprecating sense of humor. After posing with eleven sports and entertainment friends in a billboard ad for Oleg Cassini suits, Johnson remarked that he was sure people were wondering "who's that turkey up there" between Bob Hope and Mario Andretti.

Indeed, Johnson's gee-whiz manner, his Canadian accent—middle-class British crossed with American Midwest—and his fondness for practical jokes made him seem almost a hayseed in the sophisticated New York business community. Outside the stuffy world of Morris County Golf Club, Johnson was considered a regular fellow. "He is a charmer, a raconteur, a real knee-slapping kind of a guy," says Philip L. Thomas, a one-time Nabisco consultant. Not surprisingly, most of Johnson's friends were golfers, former athletes, or at least fellow fanatics. He was buddies with hockey ace Bobby Orr and football legends Don Meredith and Frank Gifford. His closest banking associate was J. Ira Harris, the bright but unbuttoned Salomon Brothers deal-maker and self-confessed baseball nut. Johnson loved Hollywood glitter, and he once kept the Four Seasons open until two in the morning, shooting the breeze with movie star Michael Douglas. Even the most straight-laced businessmen were attracted by his effusive manner. Among his more unlikely friends were Charlie Hugel, the earnest chairman of Combustion Engineering, and James D. Robinson III, the white shoe chairman of American Express.

The free spending and freewheeling made Johnson controversial in business circles, but no one questioned that he got results. Johnson had successfully transformed two stodgy old-fashioned companies, Standard Brands and Nabisco, into modern corporations, and tried to bring RJR into the twentieth century. Johnson's RJR Nabisco produced dazzling returns. At the end of Johnson's first year as chief executive, sales were up 4 percent, earnings were up 14 percent and the quarterly dividend had been hiked 30 percent to 48 cents a share. By then he had sold more than thirty operations that had once accounted for $2.5 billion in sales, bought in $1.6 billion of preferred stock and $1 billion of common, bringing RJR's return on equity to an enviable 20 percent, one of the finest in the entire food industry.

Food and liquor companies typically get involved in sports as an advertising ploy, and Johnson went Coke, Miller Lite, and Sara Lee one better, not only sponsoring a dozen events, including Nabisco Grand Prixs in tennis and golf, the Nabisco Dinah Shore golf championship, and the Planters Pat Bradley International golf tournament, but also hiring nineteen sports celebrities as the Team Nabisco to represent the company at various sports-related functions. Johnson was so keen on sports marketing that he even teamed up with Don Ohlmeyer, a former ABC sports producer, to form a television production and sports management company that, among other things, managed appearances of boxer Mike Tyson. In theory, the celebrity connection helped convince grocers to squeeze more Nabisco products onto their shelves, and although there was no hard evidence that it worked, it certainly was fun. Only in the entertainment business did executives rub shoulders with so many stars, and Johnson had considered getting involved in that too, as an investor in Michael Douglas's movie production company. In the end he decided against it; movies was quite a stretch for a cigarette- cum cookie-maker.

Johnson seemed almost out of place in the buttoned-down food and tobacco business. It wasn't just his Cassini suits and gold chain in the sea of Brooks Brothers pinstripes. What really separated him from the mainstream were his unconventional ideas. "He'd call you from Jim Robinson's country house to ask you what you thought about merging with *Time*," recalls Steve Waters, who got to know Johnson during his ten years at Lehman Brothers, Kuhn Loeb, and its successor, Shearson Lehman Hutton. Johnson worked on instinct. Often his own staffers didn't know what he was doing.

Johnson was no administrator, nor was he a particularly good judge of people. Sometimes he even lost sight of his own abilities, introducing Premier, RJR's revolutionary new smokeless cigarette long before several key factors including taste and lightability were worked out. "He thought he could sell anything," marvels a lawyer who knows him. Johnson's greatest talent wasn't marketing or schmoozing though, but corporate politics. Johnson catapulted himself to the top of Standard Brands, and maneuvered his way to the number one spot at Nabisco. Even before the Nabisco RJR merger was complete, Johnson had assessed the tobacco giant's arcane power structure and begun to put himself on course to the top.

To grease the wheels, he gave supporters generous incentives that cynics regarded as faintly disguised bribes. RJR directors got a fee of $50,000 a year for attending six bimonthly meetings, free private jet service around the world, and VIP treatment at most sports events, even some Nabisco wasn't involved in. Four key supporters—Charlie Hugel; Andrew Sage, the former president of Lehman Brothers and one of Johnson's closest personal friends; Robert Schaeberle, the former Nabisco chairman, William Anderson, retired chief executive of NCR computers—even got generous salaries to boot, with correspondingly vague responsibilities, and Johnson arranged for RJR to endow the Juanita Kreps Chair at Duke University and to fund an ethics program at Georgetown where Andy Sage was a trustee. Johnson made no attempt to whitewash the gilt treatment, and in the end that would come back to haunt him. Says a friend, "The directors liked the fact that he was 'director of transportation,' " providing private RJR airplane and limousine service around the globe. "But they didn't like him to say it." And they were mortified to see the quip repeated in the *Wall Street Journal*.

F. Ross Johnson would later denigrate an accountant as "a man who puts his head in the past and backs his rear into the future," but he started his career in 1961 crunching numbers at Canadian General Electric, the Toronto-based subsidiary of the world's greatest by-the-numbers company. His grasp of figures was hard to match. "He is the only person I've ever met who can, in five or ten minutes in a budget presentation, understand my budget better than I did after studying it for two weeks," says John Gora, president of Chuckles Gumdrops, once a Nabisco subsidiary. Johnson quickly moved into marketing, putting in time at T. Eaton, a large department store chain, and GSW, an appliance maker. Even at that early stage in his career, recalls Ralph Barford, president of GSW, Johnson was "very pragmatic," never wedded to a particular approach. If something didn't work, he'd dump it and try something else, a process that Barford, for one, won't knock: "He got results."

Those results caught the eye of Jack Banks, GSW's account officer at the Royal Bank of Canada, and in 1971 when Banks's boss, Royal Canadian chairman W. Earle McLaughlin, also a director of New York-based Standard Brands, was scouting around for someone to run the grocery company's Canadian unit, Banks suggested Johnson. There was a simple reason that McLaughlin was on the lookout for talent. Henry Weigl, Standard Brands' autocratic chairman, had scared off many of the company's promising young managers with his domineering attitude and he had weakened the company's franchise—products included such well-known brands as Chase & Sanborn coffee, Fleischmann's margarine, Royal gelatin, and Planters' peanuts—by slashing advertising, promotion, and research expenditures to improve short-term profits.

By 1974, Johnson had moved to Standard Brands' headquarters at 625 Madison Avenue in midtown Manhattan as head of the international division. A year after that he was president. Where Weigl was abrasive and rough-edged, Johnson was charming and charismatic. And he understood corporate politics, allying himself with the two powerful bankers on the board, McLaughlin, and Andy Sage, the former Lehman president. By May 1976, Johnson had lined up the board votes to oust Weigl. Johnson and his closest supporters stayed up late the night before plotting strategy. "He was very thorough," recalls O. Lester Applegate, a marketing man whom Weigl had previously pushed out. "He took every scenario conceivable and said 'if A happens this is what we do. If B happens, we do this.' "

To revive the company, Johnson hired a crew of number crunchers from General Electric and gave them free rein in implementing a GE-style planning system. Old-fashioned ideas like consumer polling and taste-testing were replaced by zero-based budgeting and planning grids. The result was best exemplified in the group's first, and only, new product, Smooth & Easy, a margarine-like gravy stick that was guaranteed not to turn lumpy when melted in a saucepan. A technological wonder, Smooth & Easy had been tested for every property except taste, and it failed in the market because housewives didn't like the flavor.

True to form, Johnson dumped the GE approach soon after the Smooth & Easy debacle. He fired his friend Reuben Gutoff as president and brought back Applegate and several long-deposed marketing executives. This time he hit the right mix. By pruning and refocusing the product line and pouring money into marketing, Standard Brands' sales and profits boomed.

Johnson kept just one relic of the GE regimen: a tight financial reporting system. Every month, unit managers were required to file detailed numbers with the controller's office. The results were distributed on a need-to-know basis, the candy chief, for example, receiving a green-covered booklet of candy numbers and the liquor chief getting one with just liquor numbers. Board members got blue books listing key totals like accounts receivable, cash flow, sales and profits, while Johnson got a red binder containing all the numbers as well as the operating team's explanation of what was going wrong or right. But that was it: no five-year planning, no detailed economic forecasting, no gazing into a corporate crystal ball.

In the spring of 1981, Johnson got a call from Robert Schaeberle, the chairman of Nabisco. Schaeberle wanted to combine the two mid-size companies into a food giant big enough to compete with Beatrice, Nestle, and Unilever. Johnson, ever focused on the bottom line, was happy to talk, and by April the two had agreed to a $2 billion stock swap merger.

It was one of those rare combinations that seemed to be as good for business as for corporate egos. Nabisco was strong in England, Japan, Italy, France, and Australia; Standard Brands was a powerhouse in Canada and Latin America. Nabisco was strong in cookies and crackers; Standard Brands was known for liquor, candy, and grocery products. Standard Brands was fast-moving and marketing oriented. Stodgy Nabisco was one of only two food companies in the country with its own fleet of trucks (the other was Frito-Lay). Because Nabisco drivers stopped once a week at every grocery store from coast to coast, the company could roll out a new product nationwide in less than fourteen days.

Actually, the only loser in the deal seemed to be Ross Johnson. He was a clear misfit in the pinstriped Nabisco culture. Surprisingly, the freewheeler got on with the squares, and Schaeberle and Johnson soon emerged as the industry's most effective marketing and management team. In 1984, after Proctor & Gamble concluded from marketing surveys that women no longer had time to bake cookies, and introduced "Duncan Hines Soft Cookies" to fill the gap, the "Siamese twins," as Schaeberle and Johnson called themselves, sprang into action, spending $50 million to develop the hugely successful "Almost Home" line in just six months. Although most watchers had expected the new cookies to cannibalize on the sales of Nabisco's own Oreos, Chips Ahoy!, and Nilla Vanilla Wafers, they didn't, and so Nabisco's overall share of the cookie market rose from 36 percent to 40 percent.

By then, takeovers were getting hot, and food takeovers in particular. In 1983, Esmark had bought Norton Simon for $932 million. Not long after, Nestle, the Swiss food giant, bought Los Angeles-based Carnation for $2 billion. Esmark had then put itself on the block and Johnson had come close to negotiating a Nabisco merger; at the last minute, he decided he didn't like the price and Esmark went to Beatrice instead. In the spring of 1985, Johnson himself became the target of a bid when J. Tylee Wilson, chairman of RJ Reynolds Industries, called with a proposal. RJR, once the country's premier tobacco company, had long since diversified into food, buying Del Monte fresh and canned fruits, Heublein liquors, and Kentucky Fried Chicken fast food restaurants. Now Wilson wanted cookies and crackers as well.

Johnson, a Davidoff cigar smoker, had nothing against selling to a tobacco giant, particularly at the top-dollar price of $4.9 billion, but he was determined to protect his shareholders against the liability risk. Smokers' widows were constantly charging that one cigarette maker or another was responsible for the death of their spouse and it was possible that some jury would go wild, awarding millions of dollars to the estate. There was no precedent for such an outcome, and, indeed, it seemed unlikely, since the courts had consistently held that the tobacco companies couldn't be liable for smoking after 1966, the year that they were required to print the Surgeon General's warning on the box. But a single megadollar reversal could force RJR bankrupt by triggering an avalanche of new suits and new rulings. Just such a legal explosion had forced asbestos manufacturer Manville into Chapter 11 in 1982. Initially, Johnson insisted that RJR pay for Nabisco entirely in cash. When that wouldn't fly, he reluctantly agreed to paper, only on condition that the notes were designed to trade above face value.

While the Nabisco shareholders were clear winners, Johnson looked to be a personal loser once again. He got the number two spot, with little hope of becoming number one since Wilson was only a few months his senior. The chemistry that Johnson had had with Schaeberle was distinctly missing. Johnson's and Wilson's management styles were totally incompatible. Wilson demanded memos, videos, and five-year plans. Johnson believed in gut decisions and flexibility. Wilson hated Wall Street; Johnson was always exploring some new investment idea. Indeed, the two nearly came to blows over finance. In the spring of 1986, just after Beatrice went private in a $6.2 billion leveraged buyout, the largest in history, Johnson had asked Steve Waters of Shearson Lehman to look at an RJR buyout. Johnson was leery of the idea himself because he didn't like debt, but he told Wilson that the numbers did look good. Wilson hit the ceiling, and the buyout idea quickly went into deep freeze.

The most visible clash came over compensation. According to one possibly apocryphal story, Wilson was outraged when Johnson suggested that RJR provide senior executives with company cars. "Goddammit," Wilson said. "These men are paid enough to drive anything they want to. If they want to drive a Volkswagen, fine. If they want to drive a Rolls-Royce, fine. They pay for it, not the company." But Wilson eventually agreed to company cars, and to other Johnson-proposed perks as well. Soon Johnson was running the tight-fisted tobacco company in the freespending way he had always run his food giants. The top thirty managers *averaged* $445,000 a year, not including the free travel, cars, and country club memberships.

That would have been enough to raise eyebrows in New York, but in penny-pinching Winston-Salem, it was beyond the pale. Local storytellers soon supplemented the real perks with ones that were more magnificent still. After Johnson left, a former RJR executive told a Winston-Salem newspaper that he had made a two-page list of the "most-discussed" expenditures. Among them: a home in Palm Springs "complete with Rolls-Royce and TV set sunken in the floor that would rise electronically"; and "a $10,000 paper clip holder." According to another story, Johnson had removed the roof of the new Atlanta headquarters building to airlift in the giant boardroom table.

The truth was slightly more mundane. Johnson insists that although he did travel in a chauffeured car, except in Winston-Salem where he drove his own jeep, he boasted no fleet of white limousines. The antiques in the RJR hangar consisted of a single fake $600 armoire; the "gym" was a treadmill-cum-weight machine. David B. Kalis, an AmEx official who joined RJR after the takeover, was sorely disappointed with the Atlanta headquarters. "It was designed by the same people who did the AmEx headquarters," he said, "and it looks a lot like AmEx," palatial certainly, but something short of Xanadu.

Johnson wasn't in charge long enough to prove his method worked, but one thing remains abundantly clear: Wilson's didn't. Under Wilson and his well-meaning but tight-fisted predecessors, Reynolds had slipped from the world's premier tobacco company to a distant number two. Philip Morris, with its marketing pizzazz and spend-money-to-make-money outlook, had rolled past Reynolds in 1976, and never looked back. By the time Johnson sold Nabisco into the RJR fold, Philip Morris claimed 40 percent of all U.S. cigarette sales, twice Reynolds's. According to Reynolds research, 25 percent of all starting smokers chose Marlboro, Philip Morris's leading brand, and since cigarette brand loyalties are so firm that 90 percent of all smokers would rather fight than switch, that meant that Wilson's Reynolds seemed doomed to slow extinction.

So was Wilson. Where Johnson knew how to make friends with his board, Wilson did everything wrong. He got his job only by threatening to quit when he heard that the board had chosen his rival Hicks Waldron instead. He hadn't done much to curry favor since. Wilson's worst mistake came in July 1986, a year after the Nabisco merger, when he passed out samples of Premier, the new smokeless cigarette that RJR had developed. Until then, the directors hadn't known that RJR was working on a smokeless, and they were outraged that Wilson had wildly overstepped his spending authority by pouring $100 million into the project without board approval. Wilson had gotten the money by misallocating cash that had been designated for other purposes.

Ever quick to exploit opportunities as they arose, Johnson made his move. He had already dropped hints that he would leave if he were not given the top job. He had already won the support of Paul Sticht, Wilson's predecessor and one-time mentor. Now Sticht and Johnson called each of the sixteen RJR directors to ask for their proxy, starting with Johnson's closest allies and ending with the four who were firmly in Wilson's camp. In mid-

August, Johnson invited Wilson into his office and announced that he had the votes to throw him out. Wilson didn't even put up a fight. Although he kept the ceremonial title of chairman of the board, Wilson "resigned" as chief executive effective January 1, 1987, ceding his power to Johnson immediately.

If the board thought that Johnson would be more conventional at the top of RJR than he had at Standard Brands or Nabisco, they were sorely mistaken. No sooner did Johnson ascend to the RJR throne than he began shaking things up. He sold dozens of ill-fitting units: Harry & David's mail order fruit, Del Monte's frozen entrees, Canadian confections. He bought the Almaden winery for $125 million, sold Heublein cum Almaden for $1.2 billion a week later, and days after formally moving into the top job, announced that he was moving the company headquarters to Atlanta. By the end of 1987 he had reorganized Del Monte three times, slashing 1,600 jobs; moved Planters/Life Savers from Winston-Salem to New Jersey and back, and sent 2,650 corporate staffers scrambling.

The policy of jerking executives from one job to another and moving business units between subsidiaries may have made for more efficient management, but some say it cost him employees that he would rather have kept. "The operating guys were scared of him," says Gerald Long, the retired chairman of RJ Reynolds Tobacco USA. "They didn't know if their jobs would be there tomorrow." Says another board member: "Ross was always in a hurry. He couldn't wait to see if something worked before he tried something else. It was unsettling." Johnson brushed that off, and so did his supporters. "Anyone who tries to change a company takes in arrows," says Beck, the Drexel banker.

Sticht, who had had such a key role in putting Johnson in the top job, was horrified when Johnson began to replace long-time Reynolds staffers with Nabisco stalwarts, and Johnson thanked him by forcing him to step down as chairman when he turned seventy in September 1987. After Johnson announced his buyout proposal, Sticht would tell friends that choosing Johnson over Wilson had been his biggest management mistake.

Not long after the Wilson ouster, Johnson got a call from Jeffrey Beck, a merger and acquisitions partner at Drexel Burnham Lambert, the investment bank famous for having pioneered junk bonds. Beck had met Johnson during the Esmark–Nabisco talks as the banker representing Esmark; he had heard all about him from his friend and former Lehman Brothers boss Andy Sage, Johnson's longtime friend. Like many other watchers on Wall Street, Beck had noticed that after the RJR take-over of Nabisco, the stock value of the combined company never jumped as high as the sum of what the two companies had been worth before, but he had waited to call until Wilson was on the way out. Beck didn't think that Wilson would be interested in Drexel's advice on what to do; Wilson was the sort of white shoe executive who didn't ken to Drexel in the first place—and besides, Wilson had been the architect of much that Beck thought should be undone.

Johnson didn't hesitate to take Beck's call. Drexel would later be tarnished by a government insider trading and market manipulation investigation, a $650 million civil settlement and a guilty plea to four criminal fraud charges. But at this time, the firm was riding high. In July, Mike Milken, the junk bond chief who would later be charged with a ninety-eight-count racketeering indictment, had been featured in a glowing *BusinessWeek* cover story; a month later, *Manhattan inc.*, the normally peppery business monthly, profiled chief executive Fred Joseph in an equally warm cover story titled "Junk Bond Baron." The insider-trading scandal had just begun with the arrest of Dennis Levine in May, but there was then no indication that Drexel was headed for trouble; although he had worked at Drexel at this time of his arrest, Levine, who had done most of his illicit dealing while at Shearson, seemed simply a Wall Street bad apple.

Johnson had been concerned about stock market values even before Beck called; that was why he had asked Steve Waters to look at a leveraged buyout (LBO) several months before. "Every dollar I earned was worth $9 [in stock market value]," Johnson complained. "Every dollar my neighbor Coke made was worth $16." So he was happy to hear what Beck had to say. He agreed to meet Beck and several of his colleagues for dinner at the Links Club on East 62nd Street in midtown Manhattan in the middle of September.

The dinner went well, at least after Marty Siegel left. Siegel, who would become infamous six months later, when he confessed to having received $700,000 for his insider tips by switching briefcases with an Ivan Boesky courier in a Wall Street alley, had invited himself, and as he was the M&A chief there was no question of saying no. But Johnson had seemed uncomfortable with Siegel and opened up only after Siegel went on to another dinner.

Beck told Johnson that he thought that the reason the stock price was so low was twofold: investors weren't recognizing that RJR was more than a tobacco company, nor were they properly valuing tobacco stocks.

The general undervaluation of tobacco companies was something that Drexel could not do much about. It was a social phenomenon, although perhaps a temporary one. After years of ineffective grumbling, anti-smoking activists were suddenly getting more aggressive. They had formed their own lobbying group to publicize the risks of smoking and to push for tighter "fresh air" laws. Half a dozen new cancer death cases had been filed, and although the cigarette makers insisted that there was no causal relationship between smoking and lung cancer, plenty of people, including the U.S. Surgeon General, viewed Reynolds and her sister companies as merchants of death. However strong were today's earnings, investors tended to discount RJR's value because of the perceived social and legal risks.

But Johnson could clarify the company by cleaning up the murky product mix, something Johnson had begun doing on his own. He was even then negotiating to sell Kentucky Fried Chicken to Pepsi-Cola and had suggested to Grand Metropolitan, the British liquor and hotels giant, that it buy Heublein. Although there were rampant rumors that Johnson was on the verge of making a major corporate acquisition—General Mills had been mentioned—Beck didn't think that that made sense. "You know, Ross," he said. "Everyone thinks you are a buyer, but I think you're a seller. What I think you need to do to get values up is sell."

In mid-October, Beck called Johnson back with a specific proposal, a tobacco master limited partnership (MLP), a tax-advantaged version of the old "carve out" that had been popular among conglomerate managers in the sixties and seventies. To draw attention to the fact that there was more to RJR than tobacco, RJR would put the U.S. tobacco assets in a partnership and sell, say, 20 percent, to the public. With a piece of paper in the market representing just the tobacco assets, investors would be forced to notice RJR's other jewels, Nabisco, Del Monte, and

Planters, and to make an independent assessment as to what they were worth.

Johnson was intrigued with the MLP idea, and for months Beck and his staff shuttled between New York and Winston-Salem crunching numbers, refining data, making presentations. By mid-February, just after the press got wind of the MLP idea, Johnson decided not to do it. Although everyone's best guess was that it would increase the stock price, Johnson's lawyers said that it couldn't be done. Under the terms of RJR's $4 billion of bonds outstanding, tobacco assets couldn't be sold or pledged to other lenders as RJR would have to do in an MLP. Worse, Congress was threatening to change the tax loophole that had made the idea attractive in the first place.

Investment bankers generally get paid only if their deals go through, and since his hadn't, Beck didn't send a bill for the MLP. Johnson, feeling guilty that he had asked Beck to do the work but had dropped the idea despite the encouraging numbers, offered to send a check all the same. Beck refused it. "I want to do the bigger deal," he said. Beck had already decided what it would be: the leveraged buyout of RJR. Even before the MLP collapsed, Beck had begun to put together some numbers for an LBO led by Kohlberg Kravis Roberts, the nation's largest buyout group and a long-time Drexel client. In March 1987, Beck sent his first study, suggesting a price of $75 a share—$63 in cash and $12 in junk notes—a premium of 28 percent over the market price of $59 a share.

Ten years earlier such a document would have gone straight into the trash. Until the mid-1980s, leveraged buyouts of large public companies were virtually unheard of. In the good old days of the sixties and seventies, takeover activity, such as it was, was friendly. Gentlemanly companies didn't buy each other and high debt was considered a sign of poor financial control. Leveraged buyouts, that is, acquisitions financed almost entirely by borrowing against the company's own assets, were limited to purchases of small family-owned companies or divisions of larger companies.

Buyouts didn't make the financial headlines until 1982, when William Simon, the former Treasury Secretary, walked away with $80 million after buying Gibson Greeting Cards from RCA and reselling it to the public a scant eight months later. Money began to pour into small deals, and then larger ones, but mega-deals were slow to follow. Although insurance companies were willing to stake enough mezzanine money, an intermediate layer of finance between the bank debt and sponsor equity, for small and mid-sized buyouts, really big deals were beyond the limit. Junk bonds, securities so risky that the rating agencies did not consider them "investment grade," would eventually fill the gap, but for a time they had an aroma too foul for blue chip investment portfolios. Even in 1985, Drexel was unable to line up just $100 million in junk so that Castle & Cooke could bid for Dr Pepper. It went instead to Forstmann Little for $650 million, mostly in bank debt.

But times had changed. Mutual fund managers, pension officers, and thrift investment departments had discovered what owning high-yield junk could do for their reported quarterly returns and threw caution to the winds. With a growing market for any and all high-yield paper, the idea of a multibillion dollar junk buyout was not so laughable, and rather than throw the study away, Andy Sage, to whom Beck had sent the document rather than to Johnson himself, filed it among the other Drexel papers he kept in a box labeled "Project Sadim." Sage had chosen the name for a very simple reason: Sadim is Midas spelled backward.

Andrew Gregg Curtin Sage II had always been more to Johnson than just a member of his board of directors. Although they came from vastly different backgrounds, middle-class Manitoba and aristocratic New York, Johnson and Sage were kindred spirits. In his day, Sage had been as controversial as Johnson. As a young partner, he had been given the job of running day-to-day operations at Lehman Brothers after Bobbie Lehman became too sick to do it, and then quit in frustration in 1973 as infighting between senior partners threatened to destroy the firm. Since then, he had continued to work as an independent adviser to half a dozen Fortune 500 companies; he had dabbled in oil and gas and venture capital, and he managed the family portfolio of stocks and bonds.

Like Johnson, Sage was something of an iconoclast. He worked at home on his own personal computer—or three identical ones, to be exact, at his houses in Glen Cove, Long Island; Jackson, Wyoming; and West Palm Beach—crunching his own numbers and typing his own memos. Sage specialized in complex finance.

Lehman Brothers had called him out of retirement to put together
a proposal for financing a $24 billion Alaska gas pipeline, then
the largest project-financing ever attempted by a factor of eight
(it didn't happen). More recently Sage had gotten interested in
factory technology; at the time of the Waverly dinner, he was
working full-time on a $2.7 billion Nabisco bakery upgrade that
included yet-to-be-designed automated machinery that was intended to be state-of-the-art for the next fifty years.

Sage had earned his banking spurs in the fifties and sixties, and
the business world had changed a lot since then. Although investment banking had long since become a deal-hungry transac-
tion-oriented business, Sage still practiced the way he had in the
old days, nurturing long-term close relationships. He was more
concerned about how healthy his client would be tomorrow than
the fee he collected today. Sage took a more active role than
most bankers. He insisted on sitting on the boards of the half-
dozen or so companies that he advised and often functioned as
the chairman's right-hand man, tackling everything from commercial banking negotiations to factory renovation. Over the
years, he had helped salvage the remains of Bernie Cornfeld's
notorious Investors Overseas Services company; restructured Ar-
len Realty; headed International Harvester's effort to stave off
bankruptcy, and negotiated the sale of American Motors to
Chrysler.

Johnson always bounced financial ideas off of Sage, and when
Beck began to send down MLP studies, Johnson asked Sage to
take a look. Sage was preoccupied with the Nabisco factory project, so he suggested that Johnson hire a former Lehman associate
named Frank A. Benevento II as a financial consultant; for his
efforts, Benevento, who had worked with Sage on the Alaska gas
pipeline, earned $3,000 a week, modest by investment banking
standards.

Benevento's job was to look at what the Beck and other investment bankers working for the company were doing, as well
as to assess proposals that came over the transom unsolicited and
generate ideas of his own. Early on, Benevento put together a
computer model of RJR, keyed to Johnson's monthly operating
report. Benevento had done an analysis of the master limited
partnership and concluded that from a financial perspective it

would work. He had looked at the leveraged buyout and concluded that that too made some sense, if a transaction so big could actually be completed. However enthusiastic Beck was about the deal, Benevento soberly noted that the largest leveraged buyout to date was Beatrice, which at $6 billion was only one-third as large as an RJR buyout would be. Still, the buyout numbers were interesting, not the least because with food company prices in the stratosphere, anyone who bought RJR, be it management or an outsider like Nestle, could almost pay for tobacco by selling food. Johnson's response to this fascinating fact was disappointing. Having personally assembled the food company over a period of fifteen years, he was frankly uninterested in selling it to buy tobacco.

So despite Benevento's suggestion that he discuss a leveraged buyout with the directors at the board meeting in Palm Springs in late March, Johnson shelved the idea. He played golf with Jack Nicklaus, watched the Nabisco Dinah Shore Invitational with the directors and grocery managers, and came home without so much as mentioning the proposal. Nor, he made it clear, did he want to hear about an LBO again. And that was that, at least for six months. Although Benevento and Beck ignored Johnson's directive and continued to remind him that a buyout made financial sense, Johnson had other ideas for getting value to the shareholders. In August, he raised the dividend a hefty 20 percent, to 48 cents a share, and he began to look at buying Wesson Oil from Beatrice. Cooking oil would mesh well with the grocery division's Fleischmann's and Blue Bonnet margarines, and it would increase RJR's presence in the more high-multiple food business.

After a meeting in New York to talk about Wesson with Beatrice chairman Donald P. Kelly and Ira Harris, Johnson's banker, Johnson decided not to buy. The $1.5 billion that Kelly wanted for the unit seemed excessive given that it earned just $100 million a year. As the talks broke up, someone mentioned golf. Kelly had never played Deepdale in Long Island, a well-known celebrity golfing hot-spot, but Johnson was a member so they headed there. On the clubhouse terrace, they talked about how lucrative the Beatrice buyout had been. Kelly, who had personally gotten 7.5 percent of the stock as part of the deal, stood to make $277 million.

Johnson joked, as he so often did, that he wanted to make

some real money. Kelly suggested that he meet with Kravis to talk about taking RJR Nabisco private.

"I'm not interested in a buyout," said Johnson.

"Dinner can't hurt," insisted Kelly, and after some ribbing, Johnson agreed. If nothing else, it was a chance to see Kravis's apartment. Everybody knew about Kravis's Renoirs.

CHAPTER 2

A Modern "Medi-chichi"

October 1987 to July 1988

Actually, the prize painting isn't a Renoir but a Sargent. Charles Stewart, the sixth marquess of Londonderry, dominates the antique-stuffed dining room. Having perfected the art of making money, Kravis has become an expert on spending it. Although he insists that he buys art because he loves it, Kravis lays no claim to being a connoisseur; and perhaps there's another reason he buys art: that is the fastest way to make new money old. Or so his father, Ray, thinks. After his first encounter with the marquess, Ray Kravis chided, "Which of our relatives is this?"

Be it deal-making, art collecting, or sports, Henry Kravis is highly competitive. He hates to lose, and rarely does. He has been publicly outbid only twice, when he lost Norton Simon to Esmark and Esmark to Beatrice, but got his revenge by buying Beatrice two years later. He ended a much-discussed search for the perfect Stubbs by buying not one, but two. After losing a game of paddle tennis to his friend Lew Eisenberg, head of securities sales at Goldman Sachs, Kravis rechallenged Eisenberg until he finally won, and has refused to play paddle tennis since.

At five feet six inches tall—Kravis claims it's five feet eight-and-a-half inches—Kravis is Wall Street's Napoleon. His company, Kohlberg, Kravis, Roberts & Co., is among the largest and most powerful industrial combines in the world. At the time of the RJR brawl, KKR controlled companies making everything from tomato sauce to machine tools; had it been public, KKR would have ranked sixth on the Fortune 500, just above General Electric. (There were those who thought that Kravis's megalomanic goal was to be number one.) Kravis's reputation is so far-reaching that, in the spring of 1988, six months before the RJR battle, he was even invited to Moscow to talk to Soviet planning officials about how to fix the stagnant Russian economy.

For all its clout and international prestige, KKR is a minuscule organization with a total professional staff of just fifteen, five of them partners: Kravis and Paul Raether in New York, and KKR co-founder George Roberts, Robert MacDonnell, and Michael Michelson in San Francisco. "The thing that's great about working for these guys is that they always have fun," says Richard I. Beattie, a trusted Kravis adviser and partner at law firm Simpson Thatcher & Bartlett. And make a lot of money. *BusinessWeek* estimated that Kravis and his cousin and Roberts took home $70 million each in 1987.

Although sharply critical of corporate waste, especially Johnson's, Kravis's own operating style is not restrained. His elegant office is almost as famous as his Renoirs. Tastefully appointed with French antiques and horse paintings—Kravis doesn't hunt— it boasts the best location and best view in midtown Manhattan. Kravis travels by limousine and private Gulfstream III jet; he eats in a private dining room, catered by his own chef. Unlike Johnson, however, Kravis pays for the ostentation from his own pocket.

He pays for an even splashier personal spread. The walls of his duplex apartment, painted celadon green because his equally high-profile wife Carolyne Roehm hates white, are covered with Impressionist canvases chosen by his Boston-based curator. There are so many paintings, indeed, that Kravis has considered buying the duplex above his as a private museum. Kravis's every need is tended by his staff of five in New York—two live in—and a selection of cooks, caretakers, and maids at his three country homes. Tales of Kravis's extravagance are mind-numbing. According to *Vogue*, guests at Kravis's Connecticut pre-Revolutionary house wake up to the smell of brewing coffee and baking croissants that has been piped to their rooms. Kravis has recently dug a lake on the grounds, complete with an island, waterfall, and a fleet of gondola ferryboats. His house in fast-money Vail,

Colorado, boasts a private ski lift. His idea of a vacation is a safari in Kenya.

He is a master of public relations. KKR is not the most successful leveraged buyout firm—its returns are only half those of almost every competitor—but it is surely the best known, and, in many circles, the most respected. Kravis is famed for his company-picking know-how but his success has, in fact, had more to do with the rising stock market; an investor would have done better by putting his money in the S&P 500 index when KKR was formed, than by investing in the partnership. Although several of KKR's deals have been spectacular failures, Kravis has managed to suppress that fact completely, even omitting such transactions from his presentations to potential investors. Kravis has long been Mike Milken's largest client, but unlike so many other Drexel clients, his name is never mentioned in the gossip or press coverage surrounding the government's three-year investigation and subsequent market manipulation case.

Indeed it is hard to find anyone on Wall Street who will volunteer anything but fulsome praise. "Kravis keeps us alive," says a sometime adviser, for Kravis paid $150 million in fees to the bankers, lawyers, and accountants on the Beatrice deal alone. "I'm not going to answer that," snapped a commercial banker when queried as to whether he had ever turned down a KKR deal. "I'm not going to say anything negative about them. [LBO lending] is a good business for us. We can't earn money lending at prime. These are the only loans where we make a spread." Often as high as four percentage points.

There is more to Kravis's reputation than the fees he pays. Impeccably dressed and carefully spoken, Kravis is usually gracious, sometimes funny. His supporters say that he is a man of his word in a world where that is no longer assumed. He likes to golf and shoot the breeze with the guys and he is fiercely devoted to Roehm and to his three teenage kids, Robbie, Kimberly, and Harrison. He is a high-profile philanthropist, having given $10 million to New York Hospital for a Henry Kravis Women's and Children's Pavilion (aka maternity ward) and $10 million for a Kravis wing at the Metropolitan Museum of Art.

Of course, the donations dovetail nicely with his high-profile social life. In recent years, Kravis had emerged as the King of what *Womens Wear Daily* calls "nouvelle society," the social group that, in another era, would have been known as nouveaux riches. Raising money for good causes is one of the responsibilities that comes with new wealth, and the Kravises shoulder their share of the burden by attending scores of charity parties. In November 1988, Kravis was elected a trustee of the Metropolitan Museum, the most socially prestigious board in New York.

Sitting on that board had other benefits: the museum is a particularly stunning place to throw a party. Indeed, Kravis hosted an intimate bash there for 110 of his closest friends just two weeks before the RJR battle began. No ordinary party this, but a recital by violin prodigy Midori, a preview of the sold-out Degas exhibit and a catered dinner all wrapped into one. "Medi-chichi," was the verdict of one veteran partygoer. "It was the grandest of the rich of New York all done up in the most extraordinary way."

No doubt the cost was impressive as well.

Kravis, forty-four, says that his father was the greatest inspiration in his life. Ray Kravis, son of an immigrant British tailor, quit a coal-mining job in western Pennsylvania and bought a train ticket to Tulsa, then the oil capital of the world, to become one of the world's first petroleum geologists. "He was a pioneer," says Kravis. "I often think, What guts he must have had." The senior Kravis invested his oil earnings in the stock market, becoming friendly with such Wall Street power brokers as Prescott Bush, the president's father and a partner at Brown Brothers, Harriman; and Sidney Weinberg, the late Goldman Sachs managing partner. The 1929 Crash wiped Ray Kravis out, but he refused to file for bankruptcy. It took him five years to pay off his debt, but by the time Henry was born in 1944, Ray had made a second fortune, this one for keeps. The Kravis family lived in the grandest house in town, and the boys, Henry and his older brother George, went to the best schools, in Henry's case, Eaglebrook, a pre-prep school, and Loomis Chaffee.

Even as a child Kravis was singularly focused. On the football field, recalls Eaglebrook linebacker Michael Douglas, still a close friend, Kravis was scrawny but undaunted, ready to tackle guys twice his size. He constantly measured himself against his father, even applying to Lehigh University, Ray Kravis's alma mater, "to show me that he could get into the same school that I did." Kravis turned Lehigh down, and went to Claremont Men's College outside Los Angeles instead. He wanted to see the West; besides, his cousin George Roberts was already there. (Publicity-shy Roberts, 45, plays a key role at KKR; those who know both say he's smarter than Kravis and takes the lead in setting strategy.)

Kravis and Roberts had been close as children, and now they got closer. During the summers, they would drive to New York together for Wall Street jobs, sharing an apartment and talking about being partners someday. They worked together at Bear Stearns, an arbitrage firm, for several years, Kravis in New York, Roberts, who hates the East, in San Francisco. Bear Stearns was distinctly third-tier as far as corporate finance was concerned, and at about the time Kravis and Roberts arrived, their boss Jerome Kohlberg, head of corporate finance, was attempting to broaden the franchise by putting together leveraged buyouts, then known as "bootstraps" because the newly leveraged company had to pull itself out of debt with its own earnings, by its bootstraps, so to speak.

The deals, while enormously profitable, were also highly risky and they were highly controversial at Bear Stearns. The trading partners wanted the activity stopped altogether. It was. In 1976, after being locked out of his office by Bear Stearns's managing partner, Salim Lewis, Kohlberg decided to go it alone and asked Kravis and Roberts to join him. "We worried a lot that we would fail," recalls Kravis. "We weren't sure if we were successful at Bear Stearns because we were Bear Stearns or because we were us." The night they resigned they went out to dinner to talk about exactly how they would begin. They agreed that "if we couldn't be successful in five years, we'd try something else."

It never came to that. Early on, they convinced Prudential Insurance to put up the mezzanine money for their deals—the layer of financing that is now junk bonds—and they were off and running. They bought A. J. Industries for $25.6 million, Eaton Leonard for $13.5 million, Rotor Tool for $27.5 million. In those days, KKR didn't get involved in price wars, dropping out when another bidder surfaced, and it cared about the cost of money: at Kohlberg's insistence, KKR canceled the $800 million buyout of Foremost-McKesson after interest rates spiraled past 20 percent at the end of 1980.

Not all the deals were winners: KKR lost $700,000 on a $700,000 investment in FB Truck Lines and $5 million when the

Foresthill timber company went bankrupt. That apparently didn't teach KKR to stay away from risky commodity companies; the firm lost big on its $425 million purchase of Bendix Forest Products in 1981. The $2 billion purchase of half of Union Texas Petroleum in 1985 was also a failure. Although Kravis likes to say that investors doubled their money in four years, even that is only a middling return of 25 percent a year, and the company remains leveraged, exposed, and unsalable. KKR took the first step toward the mega-deal in 1979 when it bought Houdaille Industries, a Northbrook, Illinois-based heavy equipment maker for $335 million, four times the previous record. "That deal revolutionized the industry," says Joseph L. Rice III of Clayton & Dubilier, another early LBO player.

KKR had always gotten its equity money from institutions rather than friends—after all, what did you tell a friend if a deal went sour?—and with their solid track record and demonstrated ability to do big deals, it was suddenly possible to raise megabucks. One particularly fertile source of cash was public pension funds in states like Oregon, Washington, Illinois, and Michigan; Midwestern bureaucrats had not previously been regarded as smart money, but certainly they had money aplenty. Between 1980 and 1986, KKR raised more than $4 billion in three blind pools.

In the early years, the three KKR partners had gotten on well, but now tensions started to develop. Kohlberg wanted the deals to stay small and ultra-friendly; Kravis and Roberts wanted to push on to larger, more aggressive transactions. They jokingly refered to Kohlberg as "Dr. No," for vetoing so many of their more aggressive plans. Then in early 1984, when Kohlberg was in the hospital recovering from brain tumor surgery, Kravis got a call from Harold Hammer, the executive vice-president of Gulf Oil, then under siege by T. Boone Pickens. Hammer had just picked up the word that Pickens planned a tender offer, and he wanted to know if KKR would make a preemptive bid.

Until then, KKR hadn't played in the takeover arena, and although Gulf's market value was twelve times the largest buyout to date—Forstmann Little & Co.'s $650 million acquisition of Dr Pepper—Kravis was eager to try. Kravis's bid of $87.50 a share was $1.5 billion above Chevron's $80 a share, but nonetheless

KKR never had a chance. Unlike Chevron, KKR wasn't making a tender offer to give shareholders cash in a matter of days; rather it planned to merge with Gulf after it got the money lined up, something that might never come to pass. Worse, shareholders were to be paid partially in junk, something that in those days wasn't worth the paper it was printed on. To underscore that point, Gulf's investment banker, Jay Higgins of Salomon Brothers, began his presentation on why the directors should turn down KKR by reading aloud the Standard & Poor's definition of a noninvestment grade security.

Kravis would never make the same mistake again. Three months after losing to Chevron, KKR made its first tender offer, a friendly $580 million bid for Malone & Hyde, the largest independent supermarket operator in the South, financed with a bridge loan from the KKR investors. By then Kravis seemed more interested in deal size than returns. Although the demand for cable operators was frenzied and prices were in the stratosphere, KKR bought Wometco Enterprises of Miami for $1.1 billion in April, the first billion-dollar buyout, and, a year later, rescued Storer Communications from a proxy fight by Coniston Partners, who wanted to break up the company. Soon after, the market abruptly cooled, leaving KKR with the dubious distinction of having bought two companies at the peak. Even after merging Wometco and Storer into SCI Corp., the nation's fourth largest cable operator, KKR couldn't get rid of it. "It was like buying the last buildable lot on the Florida Gold Coast and then finding out that it had been a toxic waste dump," said John Malone, president of Tele-Communications Inc., who looked at the possibility. KKR hadn't sold SCI at the time of the RJR fight.

In the year after losing Gulf, Kravis also joined Merrill Lynch to try his first bust-up, the dismembering of City Investing into Pace Industries, Home Insurance, and Motel 6. He plunged deep into commodities, the kind of company most unsuited for an LBO, by buying half of Union Texas Petroleum for $2 billion months before crude oil prices dropped from the mid-twenties to below $10 a barrel. In March 1987, he went hostile, more or less, when he teamed up with Don Kelly, a deal-maker and former Esmark chairman, to bid for Beatrice, the Chicago-based food giant. After announcing that the company was not for sale, the directors hinted that they might negotiate if Kravis broke his alliance with Kelly, but Kravis pressed on, winning his prize for a stunning $6.2 billion, then the largest non-oil acquisition on record.

The Beatrice purchase also marked the beginning of a new era in LBO-making. KKR had agreed to a price that was arguably too high; at any rate it was more than Kravis could borrow from bank and mezzanine investors by pledging Beatrice's assets. The only way to "pay" stockholders $50 a share was to cram $10 a share of otherwise unsalable paper down their throats. This particular paper was so bad that it didn't even pay cash interest, but, instead, accrued interest in kind, that is, in the form of more bad paper. The reason for that, of course, was that all projected earnings had already been pledged to pay bank and junk interest, but perversely it made the deal slightly less tight. Under IRS rules the interest that was accrued in kind could be deducted from income just as if it had been paid.

Although it had been near-impossible to finance, Beatrice was soon alleged to be the most profitable deal ever. Within six months of the close, word began to circulate that KKR stood to make $2 billion to $4 billion on its $400 million investment. Actually that wasn't true—investors will, at best, break even—but it didn't seem to matter. Investment banks stampeded into the fray, raising billions of dollars for new "merchant banking" partnerships to finance buyouts of their own.

Kravis's first marriage had collapsed in the early 1980s, and in 1985 he married Carolyne Roehm, the statuesque fashion designer. The newlyweds set up housekeeping in a $5.5 million apartment at 740 Park Avenue, the posh building that had once been home to John D. Rockefeller, Jr., and burst forth on the social scene, becoming almost overnight a mainstay of the *Womens Wear Daily* and "Suzy" society columns. Kravis insisted that the high profile was critical to Carolyne's fashion business, but certainly he enjoyed it too. At least the partygoing; Kravis had a formidable reputation with gossip writers, and they sometimes feared that they were in physical danger after publishing a particularly snappy item.

The high social profile was controversial, and by this time so was Kravis' LBO-making. Not only because of the size of his deals, but also because of the fees he charged. All leveraged buyout operators give themselves a free 20 percent equity stake, called the "carry," in each of their deals for finding the opportunity, and a negotiating fee for putting each deal together. In addition, KKR paid itself rich fees for "managing" each company, sitting on its board of directors, and orchestrating the breakups and refinancings necessary to get the money out. The percentage fee structure had been set in the mid-seventies, and as the deals got bigger, the numbers seemed increasingly out of line; it was one thing to pay a "negotiating" fee of one percent when the transaction was $100 million and quite another if it was $6 billion. Other LBO operators had long since cut fees or dropped them altogether, but not KKR. Robert Norris, investment manager for the $28 billion General Electric pension fund, even pulled his money out when Kravis refused to change his policy.

In some eyes, Kravis had become a creature of Mike Milken, joining the ranks of raiders like Carl Icahn, Ronald Perelman, and Norman Peltz, who owed their success to Drexel's junk bond machine. It wasn't that Kravis was directly doing Milken's bidding—or doing anything illegal—but he depended on Milken to raise the cash for his mega-deals and he had no choice but to play by Milken's rules. Kravis gave Milken five million Beatrice warrants as a kicker to help sell the Beatrice junk, only to discover that Milken had kept the warrants in his own account rather than use them to get a better price on the bonds. When Kravis bid for Safeway grocery stores in the summer of 1986, Milken, representing rival Dart Drug, negotiated a truce between the two bidders to forestall a bidding war, and then switched sides to raise the junk bond money to fund KKR's $4.1 billion purchase.

The Safeway buyout marked a milestone of another kind. Although Kravis and Roberts collected $60 million for assembling it, investors had reason to worry: leverage was a stunning 45 to 1, that is, for every $45 of debt there was but $1 of equity. Kohlberg, who was already troubled by the fees and the Milken connection, found that hard to swallow, and he gagged on Owens-Illinois. When KKR had first been approached by Owens-Illinois management, it had signed a confidentiality agreement promising not to make a hostile offer, but after the board rejected KKR's initial $55-a-share bid, Kravis wanted to do just that. He was sure he could force a deal by raising his price, the board's very public opposition notwithstanding. Kohlberg was horrified, but outvoted. As soon as the $3.6 billion transaction closed—leverage was a more modest ten to one—Kohlberg quit KKR and formed a small LBO partnership of his own. He told *The New York Times* that he would "stick with deals where reason prevails," but has refused comment since. Some watchers think that the split tolled the end of KKR's smart investing. "Kohlberg was the one who understood values," says a long-time associate. "Kravis was the one who understood raising money."

As if to prove that point, Kravis hit the road to raise $5.6 billion just weeks after Kohlberg left. Actually, he was raising $4 billion since the $1.6 billion still remaining in the 1986 partnership was rolled into the new fund as seed money. To the dismay of some investors, the new fund would be used not just for traditional buyouts, but also for "toehold" investments in potential targets, a concept that smacked of hostile raids. Following a difficult summer, the fund finally closed just after Labor Day.

One of Kravis's biggest selling points with investors had been the Beatrice aura, but by then Beatrice had gone distinctly off track. Don Kelly, Beatrice's chief executive, had auctioned off $4 billion of assets, about enough to pay down the acquisition debt, but the remaining pieces seemed totally unsalable, in part because of the towering "goodwill," an accounting liability that was enough to wipe out the earnings of any American buyer for the next twenty years. Which was why Don Kelly was doing his damnedest to get Ross Johnson interested in buying Beatrice's Wesson Oil subsidiary.

Kravis had thought about an RJR buyout even before Kelly called to say that he had been golfing with Johnson at Deepdale. Jeff Beck of Drexel had called several times to say that RJR might be available, and as early as May 1987 Kravis had asked his legal people to take a look. The only question was tobacco litigation, and Kravis was inclined to discount that. So when Kelly called to say that Johnson wanted to talk, Kravis quickly set a date, Monday, September 21, a little over a week away.

Coincidentally, several days before the dinner, Michael Douglas, Kravis's school buddy, had invited Kravis to the opening of the film, *Fatal Attraction*, and to the post-screening dinner at Tavern on the Green. Beck, also a friend of Douglas's, happened to be seated at Kravis's table. Kravis told Beck that Kelly had set up a dinner with Johnson. "What do you think?" Kravis asked.

"Well, I wouldn't have done it," said Beck, who had been the banker on the potential Esmark-Nabisco deal. "You can't get too specific with Johnson if Kelly is there. But I guess it can't hurt."

Whatever misgivings Beck had had about a meeting with both Johnson and Kelly, things went well. Johnson arrived bubbling about Premier, the new smokeless cigarette that RJR had just unveiled at a press conference the week before. He was sure that Premier was the answer to pressure from antismoking groups, and he was speeding up development so that the product would be ready for test market within a year. It worked like this, he told Kravis. Instead of burning tobacco like a conventional cigarette, Premier produced its "tobacco" flavor by heating a capsule containing glycerine and nicotine packed in a cigarette-shaped tube. Since there was no burning there was no offensive smoke; tar levels were super-low but there was still enough nicotine for a cigarette fix. Some problems remained, not the least of which was making the carbon tip flammable enough to light without a blowtorch.

Eventually the talk turned to leveraged buyouts. Kravis explained how a deal would work. Kravis made it clear that if push came to shove, KKR, as the majority equity owner, would call the shots.

"What price are we talking about?" asked Johnson.

Kravis didn't want to get too specific; talking about a price might be construed as having actually made an offer. But Johnson kept pressing and Kravis finally suggested a number in the high seventies.

"It has to be a number with an 'eight' in it," said Johnson.

"Thirty-eight?" suggested Kravis. "Forty-eight?"

Johnson laughed, and he said he would be back to Kravis soon. Kravis fully expected Johnson to say he was ready to do a deal. But when Johnson called Kelly back several days later, it was to say that he wasn't interested. He didn't like the idea of taking on so much debt.

Actually, Johnson had more or less made up his mind even before the dinner. The week before, on Tuesday, September 15, Johnson had met with Andy Sage and Frank Benevento at Nabisco's New York office, coincidentally at 9 West 57th Street, the same building as KKR, to talk about a buyout. Benevento had dusted off the studies he had done of the Drexel leveraged buyout in March and recomputed the numbers at a price of $90 a share in cash, the same 30 percent premium to market that Beck had chosen in his March 1987 buyout study.

Johnson flipped straight to the cash flow page. Even assuming the sale of all the food business, cash flow was negative for the first three years. That said it all. Johnson asked a few questions, but he quickly tossed the whole study aside. "I'm not going to start taking apart a company I took fifteen years to build," he said. Nor, echoing Kelly, did he particularly want to be that much richer than he already was. Johnson leaned back in his chair and began to wax philosophic. He talked about growing up a poor boy in Manitoba; he recalled thinking that when he was named president of GSW, he had succeeded beyond his wildest dreams. Now he earned more than $2 million a year and would retire on an annual pension of $770,000. The potential reward of an LBO wasn't worth the agony of getting there.

He did, however, want to do something about the stock price, which, although buoyed by the general market rise, remained depressed compared to stocks of other consumer products companies. Sage, who was elbow-deep in operations, suggested tightening manufacturing procedures. But Benevento interrupted to say that nothing on the manufacturing end was going to help; he suggested buying back the preferred, and Johnson volunteered that he was going to look at acquiring Cadbury Schweppes, the English candy- and mixer-maker. "We'll probably be sitting here in this same office doing this same strategic planning five years from now," Johnson said as the meeting broke up.

As it happened, a buyout probably could not have been done just then even if Johnson had agreed. Less than a month after the dinner came the first stock market crash since 1929. On October 19, 1987, the Dow Jones Industrial Average skidded 508 points in a single trading session, the largest one-day drop in history. That sent investors reeling and prompted a stampede to quality that effectively killed the junk bond market for almost six months. With no buyers for low-grade securities, many partially completed leveraged deals were suddenly on the rocks. The Thompson brothers, who had just bought two-thirds of Southland with a $4 billion bridge loan, couldn't entice investors to cough up financing to replace the bridge, and after twice sweetening the terms of their would-be permanent securities, withdrew the offer entirely. KKR, which was having similar problems with the $2 billion bridge it had used to buy Jim Walter, a Florida-based home builder, would surely have been unable to finance a giant RJR deal, even at a low post-crash price.

While Kravis scrambled to keep Jim Walter afloat, Johnson began to investigate yet another scheme for kicking up the price of RJR stock: a joint venture with a competing food company. A joint venture wouldn't trigger the same tax liabilities and good-will write-downs that an acquisition did; if each partner owned just 40 percent of the venture, neither would have to consolidate the debt on its balance sheet. Johnson called Pillsbury chairman William Spoor, who had just been pulled out of retirement to replace John M. Stafford, his failed successor, about teaming up. Spoor was vaguely interested, but the idea never got off the ground; Pillsbury would need shareholder approval to go ahead— Nabisco didn't, since the cookie and cracker units didn't constitute the bulk of RJR's total assets—and, given the management dis-array, asking for permission would have put the company on the auction block.

Johnson tried the idea on Quaker chairman William Smithburg, but Smithburg was decidedly cool, and so were Johnson's own financial people. When Benevento took a look at the idea in January, after Johnson had begun to put out feelers to partners, he was so dubious that he wrote what Johnson later referred to as the "stick it in your ear" memo, saying flatly that the idea was a loser. Johnson, ever willing to admit to a mistake, killed the plan as soon as he read that.

At about this time, rumors had begun to circulate that someone was contemplating a bid for RJR. Although Johnson thought that that might be a good thing, at least at the right price, James O. Welch Jr., an RJR vice-chairman and the head of Nabisco, was very worried, and he called Edward Robinson, the chief financial officer, to suggest that Robinson put together a "defensive LBO" that could be launched to counter a bid.

Robinson duly called Benevento and asked him to take a look. Benevento said he would, although what he was really interested in just then was something he called "Project GM," a restruc-turing that was based on the three stock system at General Mo-tors. Instead of paying all stockholders a dividend based on overall company earnings, GM paid holders of Class E and Class H stocks dividends based on the earnings of its Electronic Data Systems (EDS) and Hughes Aircraft subsidiaries respectively (ordinary shareholders got ordinary dividends). In GM's case, the three stock system had developed by chance as part of the negotiations to buy first EDS and then Hughes, but it had had the beneficial side-effect of increasing the total value of the stock. Class E traded at fifteen times earnings just like other computer service companies, Class H at an aerospace multiple of eighteen, and plain old GM at a plebeian multiple eight.

Benevento thought that the same logic could apply to RJR. In this case, all of the existing shares would be traded in for a package of one food share and one tobacco share paying dividends based on their respective earnings. The tobacco stock would continue to trade a multiple of nine, while the food stock would jump to the higher sixteen ratio where competitors like Sara Lee already traded. Of course, splitting the stock into two classes also raised embarrassing questions about why the two companies had merged in the first place, and might even suggest that the merger had failed.

Before Benevento got very far on the Project GM study—he never did get started on the defensive LBO—RJR received a buyout proposal, of sorts, from one C.D. Spangler, Jr., one of RJR's largest individual shareholders and the president of the University of North Carolina. Spangler claimed that he had talked to both his friend Richard Jenrette, chairman of Equitable Life, the nation's second largest insurance company, and the leveraged buyout department at Citibank about financing his $65-a-share offer, but when Johnson went to New York to investigate, it turned out that the money wasn't there. Spangler had apparently shown Citibank some confidential RJR financial information, but he had not asked for, much less obtained, a financing commitment.

The RJR executive committee turned the proposal down at a special meeting on March 1, but that was not the end of that. Spangler had been introduced to Johnson by Paul Sticht, and several board members were convinced that Sticht had put Spangler up to making the proposal and given him the information to show to Citibank, in order to get back at Johnson for forcing him out as chairman in September. If that were true, another RJR director, John Medlin, the chairman of First Wachovia, had also

been involved, since he had called Sticht to ask him to meet with
Spangler in the first place. Because he had reached mandatory
retirement age, Sticht was going off the board in May anyhow,
but if he hadn't been, Charlie Hugel, Johnson's friend and RJR's
chairman, would have had to ask him to leave.

Sticht's departure, in turn, precipitated another crisis, for Johnson's nomination to fill Sticht's seat was David J. Mahoney, the
former chairman of Norton Simon.

Mahoney was not the run-of-the-mill corporate leader. He was
infamous for his high-flying lifestyle, his movie star friends, and
his leveraged buyout attempts. Once considered a wunderkind
and marketing magician, Mahoney had been accused of misman-
aging Norton Simon, which boasted such indestructible brands as
Hunt tomato products and Avis rental cars, so that he could buy
it on the cheap. Although Mahoney had consistently denied any
such plans, he had in June 1983 proved his critics right by proposing to buy Norton Simon in a "management-led"—that is,
without a buyout group as a backer—LBO at just $29 a share,
fifty cents over market. Horrified, the Norton Simon directors
had put the company on the auction block, eventually selling to
Esmark for $952 million, $174 million more than Mahoney had
offered.

There were circles where Mahoney's marketing genius out-
shone that financial debacle, but the conservative RJR board
wasn't one of them. Although Johnson explained that he thought
it made sense to elect someone with packaged food experience,
Sticht opposed Mahoney and so did John Macomber, the former
chairman of Celanese chemicals and vocal Johnson critic. Given
the divisions already on the board, Johnson didn't want a director
who was not elected unanimously, and he withdrew Mahoney's
name.

Getting turned down on a director is a major defeat for a chief
executive, but Johnson was unperturbed. He quickly submitted
a second nomination, his friend Martin S. Davis, the chairman
of Gulf + Western, the publishing and movie-making conglomerate that would soon change its name to Paramount Communications. Although Davis was also controversial, he was not
infamous, and he was duly elected a director.

For all the activity, Johnson was still on square one as far as
the stock price was concerned. He had not yet solved the problem

that Drexel had raised a year and a half before: investors' failure to properly value RJR's food assets. If anything, the situation was worse. RJR's share price had dropped to $53.50 during the October crash, down from a high of $71⅞, and although the market had long since revived, RJR remained stagnant at $58 a share.

And that attracted attention, from a buyer more credible than C.D. Spangler. In January, Dan Lufkin, a co-founder of Donaldson, Lufkin & Jenrette, and former partner of Spangler's friend Dick Jenrette, sent a memo to his sometime partners Jay Pritzker, Harry Gray, and Melvyn Klein suggesting that the three look at a leveraged buyout of RJR. According to Lufkin's analysis, RJR's assets were worth enough to support a loan of $84 a share, a substantial premium to market.

Jay Pritzker was one of the few people in the world who could have bought RJR on his own. With a Chicago-based family empire valued at well over $3 billion, Pritzker had plenty of money for almost any acquisition. Although Pritzker had traditionally done small deals, turning a motley collection of near-bankrupt companies like Hyatt Hotels and Ticketmaster into an empire, he had recently toyed with the idea of something larger. After buying Braniff Airways out of bankruptcy for $70 million in 1984, he had approached Pan American World Airways, Western Union, and ITT. Even those megabuck proposals, none of which had happened, had been turnarounds. RJR was the first healthy company he had seriously considered.

It would also be the first company Klein and Gray bought as a partnership. Klein, a former Donaldson, Lufkin & Jenrette official and long-time Pritzker adviser, and Gray, who had helped pioneer the hostile takeover as chairman of United Technologies, were just beginning to raise a $550 million leveraged buyout fund, with Jay Pritzker's Hyatt Enterprises as the primary investor.

What made RJR so attractive to Pritzker and his associates was not just that it was so grossly undervalued or that its size would preclude most potential buyers from competing. Lufkin had also dreamt up a new financing wrinkle: RJR could raise money by selling interests in trademark participations. The idea was similar to the master limited partnership that Beck had been pushing to

Johnson, but instead of selling interests in tobacco assets, RJR would sell profit shares in its key brand names: Oreo, Ritz, and Camel. It wasn't an untested idea: Listerine had already successfully sold trademark shares in Europe. Like the master limited partnership, the trademark partnership also had tax advantages, although they were sufficiently arcane as to be beyond the grasp of most investors. Lufkin was sure that trademark participations would be an effective way to raise money; the only question was whether investors would be willing to buy billions of dollars worth of units on the first go-round.

So Klein and Gray began to put out feelers to RJR. Gray, an old friend of Paul Sticht, called to see what Sticht thought about the company and about Ross Johnson; Sticht was understandably cool. Klein called Ira Harris, Johnson's long-time investment banker who had recently left Salomon Brothers for Lazard Frères, a small investment bank famous for its takeover work and for its senior financial guru, Felix Rohatyn. "Ross won't do it," said Harris. "I've suggested it. Ross doesn't like leverage."

Klein was still pondering the RJR idea a couple of weeks later when he met his old friend Henry Kravis for breakfast at KKR in New York. Klein and Kravis had met in the early seventies when they were both junior bankers struggling to the top, and they had gotten on so well that Kravis had invited Klein to join KKR when it was formed in 1976. Klein had refused only because he had just promised his fiancée that they would settle in her hometown, Corpus Christi, Texas, which seemed a bit out of the way if he wanted to work for a partnership based in New York and San Francisco. Klein didn't know that Kravis had talked to Johnson about an LBO in the fall, but he thought that KKR might be interested in teaming up on it if Pritzker decided to make a bid.

Kravis wasn't. If he did an RJR deal he wanted to do it himself. But in any event, financing an RJR LBO was a moot point. "I had dinner with Ross in September," said Kravis. "He's not interested."

Two people that Klein knew and trusted had told him that an RJR buyout was a non-starter, so he dropped the idea. Instead, he began to look at Federated Department Stores, then caught in a bidding war between Campeau, the scrappy, Toronto-based builder, and the upstanding Macy's store chain, Federated's chosen white knight.

At about the time Klein met with Kravis, Johnson had decided that a stock buy-back was the answer to the sagging share price; with fewer shares outstanding, each was worth more—and logically the price would rise. It didn't. Although Johnson bought twenty million shares for $53.50 each, a total of $1 billion, the stock price stayed put.

That failure behind him, Johnson considered other options.

Maybe an acquisition was the answer. Johnson called Eric Gleacher, the head of the merger department at Morgan Stanley. As Lehman's M&A chief, Gleacher had represented Johnson on both the Standard Brands–Nabisco and Nabisco Brands–RJ Reynolds deals, and Johnson respected him. Gleacher looked at several food companies: Kraft and Sara Lee, among them. But when Gleacher came back to say that Sara Lee was a better and Kraft a worse fit, Johnson rejected the acquisition idea altogether. He thought that the price tags were too high.

Maybe teaming up with another tobacco company overseas was the answer. Foreign antitrust laws are much weaker than American ones and it was conceivable that RJR could team up with giant Philip Morris, saving them both hundreds of millions in advertising costs to compete against each other. Ed Robinson, the chief financial officer, cranked up some numbers, and Johnson called Philip Morris chairman Hamish Maxwell, who was lukewarm, given the potential antitrust problem.

Benevento had by now finished his Project GM study and concluded that it would work. According to his analysis, splitting the stock into two pieces might increase its value to as much as $69 a share. But when Benevento brought the matter up with Johnson, Johnson said that he was putting everything on hold. Two important things were about to happen that seemed likely to boost the value of the stock, and Johnson didn't want to try any more financial maneuvering until he saw how things worked out. First, a key smoking-death case, brought by one Antonio Cipollone against Liggett & Myers, maker of Chesterfield and L&M, the brands his pack-a-day wife Rose had smoked for 42 years before her death of lung cancer in 1984, would be decided by a New Jersey jury in May. In September, Premier, the smokeless cigarette, would be tested in Phoenix, St. Louis, and Tucson. Maybe the outlook for Reynolds was about to change.

Certainly Reynolds, and the other cigarette makers, could use some help. It had been an abysmal spring. Antismoking activists had scored several important victories. After convincing a number of states, including California, the largest cigarette market in the country, to guarantee the "right" to smokeless air by restricting smoking in public places and private restaurants and lounges, New York had passed an office smoking law so draconian that it had been declared unconstitutional; a weakened version, which prohibited smoking except in the confines of a private office or designated smoking areas, was scheduled to go into effect in April. The federal government had jumped into the act by totally barring smoking on airline flights under two hours long. Johnson made headlines when he yanked Nabisco's $84 million advertising account from Saatchi & Saatchi a few days later. Saatchi had developed an ad for Northwest Airlines that showed passengers cheering Northwest's even more stringent, absolute no-smoking ban.

Although Premier was supposed to address those trends, the innovative cigarette had problems of its own, not the least of which was marketing. The RJR lawyers insisted that the thing couldn't be billed as a "safe" cigarette because that implied that other cigarettes weren't safe. "Clean," the word that the lawyers suggested as an alternative, just didn't have the right ring. To make matters worse, Premier also took some getting used to. Since it didn't burn or produce ash, it didn't seem very cigarette-like to pack-a-day users; confused trial smokers kept trying to tap it in an ash tray and they were startled when the apparently unburned tube suddenly fizzled out. The fiberglass cap on the end smelled like smoldering plastic for the few seconds that it took to burn and the lighting problem still hadn't been fully solved; although the cigarette was somewhat more flammable than the earlier version, it still couldn't be lit with a match.

The Cipollone decision, at least, was good news. Although Antonio had won, the "victory" was clearly just what the tobacco companies had hoped for. The jury had ruled that Rose's smoking was 80 percent her own responsibility, and it had awarded her widower just $400,000. The $200,000 portion of that, which was due the lawyers under the contingency agreement, hardly made a dent in the $1.2 million they claimed they had spent to prepare the case. Surely, the $1 million loss would discourage rather than encourage a stampede of similar cases.

In mid-June, not long after the Cipollone verdict was announced, the rumor that RJR was a takeover target mysteriously resurfaced. That got Jim Welch excited again, and Ed Robinson again called Benevento about the defensive LBO. It seemed obvious that the $4 billion or so in mezzanine finance that RJR would need would come from a Drexel junk offering. The only question was where the equity would come from, and Benevento suggested that Johnson make some calls to see who might be willing to put up the cash quickly if the company came under attack.

By this time, Benevento and Sage had concluded that RJR didn't want to do its deal with KKR, or any other leveraged buyout specialist. Bringing in KKR would mean ceding board control and the 20 percent "carry." Instead, they believed, Johnson could keep control—and a bigger chunk of profits—by putting together the equity and mezzanine money himself.

They talked briefly about asking Drexel if it would make the equity commitment, since Drexel had already done so much work on the master limited partnership, but decided against it. In early June, the Securities and Exchange Commission had approved market manipulation charges against Drexel but, at the request of U.S. Attorney Rudolph Giuliani, it had agreed to delay filing them until the Justice Department's criminal investigation was complete. According to another rumor mill, Giuliani was planning to charge Drexel with "racketeering," and under the provisions of the Racketeer Influenced and Corrupt Organizations (RICO) law, the government would be authorized to seize Drexel's assets, including any RJR stake as soon as the papers were filed. Under the circumstances, a Drexel equity commitment didn't make much sense.

Sage and Benevento were divided on whom to ask as a second choice, but from Johnson's perspective, that was obvious: Shearson Lehman Hutton. Although not a first-tier investment bank by any stretch of the imagination, Shearson was well capitalized and eager for deals. Besides, Shearson was 60 percent–owned by American Express, the company headed by Johnson's good friend Jim Robinson—and a potential mezzanine investor. Although

Johnson wasn't exactly best buddies with Shearson chairman Peter Cohen, he had, briefly, been a director of Shearson as a favor to Robinson.

Johnson and Cohen were both directors of American Express and Johnson would be seeing Cohen at the next American Express board meeting in New York on Monday, July 25. Johnson would ask him about equity then.

CHAPTER 3

Oh, to Be a Merchant Banker

July 25 to October 6

If o-f-f-i-c-e-s-i-z-e spells success, Shearson chairman Peter Cohen wins the Wall Street sweepstakes hands down. Not only is his office big enough to hold two or three of his competitors', it is also luxurious, in a nouveau riche sort of way. The carpet is plush, the fake antiques of the best quality, and the ersatz prints of old New York look impressive from a distance. Down the hall is Wall Street's largest boardroom (conceivably the world's), so bedecked with rich paneling, fancy electronics—audio scramblers for protection against laser directional microphones—and a custom-made nineteen-foot circular table that cost $2.7 million to complete.

Success and its trappings are important to Cohen, who spent much of his business career in the shadow of his mentors. So when Shearson moved from its tacky quarters in the World Trade Center to the sparkling new World Financial Center in 1986, Cohen made sure that the new offices reflected what he had achieved. Even his detractors conceded that that was something. He had transformed Shearson Loeb Rhodes from a scrappy, tightfisted brokerage house into Shearson Lehman Hutton, powerhouse investment bank, or at least an aspiring one, by sheer force of personality.

Unlike most organization builders, Cohen has neither charm nor charisma. Associates refer to him, rather, as tough, hard-driving, and street-smart. Supercompetitive and untactful, Cohen does and says precisely what he thinks. He once described Dillon Read to a magazine reporter as a "peanut" and in the same interview mused that Merrill Lynch had passed from raging bull brokerage leader to lumbering has-been. On occasion he's even mean-spirited. Certainly graciousness is not his strong suit. After losing confidence in his merchant banking chief Peter Salomon during the summer of 1988, Cohen proceeded to humiliate him by not only keeping him off the team overseeing Shearson's bid for RJR, the largest merchant banking deal ever, but also neglecting to inform him that it was in the works. While Cohen personally quarterbacked RJR, Salomon, who had read about the bid in the newspaper, attended baseball camp in Florida. Salomon had the good grace to wait until the battle was over to resign.

Cohen does have his supporters: Jim Robinson, his boss and a usually astute critic, insists that Cohen's image problems stem from the fact that he shook Wall Street to the core. "Peter Cohen is the best manager of a large securities company in the industry, bar none," Robinson insists, Shearson's recent poor results notwithstanding. Cohen's true passion is not people but numbers, and not just the numbers on his paycheck. He passes time with Shearson president Jeffrey Lane, playing their private version of trivial pursuit: one throws out a number, $31.4 million, for example, and the other guesses what it represents, in this case Shearson's losses on tin contracts in 1986.

To friends, Cohen is bright, loyal, considerate, and even, on occasion, funny. Amid the finery in his office are prominently displayed paintings and pottery by his children, Lauren, seventeen, and Andy, twelve. At a charity auction in early 1988, Cohen paid $3,000 for a one-hour session with Ruth Westheimer, the sex therapist, and gave it to his friend Thomas Strauss, president of Salomon Brothers. For months afterward, Cohen tried to find out whether Strauss had had his session. Strauss wouldn't tell him and neither would Westheimer, claiming client confidentiality. It wasn't that he wanted to know about Strauss's sex life, Cohen insisted, but his $3,000; if Strauss hadn't gotten any advice, then Cohen deserved his money back.

* * *

Peter Cohen, forty-two, grew up in distinctly unposh Rockville Centre, Long Island. His father Sidney, the founder of the Andover Togs children's clothing company, believed you learned on the job and put his sons to work assembling packing boxes before they were teenagers. Although he was adept with corrugated cardboard, young Peter did not show much in the way of ambition. He sloughed off at school, content with mediocre grades, and earned pocket money with an occasional blue collar job—while at Ohio State he worked as a baggage handler for Mohawk Airlines—certain that a job awaited at Andover Togs after he graduated. His biggest worry was not his future but his height. At five foot six, he was sure that people wouldn't take him seriously. His mother Florence reminded her son that plenty of short people had earned respect, from Fiorello LaGuardia on down.

Sid Cohen wasn't pleased with his son's attitude and told young Peter that there would be no job at Andover Togs unless he obtained a business school degree. Cohen was rejected by Harvard, but squeaked into Columbia where, to the great annoyance of his classmate, Jeff Lane, he rarely showed up in class and didn't bother with a shave or sports coat when he did. (Cohen didn't think much of Lane either; he has since described him as "the guy with the plastic thing in his pocket to hold his pens.") After he graduated, Dad offered him $100 a week at Andover Togs. That being beneath the dignity of an MBA, Cohen headed to Wall Street instead, first as a $12,000 a year analyst at Reynolds & Co., later at CBWL–Hayden Stone, the firm that eventually became Shearson. "I wouldn't hire him," said Jeff Lane when his boss at Hayden Stone asked about Cohen. "He's a wise-ass."

In 1974, Sanford Weill, one of CBWL's co-founders and by then chairman of Hayden Stone, noticed how many fifteen-hour days Cohen worked and plucked him from research to be his executive assistant. Cohen quickly became chief hatchet-man; as charismatic Weill bought sick brokerage after sick brokerage, Cohen cleaned up the mess, mercilessly firing unnecessary employees and integrating the newcomer's confused back office into the Hayden Stone computer system. Cohen lost self-confidence only once: in 1978, he quit Shearson to work for Edmond Safra, the secretive Lebanese-born investor who owns Republic National

Bank. "I had to find out if I was just a Sandy Weill creation," he told *BusinessWeek* at the time.

Whatever he found out, Cohen returned to Shearson a year later, and he was again Weill's right-hand man when Weill sold Shearson to American Express for $915 million in 1981. Not long after that, Cohen got the power and prestige that he had been waiting for. Weill was promoted to president of American Express and Cohen ascended to the top spot at Shearson. In an unusual public display of wit, Cohen showed up at the critical board meeting with a brown paper bag containing a crown and sceptre for Weill and a gigantic pair of wing-tips for himself, a reminder of just how big were the shoes he had to fill.

There are those who believe he never did. Certainly he never attained Weill's stature as an industry leader. At first Cohen continued Weill's policy of growth, buying Robinson Humphrey, Foster & Marshall and, in 1985, Lehman Brothers, Kuhn Loeb. Unfortunately, neither of the mega-deals—Lehman and the $550 million purchase of Edmond Safra's Geneva-based Trade Development Bank that Cohen negotiated for American Express— could be counted a success. Safra left AmEx after just two years, taking many of his clients with him. By then, most of the Lehman partners had long since departed.

The Lehman exodus was particularly distressing. Brokerage companies fall at the bottom of the Wall Street hierarchy—and Shearson at the bottom of the brokers—and investment banks at the top. To get the respect that he wanted, Cohen had to make Shearson an investment bank, and buying Lehman, a premier, if ego-torn, investment bank, had been intended to do that. He had not anticipated the disdain he would get from the Lehman partners, or that snowballing defections would bring out his vindictive worst. Cohen even sued Michael Schmertzler, Lehman's chief financial officer, when he fled Shearson for Morgan Stanley (Cohen lost). Within two years of the merger, most of the senior Lehman partners had left, and those who remained were "on mental holiday," as one put it, looking for opportunities anywhere else.

In an attempt to increase the deal flow, Cohen, in 1986, hired Daniel Good, a leveraged buyout expert who had masterminded such innovative deals as Ted Turner's cashless $5 billion bid for

CBS. That only exacerbated tensions with what few Lehman bankers remained: Good's client list included such corporate raiders as Paul Bilzerian and Asher Edelman "who specialize in launching raids against the companies we wanted as our clients," as one exasperated Lehman executive put it.

The failure of the Lehman merger didn't dampen Cohen's goals of making Shearson the most powerful house on Wall Street. He could always attract business if he had bounteous capital and when Jim Robinson balked at writing a check on American Express's account, Cohen went to Japan, selling a 13 percent block to Nippon Life for $508 million, or $39.10 a share. Several months later, he unloaded another 18 percent on the public for $34 a share. At the time, Cohen explained that the reason for the public offering was to validate the Nippon price; in fact, it only proved that Nippon had overpaid. Whatever its other benefits, that transaction made Cohen an overnight millionaire: his 250,000 Shearson shares were suddenly worth a liquid $8.5 million. (In an attempt to make his employees millionaires too, Cohen had rolled all of the cash in Shearson's generous incentive bonus plan into Shearson stock; unfortunately the shares sank like a rock from the day they were issued, eventually cutting hard-earned past bonuses by more than a third.)

About the time he took Shearson public, Cohen's tight-fisted approach to office decor gave way to conspicuous consumerism. He had once caused an uproar at Lehman by announcing that he would save money by removing the free cigars from the partners' dining room; now there were not only cigars but "SL" engraved silver and a new set of Wedgwood china. It was clearly a richness based on rank. Even as Cohen was ordering a new Gulfstream III jet for executive officers, he was reminding his bread-and-butter employees to cut back on taxi use and to keep photocopying to a minimum.

It was from his newly exalted seat that Cohen launched his bid for E. F. Hutton in November 1987. The price had been knocked down to a bargain basement $29.25 a share by the October 19 stock market crash. Shearson had the money to pay, but the remaining bankers found the fact of the acquisition deeply troubling. The only way that buying Hutton could make any sense was if individual investors rushed back into the market, bucking a seemingly inexorable trend toward institutional investing. As if to prove the point, brokerage earnings had shriveled in the fourth quarter of 1987, leaving Shearson, the industry's highest fixed-cost player, with hemorrhaging losses. Income for the year was a puny $101 million, compared to $341 million in 1986.

And that made Cohen even more eager to snap up some of the generous profits that competing "merchant banks" like First Boston and Morgan Stanley were racking up on bridge loans, junk bond underwritings, and committing their own capital to deals. Cohen named M&A chief Peter Salomon head of merchant banking and boasted on the cocktail circuit of his new prowess. Henry Kravis jocularly remarked that he didn't want to see Shearson interfering in his deals, which Cohen took as an acknowledgment that Shearson had arrived: Shearson and KKR had a quid pro quo, he thought Kravis was saying: Shearson would not interfere in KKR's deals and KKR would not interfere in Shearson's. Nice as that sounded, it was not what Kravis had meant; what he thought he had told Cohen was that KKR was not going to pay anyone to be its adviser who also competed for its deals.

Cohen pressed on. In March 1988, he announced his first merchant banking initiative, a joint $1.85 billion hostile bid for Koppers, the Pittsburgh-based chemical and cement company, with Beazer plc, a British builder and Shearson client. Cohen insisted that what he was doing was no different from any other merchant banking deal (in truth, it was the first hostile), but Koppers nonetheless lashed back. In its most stinging move, the company invited national television crews to cover their "You can leave home without it" American Express card cutting-up ceremony at Koppers headquarters. Adding insult to injury, Pennsylvania State treasurer G. Davis Greene Jr., with a little prompting from his Pittsburgh friends, sent Cohen a letter accusing Shearson of untrammeled greed and announcing that Pennsylvania, then a Shearson commercial paper and muni-bond client, was moving all its business elsewhere.

Although Shearson and Beazer eventually won control of Koppers, the fallout was immediate. Steve Waters, the highly respected co-head of the M&A department, resigned immediately; already at odds with Cohen over merger policy, he had found out about the Koppers bid only when he read it on the wire and he knew once and for all that he and Cohen had an irreconcilably different idea of what was ethical in the business. Image-conscious

AmEx chairman Jim Robinson was livid. AmEx's name, its most valuable asset, had been dragged through the mud, something, Robinson made clear, that was not going to happen again. There would be no more hostile deals, he told Cohen, no more representing the sort of questionable clients like Bilzerian and Edelman.

That left Cohen in a bind. He had promised his restive bankers that he would make up for their anemic 1987 bonuses with generous bonuses in 1988, but with brokerage business in the doldrums and the pipeline deal now partially blocked, there seemed no way to do that.

So he was thrilled when Ross Johnson took him aside after the AmEx July board meeting to ask about Shearson's willingness to commit to a defensive LBO. Surely that was just the sort of leveraged buyout that Robinson, Johnson's closest personal friend, would want Shearson to be doing. And one that would put Shearson on the buyout map. How could anyone ignore the firm that had financed the largest LBO in history?

Of course, Johnson hadn't initially asked Cohen to actually do an LBO, just to make an assessment of how much equity Shearson could put in, and he had made the heinous suggestion that Drexel, not Shearson, would be raising the debt. Cohen assured Johnson that Shearson could do anything Drexel could do, and although that was perhaps farfetched, Johnson didn't challenge him. The question was hypothetical anyhow.

After the first conversation, Cohen wasn't directly involved in the project. The actual analysis fell to J. Tomilson Hill, the head of the mergers and acquisitions department. Hill was something of a maverick in the takeover arena. He was known for bidding low and bargaining up, and for aggressively pumping his story to the press. He had also been criticized for shooting from the hip, ignoring details that could sometimes kill a deal.

Meantime, Johnson was working on something else. He had decided to give the joint venture idea one last whirl, the "stick it in your ear" memo notwithstanding. In early August, he called Hamish Maxwell of Philip Morris yet again. Philip Morris, which had bought General Foods in 1985, had the same problem that RJR did: it traded at a tobacco multiple although a large portion of earnings were from food, and Johnson thought that Maxwell

would therefore be particularly interested in a deal that promised
to draw attention to food. True to form, Johnson volunteered to
run the merged Nabisco–General Foods unit, and although Maxwell didn't quite reject the idea out of hand, he was skeptical that
it would do much for the stock price.

"What have you got to lose?" countered Johnson. "It couldn't
make things worse."

Maybe not, but Maxwell decided to pass.

At about this time, Johnson was starting to worry that the
change in attitude about cigarettes that he had hoped would buoy
the stock price didn't seem to be happening. Instead of rising in
the wake of the Cipollone ruling, the stock had plummeted. Apparently investors believed the Cipollone lawyers when they announced that they had learned so much in the course of the case
that the $1 million loss would not dampen but speed further cases.
So by mid-August, Johnson was faced with a curious phenomenon. Although RJR stock was clearly less risky than it had been
in May, it was also cheaper. To a potential bidder, indeed, RJR
looked alluringly cheap.

Which was very much on Johnson's mind when he left Atlanta
for two weeks at the Castle Pines golf resort outside Denver.
Partly it was a vacation. Partly it was to entertain grocery store
buyers. He wined and dined and golfed and did his own "market"
test of Premier, distributing sample boxes to his friends for a trial
smoke. The response was unanimous: on top of all the other
technical problems, the taste was nauseating. The only thing it
would be good for was helping you quit.

Premier had been Johnson's last hope for getting the stock price
up. If, after everything else that hadn't worked, the smokeless
cigarette was about to fail, then Johnson had run out of options.
The conclusion seemed obvious: if there was no way to overcome
the tobacco stigma among public investors, then the Reynolds
Tobacco company—and all tobacco companies—should be privately owned. However much he hated the idea of leveraging up,
Johnson had no choice. He would have to give a leveraged buyout
serious thought.

Johnson called Andy Sage at his ranch in Jackson, Wyoming,
and asked him to come to Castle Pines for his final Colorado
weekend to talk. Sage did, and although he was skeptical that
Johnson would actually go through with a buyout given his long-

standing antipathy toward debt, he pointed out that if this was the course that Johnson wanted to take, he had to make his views about Shearson's role clear from the start. Johnson's buyout would be a *management* buyout, not a Shearson buyout. Shearson's job was simply to raise equity for a fee, just as Drexel would raise the junk for a fee. Johnson would control the board; Johnson would control the company; Johnson would sell what assets needed to be sold without interference from Shearson. Only Johnson really knew the business; only he would be able to negotiate the best prices.

Tuesday, September 6, the day after Labor Day, at a meeting with Hill at Shearson headquarters at the World Financial Center in New York, Sage announced that there had been a slight change in plans. Johnson had decided that he might be willing to propose a leveraged buyout if that was indeed the best financial alternative. So Shearson was to go back to the drawing board. To help with that evaluation, Sage offered to turn over to Shearson all of the various studies that had been sent in by investment bankers over the years.

Several days later, those arrived in several packing cartons. They ran the gamut, everything from the Drexel MLP studies to a Dillon Read proposal for a buyout financed by a warrant offering to shareholders, to an analysis by former Standard Brands president Reuben Gutoff suggesting that the company would go for more than $100 a share in a bidding war.

Johnson had missed the September 6 meeting in New York for a meeting in London, but as it turned out, he didn't attend that either. When he arrived at the Inn on the Park, there was a message to call the States and after he did, he headed right back to the airport to catch the Concorde to New York. His twenty-six-year-old son Bruce was in critical condition at a Westchester hospital. While driving home on the Saw Mill River Parkway the night before, Bruce's car had swerved into the embankment, crushing his head. It wasn't clear what time the accident had occurred, but the doctors guessed it had been at least three hours before another driver reported the crash. The prognosis wasn't good.

For the next week, Johnson spent most of his time at his son's bedside. Bruce did not come out of the coma but his condition did seem to improve, and by Monday, September 12, he seemed stable enough that Johnson was willing to leave the hospital to talk to Sage and Benevento about what Shearson was doing. However esoteric the financial presentations were, they would provide a welcome relief from the agony of the sickroom.

When Johnson got to Nabisco's New York office at 9 West 57th Street at two o'clock in the afternoon, Sage explained that Shearson would be recommending an LBO at the final presentation the next day. Johnson would have to make some kind of decision about either going ahead or trying to come up with yet another alternative.

"If we're going to think about this, I've got to get comfortable with the numbers," said Johnson. He closed the door to the office, rolled up his shirt-sleeves and sat down with Benevento.

They worked through the cash flow, keying the buyout numbers to the numbers in the RJR monthly report. As an operating executive, Johnson was most concerned about what the price level and the corresponding debt meant in terms of the day-to-day functioning of the company. Every $1 a share he paid translated into $10 million a day of debt service. Where you ended up, of course, depended on how much you got for selling assets. Johnson wrote his own estimates for what it would bring on the auction block next to the name of each food unit listed in the monthly book. Those guesses totalled $11.8 billion. Johnson also guessed that he could get $1.5 billion for the international tobacco company, bringing the total for divisions to be sold to $13.3 billion. Later, Shearson used that estimate as its worst-case scenario.

After three hours, Johnson finally felt comfortable. He might ultimately decide not to do an LBO, but he truly understood what Shearson was talking about.

Shearson did, indeed, recommend a buyout at the Tuesday meeting.

Sage said that Johnson was only interested on his own terms: control of the board and of corporate transactions.

Cohen didn't flinch; indeed, he seemed to regard giving the reins to Johnson as an advantage. The only thing he didn't like was Sage's suggestion that Shearson talk to Drexel about the junk. Cohen had said back in July that he didn't think Drexel needed to be involved, and he hadn't changed his position since.

So they agreed that Hill would buckle down with his team to

prepare a thorough analysis by early October. That wasn't a lot of time, but Johnson wanted to be able to say something to the directors at RJR's October 20 board meeting. With Thanksgiving and Christmas coming, that would be the only meeting until 1989 at which the directors had the luxury of just kicking around an idea. The last thing Johnson wanted to do was make the board feel rushed.

So, after the meeting, Johnson called his friend Charlie Hugel, chief executive of Combustion Engineering and also chairman of RJR. "We're going to do a buyout," he said.

"Why?" asked Hugel.

"The market doesn't properly value tobacco," said Johnson. And besides, he and the other members of his group were going to make a lot of money fast.

"That's dumb," said Hugel. "It's dumb for you personally and it's bad for the company." Johnson wouldn't be able to run RJR in the way he was accustomed; there would be no airplanes, no golf tournaments, no time to try new things; the focus would be debt, debt, debt. Worst of all, a buyout meant taking the company apart. Hugel believed that putting RJR together had made sense and that putting the pieces on the auction block now was the height of stupidity.

After a long talk, Johnson said that he agreed. He called Sage to say that he had changed his mind. The LBO was dead.

By mid-September, a leveraged buyout of RJR was far from Henry Kravis's mind. He had his hands full trying to buy two mega-companies simultaneously, Macmillan publishing and Kroger grocery stores, and with the first bad press he had gotten in his fifteen years as an acquirer.

Actually, things had gone quite as intended for several months. Kravis had picked up a 4.9 percent toehold in Texaco, the ineptly run oil giant then under siege by Carl Icahn, in hopes that management would invite him in as a white knight. Instead, president James Kinnear announced that Kravis's investment signaled confidence in his team. Forced to choose between bad management and backing a raider, Kravis dropped out. Weeks later, he almost didn't get Duracell, the battery company being auctioned off by Kraft foods, because Duracell management worried that his plan was so highly leveraged that the company would quickly go belly-up. Kravis upped his offer by throwing in another $150 million of equity. That did the trick, although watchers noted that the price was at least $150 million too high. Be that as it may, investors had reason to be skeptical: according to KKR's own estimates, the return would be just 28 percent a year if everything went right, well below the 60 percent best case that buyout operators usually shoot for.

The Macmillan saga had begun even before the ink was dry on Duracell when Robert Bass, a Texas investor and 10 percent holder, had put the company in play by making a tender offer to protect against a rumored LBO at a low price. Macmillan management had responded with a complicated "restructuring" that was quickly struck down by a Delaware court as unfair to shareholders, since it left the company's most valuable asset, its electronic information unit, in the hands of management. Robert Maxwell, an aggressive Brit, had entered the fray in August, and Kravis had joined the battle shortly after that, as a white knight.

Maxwell had continued to bid after a KKR merger agreement was signed, and the board had been forced to nix the deal and put the company on the auction block. KKR had won that round too, although Maxwell had hauled them back to court charging that Bruce Wasserstein, the investment banker who had run the auction (that he had run the auction at all was somewhat peculiar since he was representing management, not the board) had unfairly tipped off Kravis by telling him he needed to raise his bid. Although the judge had criticized Wasserstein for rigging the auction, he had let the deal stand, given the small difference between Maxwell's and Kravis's price. Maxwell raised his bid again, and appealed. A second hearing had been scheduled for November 2.

On September 20, a week before the first Macmillan decision and twenty-four hours after the scrappy Haft family had launched a $55-a-share raid on Kroger, the Cincinnati-based grocery chain, George Roberts had decided to step in. After Kroger chairman Lyle Everingham refused his phone call, Roberts sent a letter offering to buy the company for $58.50 a share.

Although Roberts claimed that the offer was intended as friendly, the Kroger board didn't see it that way, and for the first time since KKR had been formed, Kravis and Roberts found themselves in an uncomfortable spotlight. Should state pension funds be backing raiders?, articles asked again and again, painting Kravis with the same brush as greenmailers Saul Steinberg and Carl Icahn. Roberts had further riled management with a second unsolicited letter upping the ante to $61 a share. "Friendly, bullshit," said one Kroger adviser. "Kravis made a public offer and he raised it twice. He did everything except tender, and we don't understand why he didn't do that."

The second letter had just gone out when Jeff Beck of Drexel called Kravis to schedule a meeting. When the two sat down at KKR late in the afternoon on October 3rd, Rosh Hoshannah eve, Beck told Kravis that it was time to get aggressive about RJR. Although Beck hadn't said so to Kravis, he was pushing a move on RJR because he had begun to sense that Johnson was doing something on his own. For two years now, Beck had been talking to Johnson regularly. Johnson had always been prompt to return Beck's phone calls. Suddenly Johnson wasn't. In fact, he didn't return them at all. Jim Welch, the vice-chairman and Nabisco chief did, and Welch gave only vague answers to Beck's pointed questions about why Johnson wasn't pursuing a leveraged buyout.

At the meeting in Kravis's office, Beck warned Kravis that Johnson would want to keep control even after the company went private.

"No," said Kravis. "He can't do that. Not if we buy the company."

"Well, maybe there's some way to structure the deal so that he has a majority of the directors," said Beck.

"No," said Kravis. "We have to have control of the board."

Beck called back a couple of days later to say that Johnson, through Welch, had agreed to meet. Kravis gave him two dates he was free in late October, and Beck said that he'd be back in a couple of days with a firm appointment.

Jeff Beck wasn't the only one who had gotten wind of goings-on at RJR. So had Steve Waters, a merger partner at Morgan Stanley, and the former co-head of M&A at Shearson Lehman. It wasn't that Waters had talked to any of his former Shearson colleagues. He just knew Johnson.

Until he quit in March, Waters had been Johnson's contact at Shearson. Waters had been part of the Lehman Brothers team that negotiated the sale of Standard Brands to Nabisco and he had been the top adviser on the sale of Nabisco Brands to RJR. More recently, he had looked at various acquisition projects for Johnson at RJR Nabisco, although none had panned out.

After Waters left Shearson in frustration over Cohen's policies, Johnson remained friendly. He had called Waters the afternoon he resigned to offer him a desk and telephone at Nabisco's New York office. Although Waters had turned him down, since allying himself with a client didn't seem like a good idea, Johnson had told Waters to let him know if he had any ideas for RJR. "If you say it's important, I'll always return your call," said Johnson.

Johnson had kept his word. In early June, after Waters had landed at Morgan Stanley, the elite investment bank where his one-time Lehman Brothers boss Eric Gleacher was now head of M&A, Waters had called Johnson and Johnson had given him an assignment, to look for acquisition opportunities in Europe. (In the spring, of course, Gleacher had looked at several domestic acquisitions for Johnson.) During the summer, Waters had become convinced that Johnson wasn't a buyer at all but a seller, and he asked Morgan Stanley merchant banking group to look at the possibility of an RJR leveraged buyout. Morgan's analysis showed that at a price of $85 to $90 a share the returns on an LBO investment were extremely attractive, but the firm nonetheless decided not to make a proposal: Morgan Stanley didn't want to own a tobacco company.

By the end of the summer, Johnson was suddenly not available to meet with executives from companies that he'd asked Waters to talk to. Johnson's secretary Betty called to cancel a meeting with Waters himself; when Waters's secretary Debbie had tried to reschedule, Betty refused. Johnson was tied up for three weeks, she said. She'd call later.

That might not have piqued Waters's interest were it not for a curious coincidence. Waters happened to be as close to Henry Kravis as he was to Johnson. He had worked extensively with Kravis at Shearson Lehman, selling him Jim Walter and Stop & Shop and helping him to sell the Beatrice bottled-water unit to Perrier. The day after he left Shearson, Waters had breakfast with Kravis to talk through his alternatives. Kravis later called the heads of several Wall Street firms to pave the way for a Waters interview and talked to him about offers as they were made. When Waters landed at Morgan Stanley, Kravis shifted some of his business there.

Unlike Beck, Waters hadn't been thinking of teaming up KKR and RJR. Kravis had consistently told Waters that tobacco was something that KKR didn't want to own, along with liquor and gambling. But when the two met for one of their occasional breakfasts at KKR on Wednesday, October 5, Kravis brought the matter up. "Have you kept in touch with Ross Johnson?" he asked.

"Yes," said Waters. "But you've always said you weren't interested in a tobacco company."

"I've rethought," said Kravis, partly because other bankers had suggested that he take a look. "See if you can set something up."

Waters called Johnson as soon as he got back to the office and left a message that it was important.

Although Johnson had promised to return messages marked important, he didn't call. Instead, Jim Welch did.

Waters explained that Kravis wanted a meeting.

"That's interesting," said Welch. "We'll think about it and call you back."

CHAPTER 4

It Happened So Quick

October 7 to October 19

Jim Welch never did get back to Steve Waters about a KKR-led LBO, nor did he set a firm date with Jeff Beck. It wasn't that Ross Johnson wasn't free. Johnson had other things on this mind. Like the LBO deal with Shearson. On Saturday, October 8, just three days after Kravis's breakfast with Waters, Johnson and Welch had scheduled a meeting with Tom Hill and Peter Cohen to review the numbers and make a final decision on going forward with a bid.

Before that session, on Friday, October 7, a team of Shearson lawyers led by Jack Nusbaum of Willkie, Farr & Gallagher, Shearson's outside counsel and a close friend of Cohen's, met with the RJR lawyers in Atlanta to talk about tobacco and what they truly thought about the legal outlook. The legal status of tobacco was the key to the deal. If investors were overreacting to the possibility of snowballing cancer judgments, as Johnson claimed, then a leveraged buyout was a fantastic opportunity. If Johnson was wrong, it would be a nightmare. Shearson had to be sure before committing to do the deal.

The lawyers' meeting went well, and so did the Saturday meeting on the buyout. Shearson's numbers weren't much different from the ones that Johnson had worked through with Frank Benevento that Tuesday in New York. The only thing that had changed were the estimates of what Shearson could get by selling the food companies; Hill's numbers were much higher than the ones Johnson had used. That greatly improved projected cash flow and it made the returns to equity investors sweeter. In defense of those rather generous estimates, Hill noted that food company prices just kept going up. That very week, on Tuesday, October 4, Grand Metropolitan, the same company that had bought Heublein from RJR, had bid $60 a share for Pillsbury, a fabulously high twenty-four times earnings, for a company which, unlike any of the RJR food units, had deep-seated operating problems. Hill knew whereof he spoke: he was heading up Pillsbury's defense team.

Although Hill had done all of his calculations assuming a buyout price of $72 a share, partly in paper, he warned Johnson that the management group might have to pay more. Johnson didn't respond specifically, but over the past couple of weeks both he and, more particularly, Sage, had made it clear that there was a price at which he didn't want to own RJR. Sage hadn't said what that price was; Hill guessed it was in the eighties. Certainly it would not be overgenerous. As a buyer, Johnson had consistently been stingy. Indeed, when Hill had floated the idea of a white knight bid for Pillsbury, Johnson had laughed; he thought that Pillsbury was worth in the mid-$50s a share, less that the $60 a share Grand Met had already offered.

Hill said that if Johnson did bid, he might draw in a competing bidder. Of course, there were very few potential competitors who could afford the $17 billion-plus price tag. Hill had divided them into three groups: food companies, tobacco companies, and what Hill referred to as financial companies. In the food category, only two companies seemed to have the wherewithal for a bid: Nestle and Unilever. Both had been expanding activities in the U.S. in recent years. It wasn't clear, though, that any publicly traded company, and both Nestle and Unilever were, would be willing to buy a tobacco company, given the controversy over smoking.

That would presumably not loom so large for a company already in the business, but none of the big cigarette makers seemed likely to get involved. American Brands (Carlton, Tareyton, Pall Mall) was too small. Philip Morris (Marlboro, Benson & Hedges, Virginia Slims), which had not yet launched its bid for Kraft, seemed determined to expand further into food. British American To-

bacco (Kool, Viceroy, Raleigh) seemed to be interested in financial services: that spring it had bought the Farmer's Group
insurance company. Hanson Trust, the owner of Imperial Tobacco, Britain's largest cigarette maker, seemed a distinct possibility: not only was Sir Gordon White, the company's takeover
strategist, known for his wily breakup-minded approach, but the
company also had a $6 billion cash hoard. Still, Sir Gordon had
always bought for bargain prices, and it wasn't at all clear that
he would be willing to get into a bidding war with Shearson.

As far as Hill was concerned, the most worrisome class of
bidders was the financial type. Unlike Shearson, both KKR and
Forstmann Little, another buyout group almost as big as KKR,
seemed to have the cash on hand for the equity piece of the bid.
Both had the know-how to do it quickly. No one had told Hill
about the calls from Waters and Beck, and he volunteered that
he was inclined to think that KKR wouldn't bid; in the wake of
the Kroger debacle, Kravis and Roberts would surely not want
to oppose a management offer.

"I've talked to Kravis," volunteered Johnson, who, being an
operating man, was much more worried about Nestle and Unilever, in any case. Kravis had told him that KKR didn't do hostile
deals.

The last question was what to do next. Typically, a ceo doesn't
tell his directors that he is looking at an LBO until the money is
lined up and ready to go. Hill was pushing that as the wisest
strategy. Johnson should "jam" the board, making an offer with
a twenty-four-hour fuse. That might scare the board into signing
an agreement, and with an agreement in hand, no one was likely
to launch an opposing bid.

There was no way Johnson was going to jam his board. That
wasn't the way he operated. Period. Instead Johnson wanted to
float the idea informally at the October board meeting to see what
the directors thought. If they were receptive, he would go ahead
with a formal bid.

Although Johnson strictly forbade Shearson to actually raise
any money, he did want to have a sense that raising this much
money would be possible. At $72 a share, the price Shearson was
using as a working number, buying RJR would take $17 billion.
Shearson was going to put up about $1.5 billion of equity; James
Stern, the head of Shearson's fledgling junk bond department,

said that it would be difficult to place $1.8 billion of junk bonds, which left a stunning $14 billion to be syndicated by the banks. No one at Shearson had any idea if that were possible, but Cohen agreed to find out.

On Monday, October 10, Columbus Day, Cohen called Charles Sanford, the chairman of Bankers Trust Co., to make an appointment; John Reed, the chairman of Citibank, had taken the day off, so Cohen didn't reach him until Tuesday. At separate meetings on Tuesday and Wednesday, Sanford and Reed both opined that there was some finite amount that could be raised in a syndicated loan, but neither could put his finger on what it was. They did, however, agree that it was larger than $14 billion.

By now it was Wednesday afternoon, October 12, only a week before the board meeting. And as far as Johnson was concerned there was one key matter that had to be taken care of before he talked to the directors: the so-called management contract agreement that laid out how the spoils would be divided between Shearson and Johnson. So, first thing Thursday morning, Sage, Johnson's chosen negotiator, met with Jim Stern at Nabisco's New York office—the Shearson people always referred to it as the "Cookie Palace," although in fact the furnishings were not particularly splendid—to bang out the terms. Unlike most executives contemplating a buyout, Sage did not see himself as a supplicant thankful that Shearson had given him the opportunity to go private and make a fortune, but as a principal, and his question was not how much equity Shearson was willing to give him as a sop, but what rate of return Shearson needed for Sage to attract the firm's money to his buyout. Sage reminded Stern that he had talked about a 40 percent return in earlier meetings and that was what management proposed to give him: Shearson would get 40 percent on its equity; beyond that everything belonged to Johnson.

Stern was horrified. That wasn't how things worked. Shearson had the money, not Johnson, and Shearson would call the shots. Stern was certainly happy to give Johnson a small incentive stake, but nothing along the lines Sage was proposing.

That's the deal, insisted Sage. Either you agree or we go somewhere else.

Stern and, more importantly, Peter Cohen, who was ultimately making the decision, didn't want Johnson to go somewhere else. Given Johnson's record at selling and restructuring companies, surely he could be trusted to run RJR properly, which meant that ceding board control and veto power wasn't particularly risky. "We can't have a 40 percent cut-off on profits," said Stern. "You get a piece of equity. Not everything over 40 percent."

That point was not debatable. "It's your number," said Sage. "You told us in the meetings that you needed a 40 percent return. We're giving you a 40 percent return. If you're saying that you need a higher return to place the equity, we can talk about that."

Stern had used a 40 percent number, but not in context. "We said 40 percent was a sort of ball-park estimate for what we'd get in a leveraged buyout, not what we thought we could get as a return." But the problem wasn't so much the 40 percent number as the concept. If Shearson was going to be an equity investor, he explained, there could be no ceiling on the upside.

Sage held his ground, and Stern decided to get some help. Cohen was at an American Express management conference in Tucson and couldn't get involved in the negotiations, so Stern called in Tom Hill, the M&A chief, in hopes that Hill would be able to talk some sense into Sage. Hill couldn't. Sage just repeated what he had said to Stern: if Shearson didn't agree to the terms, Johnson would take his deal elsewhere.

"A management deal this generous is going to be a public relations disaster," said Hill. "The bad press will kill the whole transaction."

Sage laughed. That was the feeblest negotiating line he'd ever heard. They were working out a split between management and Shearson, not between management and the shareholders. What management didn't get simply went to Shearson; the split between management and Shearson didn't affect what price the shareholders got. There was no logical reason that it affect the board's decision to sell the company to Johnson or anyone else. No one had ever suggested that KKR's getting a 20 percent carry would kill one of their deals.

Over the next two days, Hill tried everything he could think of to make Sage change his mind. He put together a chart showing what management teams had earned in other buyouts. He all but begged.

Sage wouldn't budge. The only change he was willing to consider was to drop the fixed return for a ratcheting scale: as Shearson's return increased, so did Johnson's percentage stake.

Stern wasn't buying that, and Friday afternoon in desperation, he called Cohen in Tucson to suggest that Jim Robinson get involved.

If anyone was going to be sensitive to how public opinion could kill a takeover, it was Jim Robinson. As Cohen had discovered when he attacked Koppers, public criticism was Robinson's Achilles' heel.

Robinson had learned the hard way.

In 1979, after failing to buy Book-of-the-Month Club, Philadelphia Life Insurance, and Walt Disney Productions, he launched an offer for McGraw-Hill, the book and magazine publishing company. Harold McGraw roared back with a $500 million breach of trust suit, charging that Roger Morley, AmEx's president and a McGraw-Hill director, had abused McGraw's confidence by attending board meetings even as he was planning a raid. Just in case anyone had missed the legal action, McGraw also took out two-page newspaper ads across the nation charging AmEx with corporate immorality.

Robinson backed off, only to be hit again. Sensing that the bad publicity had been the key to McGraw's success, Citicorp didn't bother with a lawsuit. It simply ran a series of full-page newspaper ads shrieking in one-inch type that AmEx's advertising was false and deceptive; Citi's travelers checks were just as easy to refund as the AmEx ones, and less expensive. Not surprisingly, Robinson withdrew the offensive Travelers Cheque ad.

And began to rebolster AmEx's image.

Protecting the AmEx aura is critical to the company's success. After Coca-Cola, American Express is perhaps the best-known name in corporate America, and it is the primary reason that people are willing to pay more to carry the company's Travelers Cheques and cards than the equally serviceable competition. Under Robinson, AmEx boasted what was arguably the best advertising and public relations teams in the business. Everybody understood that you "don't leave home without it"; everyone knew how many celebrities had been "cardmember since" when. Robinson gave a new meaning to the words "quality of service."

"Quality is our only form of patent protection," he explains. "I want quality written on my tombstone."

Even if he hadn't had the bad experiences, Robinson would have been image-conscious. It was in Robinson's blood. The scion of a wealthy Atlanta banking dynasty, Robinson was everything Ross Johnson and Peter Cohen weren't: polite, polished, patrician. He'd gotten his first job, at Morgan Guaranty Bank, then a bastion of Social Register rectitude, on the recommendation of World Bank president Eugene Black, a family friend. Later he worked at White, Weld & Co., an ultra white-shoe investment bank. Robinson had talent too, rising to the top of American Express at the tender age of forty-two. With the notable exception of McGraw-Hill, he had made his mistakes in private.

By the fall of 1988, Robinson was riding high. AmEx earnings were well on their way to $1 billion for the year, after a difficult 1987. Travel Related Services—cards, cheques, and vacations—was racking up its best year ever; the new Optima credit card had become the number six card nationwide after only eighteen months on the market; problems at Warner-AmEx cable, Shearson, Fireman's Fund, and IDS had been solved or sold.

Cynics believed that there was another reason that Robinson wanted to keep AmEx's name out of the takeover arena: politics. Although he repeatedly denied having political ambitions, in the year before the RJR bid Robinson had certainly acted like someone angling for office. He had given speeches outlining his position on such hot issues as bank regulation, trade policy, and third world debt. His friend Felix Rohatyn, a partner at Lazard Freres and well-known financial guru, had been widely quoted as recommending Robinson as Treasury Secretary to whoever won the presidential election in November (Vice-President George Bush was running against Massachusetts governor Michael Dukakis). Another unstatesmanlike episode along the lines of Koppers would kill any hopes Robinson had of attaining public office.

Like Henry Kravis, Robinson was active on the social circuit. He once confessed to the *Wall Street Journal* that he and his second wife, Linda, a public relations consultant and former political strategist, spent a quiet evening at home together one-and-a-half nights every other week. Indeed the Kravises are close friends of the Robinsons; Lake Hill Farms, the Robinsons' thirty-five-acre Connecticut retreat, is just down the road from the Kravises' pre-Colonial mansion, and Kravis and Linda Robinson are joint owners of two show horses.

Robinson had met Johnson back in 1975, the year that Robinson had been made president of American Express and Johnson president of Standard Brands, but they hadn't gotten close until 1981, when Treasury Secretary Donald Regan asked them both to work on the Savings Bond drive, Robinson as head of the national sales effort and Johnson as team captain for New York. Soon the two were fast friends.

So it was no surprise that when Stern and Hill started jerking Sage around, even sending him a draft management contract that bore little relationship to the 40 percent system that Sage thought had been agreed to, Johnson called Robinson. "We're trying to get this negotiated," he said, "and your M&A guys are being impossible."

Robinson said that he didn't know anything about it, but he would find out. He called Cohen and repeated what Johnson had told him. Whatever Robinson meant to communicate, the message seemed clear. Cohen called Johnson and the two quickly agreed that Johnson's equity stake would be tied to the return Shearson got. It wouldn't be the Johnson gets everything over 40 percent that Sage had suggested, but Cohen said he would design a system that worked. A couple of hours later, Cohen sent down a schedule tying Johnson's return to his performance; as the numbers worked out, Johnson ended up with roughly the same thing under the Cohen scheme as he had under the Sage scheme, at a price of $75 a share. That was acceptable, and over the next two days the Shearson and Johnson lawyers turned the grid into a complex fifteen-page document.

With that Johnson was ready to go. If Johnson had any premonition of what was to come, he didn't show it. He spent the weekend before the meeting relaxing at his condominium in Jupiter, Florida, just north of West Palm Beach. He had invited Steven F. Goldstone, his lawyer from Davis Polk & Wardwell, Reynolds Tobacco's long-time outside counsel, to come along to brief him on the legal implications of making a bid. Goldstone was a curious choice to be the legal point man on this deal. He was a litigator not a corporate lawyer, nor did he know much about the company, having met Johnson only a few months earlier. Goldstone's previous claim to fame was having advised Donaldson, Lufkin & Jenrette to defy a judge's order to testify in the Nucorp securities fraud case; charges against the defendants who showed up were dropped, leaving DLJ solely responsible for the claimed $100 million in damages by default judgment.

In addition to the RJR buyout, there was one other matter that Goldstone wanted to clear up in Jupiter. He knew that Johnson had looked at Pillsbury over the summer and he knew that Hill had just asked Johnson if he wanted to bid. Since Davis Polk was representing Morgan Stanley, Grand Metropolitan's banker, the firm couldn't work for Johnson if he decided to bid. Johnson laughed. "At that price, I wouldn't go near it," he said.

In the past, Johnson had always been careful not to surprise his directors, calling them frequently in between board meetings to find out what they thought about various schemes. When he was thinking of something unusual or controversial, he always called each director in advance to make sure any objections got raised and problems solved before the meeting began. He'd done that with the Mahoney nomination, for example, and had withdrawn it before it was formally proposed, when he realized from his phone conversations that it wouldn't fly.

With the buyout proposal, however, Goldstone insisted that he couldn't do that. Partly it was because it had come up so quickly that there wasn't time. Partly it was because Goldstone didn't want the word to start leaking out before the meeting. Nor would Goldstone endorse Johnson's plan to have Harold Henderson, RJR's general counsel, talk to the board about its legal position. As a member of the management buyout group, Henderson was totally inappropriate as an adviser, Goldstone told Johnson. The board needed a lawyer of its own.

However, Goldstone also didn't want Johnson to keep the board totally in the dark. That could be risky: when JWT Group chairman Joseph O'Donnell had sprung an LBO on his board cold in February 1987, he had been fired on the spot. So on Wednesday, October 12, eight days before the meeting, Johnson called the three non-management members of the executive committee: John Medlin of First Wachovia Bank, John Clendenin of BellSouth, and Charlie Hugel. Medlin and Clendenin were noncommittal. Hugel, who happened to be in Seoul on business, asked again if this was really what Johnson wanted to do. Johnson said it was, and this time Hugel didn't argue: Johnson's mind seemed made up. "I'm going to be discussing the buyout at the board dinner October 20," he said. "I'd like you to be chairman of the Special Committee."

Of course, Hugel agreed. As chairman of RJR Nabisco he was the most appropriate person to chair the subcommittee, and he was perhaps the best qualified. "I'm good at running organizations," he boasts. "After all, I ran the phone company."

Whatever his other virtues, Charlie Hugel is practical. So practical, in fact, that in his five years at Combustion Engineering he has never used the giant fireplace that his predecessor installed in the otherwise ultramodern chairman's office. "Fireplaces aren't efficient," he says. At least not for supplemental office heating. Nor are they efficient for home heat: Hugel has never used any of the three stone fireplaces at his vacation house in New Hampshire; although he is widely known as a man who chops wood in his spare time, that is strictly for the fun of it.

Earnest and hardworking, Hugel cared that people liked him. He spent so much of his time traveling to Combustion Engineering sites to make friends with employees that he started taking his wife Nina along, "otherwise I would never see her," and he smarted for months after *Forbes* magazine labeled him a "tyrant." No one could ever accuse Hugel of not trying to do the right thing. Doing right was at the top of Hugel's list of priorities, and he tried hard. All of which made Hugel an unlikely candidate to be one of Ross Johnson's closest friends—a fact Hugel acknowledges. "I like Ross," he says, although he finds Johnson's imprecision trying. "Ross sometimes hears what he wants, not what you said. Listen closely when he talks to you. When he starts mumbling, he's stretching the truth."

Like Johnson, Hugel came from a very modest beginning. Hugel's father "ran off" when he was a child and his mother raised him in poverty in Plainfield, New Jersey. Young Charlie planned to be a mechanic, but he was such a bright student that his teachers insisted that he set his sights on college and a white-collar job. After an extra year in high school to make up for the slow beginning, he enrolled in Lafayette College as a psychology major;

he didn't know much about psychology but it seemed like the way to the top. In 1952, after a stint in the army, he signed on at American Telephone & Telegraph as a student engineer. Again, his brillance shone through. Although he had no previous technical training, he was soon recognized as the leader that he was and plucked from the lab and put on the management fast track. He ran New England Telephone, then Ohio Bell, then Bell Labs, and was selected to figure out how to break the company apart in 1981.

Hugel was clearly in line to run the deregulated AT&T, but instead of doing what everyone expected, he jumped ship, accepting an offer from Combustion Engineering chairman Arthur Santry to become his deputy and heir apparent. At the time, Hugel, an electrical engineer, was a novice at building bridges and nuclear reactors, but fortunately it didn't take that kind of know-how to solve Combustion Engineering's biggest problems. Hugel quickly announced that Combustion Engineering was withdrawing from the low-margin oil service business and refocusing on instrumentation and calibration equipment. In five years, Hugel slashed the payroll from 42,000 to 28,000, only 14,000 of whom had worked for the company when he got there.

Hugel had been a Nabisco director at the time of the Standard Brands merger and he had come to admire Johnson's savvy. The two got on so well that after Johnson forced Sticht to step down as chairman in September 1987, it was almost logical to choose Hugel as a successor. "My background is in operations and developing people," Hugel said at the time. "Ross's is financial. He has always bounced ideas off me, now he's formalizing that relationship." There was, of course, another pressing reason for Johnson to put Hugel on top rather than taking the job himself. Johnson's struggles with Wilson and Sticht had left the already fractured board even more deeply torn. Johnson's appointing Hugel seemed likely to soothe the wounds.

In the eyes of many, it was also a blatant exercise in buying votes. Johnson paid Hugel $155,000 a year in chairman's fees, on top of the $50,000 a year he already got as a director, and made him the only double chairman in the Greenwich country club set. Johnson included Hugel on the VIP list for all of RJR's celebrity events, told his New York secretary to keep Hugel supplied with theater tickets and anything else he wanted, and picked up the entire tab when Hugel used the Combustion Engineering plane to get to RJR events instead of just the cost of a first-class ticket.

As an engineers' engineer, Hugel was arguably out of his depth as chairman of a marketing-oriented cookie cum cigarette company, and clearly underwater when it came to presiding over a company auction. Auctions were something Hugel knew next to nothing about. Indeed, his only previous experience with takeovers had been in 1982. As a director of Martin Marietta, he had presided over the most infamous takeover battle before RJR, the successful Pac Man bid against Bendix Corp.'s hostile raid. He had gotten a refresher course in August 1988 when, with the other directors of the Primerica insurance conglomerate, he was asked to consider a friendly offer from Sandy Weill's Commercial Credit. Needless to say, neither situation was remotely like this one.

Hugel had been supportive of most of Johnson's RJR moves, even controversial ones like pulling out of Winston-Salem, but he wasn't likely to help much when it came to a buyout. As he had told Johnson when Johnson first floated the buyout idea, Hugel firmly believes that buyouts are weakening American industry, since they divert critical management attention from the emerging challenge of European competition. Hugel was baffled that Johnson, who had always been such a conservative financial manager, could be talking about leading one.

But his was not to ask. Johnson had given him the job of chairman of the Special Committee and Hugel was going to be prepared. The first step was choosing a lawyer, and Hugel began to look for one as soon as he was back in his office from Korea on October 17. He asked several friends to make suggestions of possible lawyers and culled a short list of the names that everyone had mentioned. Then he bounced each of those off of several lawyer friends, including Combustion Engineering's general counsel, to be sure that whomever he selected would be compatible. The most compatible of the prestigious was Peter Atkins of Skadden, Arps, Slate, Meagher & Flom, a large New York firm that was particularly known for its take-over work.

Atkins turned out to be a decisive choice. Coincidentally, he had also represented the Special Committee of Fort Howard Paper Company, when the board had received a "proposal to make a proposal" for a management LBO in June 1988. He had advised that there was no need to put out a press release announcing that management was looking at a buyout and had been criticized by a Delaware judge for doing so, since not making an announcement effectively blocked other bidders from knowing that the company was for sale until after the management deal was signed.

In the course of searching for a lawyer, Hugel had picked up another key piece of information: Shearson was talking to the banks. According to one lawyer Hugel talked to, the syndication process was well along. Hugel assumed that that meant that Johnson would be making a formal, fully financed proposal at the board meeting, and that so many bankers now knew what was going on, that word of the bid was in danger of leaking out. Given that Johnson was that far along, Hugel decided to take care of a few additional preliminaries. He settled on Lazard Frères and Dillon, Read as the board's bankers pending board approval and he selected the other members of the Special Committee.

Marty Davis, the Gulf + Western chairman, whom Johnson had nominated to his board after the rejection of David Mahoney, got his first warning of the bid on Monday, October 17, two days before the board dinner, when Johnson called him to say that he was looking at a leveraged buyout and he wanted Davis to serve on the Special Committee. "Charlie Hugel will be calling you," Johnson had said. Several hours later, Hugel had called to confirm that Davis was on the committee and to ask what Davis thought of Peter Atkins. Davis said "top-notch," although by then he had picked up the word that Hugel had already talked to several other lawyers about representing the committee.

Davis wasn't sure what was going on, but it didn't smell good. Surely this wasn't the way to pick an independent committee, or the committee counsel. Hugel ought to be choosing the members, not Johnson, and the committee ought to select its own counsel at the first meeting. Davis was frankly surprised that he was on the committee at all. He was hardly an expert on the company. He had joined the board only in May; since then there had been only one board meeting. Did Johnson think that Davis would put friendship over responsibility and give him his vote?

That was not the sort of thing Davis did. Indeed, even before Johnson's call about the buyout, Davis had begun to think that joining the RJR board had been a big mistake. Although he and

Johnson had been friends since the mid-seventies, when they had both raised money for multiple sclerosis research, they had very different ideas about how to run companies, and Davis had been shocked to see first-hand what Johnson thought was an appropriate use of corporate cash. There was the "air force," waiting to whisk directors to London or Paris or Atlanta. Davis refused to fly corporate when he could fly commercial, so he hadn't seen the RJR hangar at Hartsfield Airport in Atlanta, but he had heard that it boasted such amenities as golf club caddies and antiques. For his part, Davis had sold all but one of twelve corporate jets he had inherited when he became chairman of Gulf + Western in 1983, and he left that one in California for the movie executives to use. When he invited a reporter to "breakfast," he noted that he could offer bad coffee, decent tea, and a working toaster to heat up what she brought to eat.

The dinner meeting at the Waverly Hotel in Atlanta was even worse than Davis had imagined. It was not the "informal chat" that Johnson had mentioned on the telephone. Johnson had come "loaded for bear," with a team of lawyers and investment bankers and a price of $75 a share. Nor was the brief board session after the dinner inspiring. Davis, being new to the company, didn't have a handle on what RJR was worth; but neither did anyone else. When Davis asked what the cash flow was, for a rough estimate of how high the buyout price could go, he just got silence. The directors seemed more concerned with their fees and status in the community than with the RJR shareholders. Ronald Grierson, the vice-chairman of British General Electric, moaned that he would never be able to explain the buyout to the queen.

The committee that he was a member of was odd at best. Presumably Hugel and Albert Butler, a Winston-Salem real estate developer, had been chosen, like Davis, for the certainty of their votes. William S. Anderson, the retired chairman of NCR, was unlikely to rock the boat, and he added a patina of experience to the group, having pioneered the concept of a board's duty to "stakeholders," people like employees or customers who weren't ordinarily put in front of the shareholders, the company's owners. John Macomber, the former chairman of Celanese, had probably been included because he would have complained that the committee was stacked if he hadn't been on it. Macomber and Hugel were barely on speaking terms, a fact that was sure to make committee meetings more interesting.

The only thing that Davis thought went right that night was Hugel's announcing that he was going to call both Dillon and Lazard to ask them to represent the committee. Although Davis had never worked with Dillon before, he was a close friend of Lazard partner Ira Harris, and he knew that Harris could be trusted to give good, ethical advice.

Clearly this board was going to need a lot of that.

Coincidentally, AmEx chairman Jim Robinson was in Atlanta on Thursday morning. Coca-Cola, Atlanta's other Fortune 500 company, happened to have its board meeting on the same day as RJR's, October 20, and Robinson, a director, had come south to attend. At eight o'clock, while he was still at his hotel, Robinson got a call from Peter Cohen saying that there would be an RJR buyout announcement on the wire within the hour.

"What?" asked Robinson, who didn't know the structure of Shearson's deal, much less the terms of the management contract. "How did this happen so quick? I thought it was going to be awhile."

"The lawyers said that it was far enough along to disclose," said Cohen. He read Atkins's press release, and promised to have a term sheet on Robinson's desk by the time he arrived back in the office the next morning.

Robinson didn't call Johnson. He headed to Coca-Cola as planned. Although the timetable had been speeded up, Robinson assumed that everything was under control.

CHAPTER 5

Protecting the Franchise

October 20 to October 23

Henry Kravis, of course, didn't know that Ross Johnson was looking at a buyout, much less getting ready to propose one. Kravis had decided to contact Johnson only in the faint hope that Johnson had changed his mind about a buyout in the year since their dinner. When he had asked both Jeff Beck and Steve Waters to set up a meeting with Johnson, Kravis had half expected that Johnson would say no, and when there was no response, Kravis took the silence to mean that Johnson hadn't changed his mind. It did not occur to Kravis that Johnson was looking at a buyout with someone else, much less an upstart like Shearson.

So after the meetings with Beck and Waters in early October, Kravis turned his eye to other things. By Thursday, October 20, he had given up on Kroger and was considering a white knight offer for Kraft, which had just received a hostile $90-a-share offer from Philip Morris, a total of $11.5 billion.

Kravis doesn't have a stock ticker in his office, so he didn't know that the RJR announcement had crossed the tape until his lawyer, Dick Beattie, of Simpson Thatcher called at nine-thirty. "You're not going to believe this," said Beattie. He read:

> RJR Nabisco Inc. said certain members of its management, including F. Ross Johnson, president and chief executive,

and Edward A. Horrigan, Jr., chief executive officer of the company's tobacco subsidiary, have advised the board that they intend to seek to develop with a financial partner a proposal to acquire the company in a leveraged buyout.

The executives said they contemplate paying about $75 a share cash, for an indicated value of $17.6 billion. The company said any proposal, if made, would be reviewed by a special committee of outside directors which has been established by the board. Charles E. Hugel, chairman of that committee, said no determination has been made regarding the acceptability of any proposal made at such a price level.

Kravis was stunned. He'd given Johnson the buyout idea at the dinner in September 1987. He'd asked both Beck and Waters to set up a meeting only weeks before. Surely Johnson owed it to Kravis to come to him first when he decided to try.

As it was, the offer was puzzling. Seventy-five dollars a share was incredibly low, just twelve times the $6.25 a share that stock analysts were estimating RJR Nabisco would earn in 1988. By contrast, Grand Met had offered twenty-four times earning for Pillsbury a fortnight ago, and Philip Morris had offered twenty-three times earnings for Kraft at the beginning of the week. Kravis himself had paid forty times earnings for Beatrice in 1986. Indeed, the $75 price was so low that Kravis figured that it could be paid entirely in cash; by his estimate the company's assets were more than sufficient to support a bank loan that size—and the return to equity investors could soar well over 50 percent.

Most puzzling, though, was the fact that there was an announcement on the wire before Johnson had signed a deal. Presumably Johnson was so close to a contract that it wasn't possible for someone to come in with a competing offer. Otherwise, Johnson had just put his company in play. "They teed the company up" was how one of Kravis' advisers put it later.

Kravis dialed Jeff Beck and then Steve Waters, the two investment bankers who had been trying to line up an RJR buyout for KKR, to find out what was going on.

Like Kravis, Steve Waters had begun the day Thursday thinking about Kraft. Philip Morris president Hamish Maxwell had called

Bob Greenhill, Morgan Stanley's vice-chairman and a renowned takeover strategist, to ask if Morgan Stanley could join the Philip Morris advisory team. Morgan Stanley couldn't, because the firm had just finished an assignment for the Kraft pension fund, but Greenhill had had another idea: maybe Morgan Stanley could represent someone as a white knight. So Waters and a team of senior takeover strategists were in a conference room down the hall from his office looking over the numbers to decide if a rescue made sense—and for whom—when Waters's secretary, Debbie, knocked on the door to say that Eric Gleacher, the M&A chief, wanted to see him immediately.

"What's going on with RJR?" Gleacher asked as soon as Waters walked into his office. He pointed at the announcement on the Quotron screen.

Waters just stared. Johnson was making a buyout proposal? At $75 a share? $75?

Before Waters and Gleacher had time to talk, Debbie was back with three messages, one from Kravis, one from Raether, one from Kravis and Raether together. Waters called right back to assure them that Morgan Stanley didn't have anything to do with the announcement. Then he called Johnson in Atlanta and left a message saying that it was important. Johnson had, after all, promised to return "important" calls. But Johnson didn't call back. Jim Welch did.

"Who's doing this deal?" asked Waters.

"I can't tell you," said Welch.

"What about us?" asked Waters.

"We're working this through," said Welch. "Stay tuned."

Indeed. Waters wanted an assignment, not a pat on the back. By now, it was obvious that Johnson wasn't going to hire Morgan Stanley. If he had intended to do that, he would have called before making his announcement. Maybe KKR or the Special Committee needed a banker. Gleacher and Waters agreed that Waters would call Kravis and that Gleacher and would have Morgan Stanley chairman Parker Gilbert call Charlie Hugel. In the meantime, Gleacher would find out why Shearson had chosen the low, $75-a-share price.

Tom Hill had flown up from Atlanta that morning, and he had just gotten to his office when Gleacher called.

"What's this seventy-five?" asked Gleacher, Hill's former boss.

"We wanted to put a cap on the market," said Hill.

"Huh?" said Gleacher. That wasn't standard jargon.

"We wanted to let the stock trade up and lock in our profit," said Hill.

Gleacher wasn't quite sure what Hill meant. Letting the stock trade up to lock in a profit was not a strategy he had ever heard before—or one that seemed to make any obvious sense. "I guess I'm in a fog this morning, Tom," said Gleacher, "but I didn't get that. Could you run it by again?"

Hill couldn't. "I've got to get another call," he said.

After he put down the phone, Gleacher decided that what Hill had been trying to say was that he had thrown out the low $75-a-share price to get the market thinking about how much RJR was worth. After the stock settled at, say, $83, Shearson would up its price to $84, and walk away with the company at a bargain basement price. The problem with that strategy was that it only worked if you didn't get caught. If another bidder surfaced with a more reasonable bid of, say, $90 a share, Hill would be out of the running. And Gleacher didn't see how Hill could think he wouldn't get caught. Not with Kravis already trying to set up a meeting with Johnson.

Meanwhile Jeff Beck was sitting in a conference room at Skadden Arps with a team of Drexel and Shearson bankers trying to devise a way for Pillsbury to escape the clutches of Grand Metropolitan, a task that was complicated by the fact that none of the bankers there was convinced that Pillsbury was worth anything close to the $60-a-share offering price. Although Tom Hill had previously been a leading adviser, he was strangely absent from this meeting. In his place was John Hermann, a junior Shearson M&A executive.

While the others talked about Pillsbury, Hermann strode over to the stock ticker in the corner and stared at the news briefs. "The largest deal in history is coming over the tape," he said suddenly. "And we're doing it."

"What's the company?" asked Beck, suspecting the worst.

"RJR," confirmed Hermann.

"What's the price?" asked Beck.

"The price," began Hermann. Then he corrected himself. "The indication is $75 a share."

Beck was stunned. Seventy-five dollars a share? That was pre-posterous; when he'd looked at an LBO for Johnson a year and a half ago, he had started at $75 a share, and food company sale prices had jumped substantially since then. Beck found a tele-phone and dialed Kravis. Kravis, of course, had just talked to Steve Waters.

"This caught me completely by surprise," Beck explained. "I don't know what's going on. It's Shearson's deal. Drexel isn't involved."

Then Beck called Johnson in Atlanta. Johnson's secretary said he was in a board meeting, but Beck said he'd hold indefinitely. Finally Jim Welch got on the line.

"Why?" asked Beck. That is, why was Johnson doing this deal without Drexel? And why had Welch told him to set up a meeting with Kravis even as he was planning the bid with Shearson?

Welch didn't have an answer. "There will be something here for you," he said.

"Kravis isn't going to go away," said Beck. "You should meet with him right away. This afternoon."

Welch said that they had things under control.

Beck called Kravis back to say that he didn't have any clarifi-cation. Although Kravis didn't say anything about hiring Drexel, Beck assumed that would happen; KKR always used Drexel for its deals.

Later, Welch called Beck.

Beck thought Welch wanted to hire him, but now Beck was no longer interested. "We have other obligations," he volunteered.

Welch seemed crushed by his tone. "We expect Drexel to ap-plaud this transaction," he said.

Applaud this transaction? What about get an assignment? "Jimmy," began Beck.

"I'm too old to be called Jimmy," said Welch.

"Well, I'm too old to be called Jeffy," said Beck.

The battle lines were set.

By late afternoon, Kravis had hired both Waters and Beck and he was considering hiring two other firms as well: Merrill Lynch, which was number two to Drexel in junk bond underwriting and could raise the necessary junk bond financing if the rumors of a pending RICO indictment knocked Drexel out, and Wasserstein, Perella & Co., the M&A boutique that had been founded six months earlier by First Boston whizzes Bruce Wasserstein and Joseph Perella. Wasserstein was one of the sharpest, most aggressive, bankers around. He might have some sage counsel on this deal, and, more importantly, adding him to the KKR team kept him from working for someone else.

By Thursday afternoon, James Maher, the co-head of the investment banking department at First Boston Corp., realized that he was the odd man out. There were three major merger deals going on: Pillsbury, Kraft, and RJR, and he wasn't involved in a single one. Every other major M&A house was: Goldman Sachs was defending Kraft; Lazard was representing the RJR Special Committee; Morgan Stanley was on board at Grand Met; Wasserstein, Perella was both team captain for Philip Morris and a coach on the Pillsbury defense.

And First Boston belonged in that tier. Until February, when Wasserstein and Perella had walked out in a power struggle, First Boston had been the unquestioned leader in the business. First Boston had invented such modern takeover tactics as the two-tier tender offer (Du Pont offered stockholders $87.50 a share for 40 percent of Conoco and $75 a share for the remainder), the "Pac Man" counter tender (NLT defended itself against an offer from American General by making an offer for American General) and the "crown jewels option" defense (Marathon fought off a hostile raid by Mobil by giving U.S. Steel an option to buy the Yates oil field, its prize asset, at a bargain basement price). Many of the people who had worked on those deals were still at First Boston. Despite the departures of Wasserstein and Perella, Maher was confident that First Boston was as good as it ever had been.

Nonetheless, Maher was fighting whispers that the sparkle had gone when the Wasserella, as Wasserstein, Perella was known in the M&A trenches, crew jumped ship. The pace of assignments had slowed down, with many of First Boston's clients opting for Wasserella, or at best a team of Wasserella and First Boston to handle the deal. Pillsbury, for example, had hired Wasserella, Shearson, and Drexel in addition to First Boston.

Maher knew that First Boston had something that Wasserella didn't: merchant banking capability. To be sure, Wasserella had raised some money and talked about doing deals, but the boutique didn't have the clout or experience in junk bond markets that First Boston did, or the deep pockets. In fact, almost no one on the Street could measure up. First Boston had pioneered the concept of a merchant bank, putting its own capital into deals like Congoleum and Joyce Beverages long before newcomers like Morgan Stanley or Merrill Lynch, two of First Boston's current competitors, had stumbled onto the business.

By contrast, Shearson didn't have a clue as to what merchant banking was all about. It had never done one of these deals. It didn't even have a junk bond department. Nor did Lazard or Dillon Read, the advisers to the Special Committee. Indeed, both those firms prided themselves on their refusal to play in the junk bond arena or to put money into deals that they strategized. And therein lay Maher's opportunity. Thursday afternoon, Maher called Charlie Hugel to suggest that First Boston, with its buyout expertise, would be a wise addition to the Special Committee team.

Hugel didn't think so.

Unfazed, Maher called Tom Hill. Shearson was looking for equity, he noted, and First Boston might be willing to partner up. First Boston could contribute cash, bond underwriting capability, and merchant banking know-how. It seemed to Maher he was making an offer too good to refuse.

Hill told Maher he'd talk to his people and call back, but in truth, figuring out whether to team up with First Boston wasn't at the top of his list. Kravis was.

At the Pillsbury defense meeting Thursday afternoon, Jeff Beck had hinted that something was up on RJR, and Hill wanted to find out what that was all about. Beck hadn't been precise; he had simply told Hill that "I think you're going to have competition," but knowing how close Beck was to Kravis, both personally and professionally, Hill figured that that meant KKR.

Given the controversy over KKR's bids for Macmillan and Kroger, Hill didn't think that Kravis would make an unsolicited bid for RJR, but who knew? There was no question but that Kravis had the money to make an offer and the ego to want in. The last thing Hill wanted was a bidding war; that would push RJR's price well above $75 a share. Was Kravis looking to start a fight or did he simply want an invitation to join Shearson?

Perhaps Hill could "smoke Henry out." So as soon as he got to his office Friday morning, Hill called Kravis.

"I see you're our competitor now," said Kravis, who figured that as long as Hill had called, *he* would smoke him out.

"Yes," said Hill carefully.

"We might be interested too," said Kravis.

Hill knew that he had to take Kravis seriously. If Kravis was determined to get RJR, it would be better to cut him in than to do battle. He called Cohen to get the go-ahead to set up a meeting.

Cohen was skeptical. He didn't think that Kravis would come in: they had agreed that they wouldn't interfere in each other's deals, hadn't they? Having a meeting would make Cohen look weak.

Hill was adamant, and Cohen finally called.

Kravis took the fact that Cohen wanted a meeting to mean that he was worried—and that meant Kravis was in no hurry. "What about Monday?" he suggested.

"No," said Cohen. "It has to be today."

Kravis agreed: he had nothing to lose.

Cohen and Hill arrived at KKR's offices close to six. What exactly was said at this meeting is in dispute. At the time, Cohen and Hill insisted that Kravis had opened the session by saying that he was angry that Shearson had stepped on his turf and intended to move aggressively to "protect my franchise." Kravis denies that he used the term franchise, and Cohen and Hill, now eager to mend fences, refuse further comment. Nonetheless, Kravis, angry that an upstart like Shearson was playing on his turf, clearly subscribed to the franchise concept, and likely he did not mince words.

After that, everyone agrees that Kravis asked Cohen: "Why are you doing this?"

"This is where the business is going," said Cohen.

Kravis reminded Cohen that he had talked to Johnson about a leveraged buyout a year before. "I don't think you're going to buy this company for $75 a share," he said.

Cohen suggested that they think about things over the weekend and talk again on Monday.

Kravis agreed.

And that was that.

Cohen and Hill went straight to Hill's apartment on East

Seventy-first Street and called Johnson in Atlanta to say that
Kravis—"Tiny Tim" was how they referred to him, although both
Cohen and Hill are Kravis's height—was very interested in RJR,
but that he might be willing to make a joint offer. Then they
called Jim Robinson at his farm in Connecticut with the same
message.

"Do you want me to call Kravis?" asked Robinson. Kravis was,
after all, a personal friend.

"No," said Cohen. "We're meeting Monday. There's no need."

At seven-thirty, Cohen headed home. Although the Shearson
go-fers would be holed up at Bankers Trust over the weekend
trying to hammer out the basics of a loan agreement, he planned
to spend the weekend watching his twelve-year-old son Andy play
interschool football on Randall's Island.

Kravis too had gone home thinking that he wouldn't have to
focus on RJR again until Monday. Although time was usually of
the essence in a takeover deal, Kravis had the clear sense from
the Friday meeting that Shearson was a long way from lining
up the money to make a bid. Shearson seemed to have neither
the $2 billion of equity cash nor the $15 billion of bank debt.

By Saturday afternoon, though, the outlook had begun to
change. Steve Waters, who still had plenty of friends at RJR,
called to say that he had picked up the word that Shearson planned
to have a deal signed within a week. Another adviser reported
that the boards of both Shearson and American Express had
scheduled special meetings for Tuesday in New York, presumably
to approve a formal offer for RJR, or even a final agreement with
the board. In the middle of the afternoon, one of the bankers
reported that Shearson was demanding exclusive financing from
Bankers Trust and Citibank, its lead banks. When Kravis had
called Bankers Trust, KKR's long-time lead bank, to try to verify
that himself, he was told that Robert O'Brien, the head of the
LBO department, wasn't available because he was in an all-day
meeting with Shearson.

Suddenly it looked like Kravis would have to move quickly if
he wanted to keep his place at the table. So at the last minute,
he changed plans and called a meeting with the investment bankers and lawyers on Sunday afternoon, to talk over what to do.
Kravis had not intended to make a decision Sunday, but when

he sat down with the team in the big conference room at KKR, the advisers made it clear that they wanted some action.

Oddly, the discussion focused not on value but tactics. Eric Gleacher thought Kravis should immediately announce a tender offer direct to shareholders. Under SEC rules, Kravis would be free to buy 20 days after he began, a fact that would pressure Shearson to show its hand. Bruce Wasserstein agreed. Indeed, Gleacher and Wasserstein seemed to agree on everything that afternoon, although Gleacher prefaced every remark with "of course I haven't talked to Bruce about this," and Wasserstein noted with each recommendation that "of course I haven't talked to Eric about this."

Kravis was wary of doing anything that was overtly hostile. Both a tender offer, and Gleacher's proposed "weaker" alternative of sending Hugel a letter offering to make an offer, seemed awfully close to what KKR had tried, and been blasted for, with Kroger. And the last thing Kravis wanted to do was reinforce the perception that he was hostile, ready and eager to launch raids. That would clearly destroy his ability to woo managements to sell their companies to him on the cheap. If Kravis was worried that by going hostile he wouldn't have access to RJR's books, he didn't say so.

Nor did anyone else. Wasserstein responded that a tender offer wasn't hostile in this context. Kroger had been forced into play, he argued, while RJR had voluntarily put itself on the block by endorsing an LBO proposal from management. According to every legal precedent, Hugel was now obligated to hold an auction to guarantee that the shareholders got the best price. That he intended to do so was clear from his actions: he had formed a Special Committee, hired two investment bankers, and brought in Skadden Arps, one of a handful of law firms that specialized in auctions and other takeover-related matters. Skadden, indeed, was famous for its aggressive approach to finding other bidders.

In that context, a tender offer wouldn't be hostile at all. Indeed, Gleacher argued, it might be just what the board was looking for. If management was trying to railroad through the lowball $75 a share proposal by arguing that no one else was big enough to bid, a KKR tender would be a welcome event. It would establish once and for all that the shareholders would get the most money in an open-bidding war.

That line of thinking led to price. No one had done more than glance at the public information at this point—the annual report and several routine financial filings—but you didn't need to do that to know how much you could bid: $90 a share. Shearson had already determined that you could line up bank and mezzanine financing for a cash bid of $75 a share; you could easily force the shareholders to swallow another $15 a share of cram-down paper.

Gleacher insisted that there were two reasons to bid so high. First, a high bid would underscore that Johnson had tried to steal the company, perhaps driving a wedge between Johnson and his board. Second, it might force Johnson to withdraw altogether, out of embarrassment, tightfistedness or both. Indeed, Gleacher was confident, and Wasserstein agreed, that $90 a share was so high that it would blow Shearson out of the water, and KKR would have the company by default.

Besides, Wasserstein said, bidding sent the right signal to Cohen. Wasserstein was sure that Cohen had no intention of doing a deal with Kravis; he was pretending that something was possible so that he could stall Kravis from working on his own bid. If Kravis tendered, stalling would be moot. With KKR out in front, Cohen would come begging to be part of their deal.

Still Kravis hesitated. A tender offer was generally regarded as hostile.

Well, said Drexel's Leon Black, playing devil's advocate, there was an alternative. Kravis could wait until Shearson actually had a deal signed up, and then bid.

Kravis laughed. That might be the way to go if you were determined to pay the lowest price, but it would forever ruin his reputation as a friendly bidder.

About six, the meeting recessed so that Kravis could talk to Roberts. The KKR people—Kravis, Raether and several associates, and Beattie, KKR's lawyer—went to Kravis' office to call San Francisco. The investment bankers waited in the conference room. It was dinner time, but there was no chef and nothing readily heatable in the kitchen, so they ordered out for pizza.

The strategy meeting resumed about an hour later. Kravis was leaning toward making a bid, although he was still nervous that bidding would be considered hostile. Gleacher had already thrown out a price of $90 a share. Now they talked about that.

The logic seemed watertight. Clearly the company was worth at least $90. By bidding $15 a share more than Shearson, KKR would demonstrate how serious it was, and how good an auction would be for shareholders.

The meeting recessed again about eight-thirty so that Kravis could call California again to make a final decision. An hour later, Kravis walked into the conference room to announce that they were going ahead. KKR would bid $90 a share Monday morning.

There were a dozen loose ends to tie up. Beattie and Tom Daly, Kravis's public relations man, drafted a press release and a letter to Hugel explaining that the bid was intended to be friendly. Some of the other lawyers began working on the tender offer documents.

Wasserstein got a call from someone at Philip Morris—Wasserella was, after all, Philip Morris' chief strategist—saying that Kraft had announced a defensive restructuring that it claimed was worth $110 a share, $20 a share more than the Philip Morris offer. Then he made some phone calls of his own.

Ross and Laurie Johnson spent the weekend playing golf in Chattanooga. Late Sunday afternoon, they flew into New York, and after dropping their clubs and luggage at their apartment at 800 Fifth Avenue, they headed to Museum Tower for dinner with Jim and Linda Robinson. By this time, the RJR leveraged buyout had become headline news, featured everywhere from the front page of *The New York Times* and CBS Evening News to local papers in North Carolina, Texas, and Rhode Island, and Johnson had hired Linda Robinson as his public relations representative. Naturally, the four talked about the deal.

Actually, Jim and Ross had already talked several times over the weekend about what to do. Johnson had been skeptical about teaming up with Kravis from the time Cohen had first mentioned it Friday evening. Johnson had chosen Shearson over KKR in the first place because Shearson wouldn't take a carry, making the profits to management—and investors—proportionately higher. He didn't think that Kravis would bid; when they had had dinner the year before, Kravis had made it very clear that he didn't do deals without the support of management.

But the Robinsons insisted that, on the right terms, a joint deal made business and public relations sense. It could mean winning the company at a lower price, without the spectacle of a bidding brawl.

By ten-thirty, Johnson had agreed to give it a try. Jim Robinson called Cohen to say that they were agreed. "Should I call Henry?" he asked again.

"I don't see why," repeated Cohen. "We're meeting tomorrow morning anyhow."

At midnight, half an hour after the Johnsons had left, the Robinsons' phone rang. It was a reporter for Linda. He had just heard—he wouldn't tell Linda from whom—that Kravis was going to make a tender offer the next morning at $90 a share. Did Linda have a comment?

Linda didn't. She never commented on rumors. But she was shocked. As soon as she got off the line, she called Cohen.

He wasn't worried. "They're bluffing," he said. After all, he reminded her, "I'm meeting with Kravis on Monday to talk about a joint bid."

CHAPTER 6

The Once and Future(?) King

October 23 to October 24

While Henry Kravis and his investment bankers were meeting at KKR headquarters at 9 West 57th Street Sunday afternoon, another group of investment bankers was meeting seven blocks away at 834 Fifth Avenue, the home of Salomon Brothers chairman John Gutfreund.

For Gutfreund as for Cohen, the leveraged buyout of RJR was potentially a key deal, and Gutfreund was scrambling to get involved. Gutfreund didn't have Ross Johnson on his team, of course, nor would he have, if agreeing to the Sage version of the management contract had been necessary. Unlike Cohen, Gutfreund would have responded to Sage's 40 percent or walk line by telling him to start walking. Gutfreund had made his share of mistakes over time, but putting expediency before sensible deal making was not one of them.

Unlike Cohen, Gutfreund isn't into conspicuous corporate consumption (home is a different matter: the Gutfreund apartment, which cost $20 million to decorate, boasts, among other things, a panel of Monet's Giverny "Water Lilies"). Although he has a small office, he usually works at a simple desk on Salomon's open trading floor. Nor is he impressed by banking's position at the top of the Wall Street hierarchy. A brilliant trader whom *BusinessWeek* had once crowned the "King of Wall Street," Gutfreund got Salomon into investment banking only because everyone else was making so much money in M&A. Nonetheless, after a day spent meeting with his corporate finance team, he would return to the trading floor for a game of liar's poker with whichever of his fellow bond men happened to be around. "This is a trading firm," says a senior banking executive shortly before the RJR war broke out. "When Morgan Stanley ran out of space, the traders moved across the street. When Salomon ran out of space, the bankers moved across the street," to the former American Express headquarters at 2 New York Plaza.

Although his social-climbing second wife, Susan, was often the talk of the town—who could forget her being sued by her upstairs neighbor for hoisting up her twenty-two foot Christmas tree from his balcony without permission, or serving spun-sugar apples at a birthday party for Henry Kissinger, made with a technique that the chef had learned from the glassblowers of Murano—but "Solemn John," as the gossip columns referred to him, was the very antithesis of New York glitz. Indeed, when Montefiore Medical Center was hit by a strike in 1984, Gutfreund, a director, quietly spent weekends working as an orderly in the kitchen until the contract was renegotiated. "You do what you have to do," was all he would say of the experience afterwards.

But Gutfreund and Salomon had fallen on hard times. In the past year, Gutfreund had presided over one disaster after the next: fending off a raid by Revlon chairman Ronald O. Perelman, sustaining a $75 million loss in the October 1987 stock market crash, and surviving a scathing round of bad publicity that included a *New York* magazine cover story attributing Salomon's problems to Gutfreund's having belatedly discovered his "sexual vitality" with his wife, Susan. Gutfreund pledged to regain Wall Street's crown by transforming the bond house into a merchant bank.

The initial results were not encouraging. Executives quit, morale sank, clients defected. In January 1988, Ira Harris, Salomon's best-known deal-maker, left Salomon for Lazard, taking many of his clients with him. The first two buyout deals, Revco drug stores and TVX broadcasting, quickly went bankrupt, and the day before the RJR announcement, three key traders threw in the towel, apparently in response to Salomon's dimmer prospects. "Salomon is bonds," said one "Streeter" when he heard the news. "Without

Coatsey [the government bond trading chief E. Craig Coats, Jr.], Salomon will collapse."

Nothing so dramatic was in the cards, of course, but Gutfreund was desperate for a merchant banking success, and RJR looked like the perfect opportunity.

Time was when Gutfreund, fifty-eight, was the toughest, most decisive man on the Street. An Oberlin literature major, he had toyed with teaching but ended up at Salomon Brothers because his father, a Westchester trucking executive, was a friend and occasional golfing partner of Salomon's then-chief William A. "Billy" Salomon. He quickly rose to the top, displaying a singleness of purpose and a foul tongue that cowed even the firmest opponent. A trader to the core, he made decisions quickly and never looked back; friends laughingly explained that when dining out, Gutfreund always ordered the first special that a waiter listed, never waiting to hear what the others might be.

In those days, underwriting had been controlled by a handful of old-guard firms like Morgan Stanley and Goldman Sachs, but Gutfreund, a premier bond trader, sensed that the established relationships between such firms and corporate America were weakening, that Salomon's trading expertise and its strong relationships with bond buyers could make it a powerful underwriter, and he began to line up deals. Although Gutfreund was eager for business, he played hardball all the way. One managing director remembers calling Gutfreund, then head of the syndicate department, to say that a client, a major bank, had refused to give him certain financial information. "Tell him that he can either cooperate or shove the offering up his ass," said Gutfreund. The client cooperated.

Three years after becoming chairman in 1978, Gutfreund enraged many partners by secretly negotiating to sell Salomon for $554 million to commodity-trading giant Philipp Brothers. When the market for stocks and bonds soared while commodities collapsed, Gutfreund won control of the entire operation. Access to Phibro's capital, combined with a controversial Securities and Exchange Commission ruling known as 415, catapulted Salomon to the top. By virtually eliminating paperwork and shareholder notification, 415 turned underwriting into an almost-instantaneous auction run from the trading floor, and Salomon, with its trader-oriented predilection for quick decisions and thin margins, quickly became the nation's leading underwriter of corporate stocks and bonds.

Gutfreund pushed Salomon as if he thought his luck would never change. In 1985 the payroll leapt 40 percent. By the time he was dubbed the King of Wall Street that December, internal systems had so deteriorated that Gutfreund no longer even knew which departments were making money. It scarcely seemed to matter. To capitalize on London's Big Bang, Salomon opened the world's largest trading floor a couple of blocks from Buckingham Palace, and it announced plans for a controversial Manhattan palace of its own, two towers looming over Columbus Circle, to be built in partnership with Mortimer Zuckerman.

In retrospect, Salomon was only a pretender to Wall Street's throne. The firm was a one-trick pony, and the trick was trading. It had never developed the long-standing hand-holding relationships with clients, be they corporate executives or raiders, that brought deals in and made them work. "But hell," says investment banking chief Jay Higgins. "We were making half the money on Wall Street. Who was going to try to fix something that wasn't broken?" In the two years following his coronation, Gutfreund saw just how broken Salomon was. Competition pressed profit margins to the bone, the anticipated markets for commercial real estate-backed bonds and other exotic securities didn't develop, and Salomon began to lose customers. By 1988, Salomon had ceded its place at the top of the underwriting rankings to plebeian Merrill Lynch.

The question of merchant banking came up even before King Salomon began to wobble. As early as 1984, some of the younger partners began to press Gutfreund to open a junk bond trading desk. Henry Kaufman, the firm's highly respected chief economist, was violently opposed, saying that what Salomon did best was trade blue chip stocks and bonds, while low-quality securities threatened the very foundations of the U.S. economy. After a bruising internal fight, Gutfreund finally took the plunge, but by putting the entire merchant banking operation on the trading floor, he was asking for trouble. The problem went deeper than "class" warfare. Trading and banking were simply different disciplines. Traders make hundreds of decisions a day, betting on minute moves in interest rates, in hopes that they will be right

51 percent of the time. Bankers, by contrast, invest the firm's capital for years, not minutes, and their risk is that the company they are buying will go belly-up, not that the thirty-day T-bill will drop six basis points (six one-hundredths of one percent).

By now, of course, it was clear that the wind had gone out of the trading sails. Faced with hemorrhaging losses, Gutfreund had closed the firm's municipal bond department, the largest on Wall Street, and pulled out of commercial paper. Although the departure of the top traders in October was a symbolic hit, it was, perhaps preordained. If Salomon was to become a merchant bank, the trading ranks would have to thin, and Gutfreund had said again and again that the future was merchant banking.

With the RJR announcement, the future seemed to be now.

Hours after the first story crossed the wire Thursday morning, William Strong, a Salomon corporate finance executive, called Hanson Trust about forming a partnership. Strong didn't yet have a formal proposal, but he needed an indication of interest. Hanson was in many ways an ideal bidder. Not only did the company already own Imperial Tobacco, England's largest cigarette manufacturer, and a motley assortment of English and American food and industrial companies, it was also renowned for financial savvy. Its founders, James Hanson, now Lord Hanson, and Sir Gordon White, were always willing to try something different. Sir Gordon had even done the Americans one better when he went after the Smith-Corona conglomerate in 1985, going into the market to buy control after company executives refused to consider his bid. By October 1988, Hanson had a formidable war chest: $6 billion in cash plus a $7 billion credit line. Although he didn't know anything in particular about RJR, Sir Gordon sent back the word that he wanted to take a look, and Strong scheduled a meeting for Monday morning at Hanson headquarters at 410 Park.

Then the Salomon team buckled down for a weekend of work. Before they met with Hanson, they had to have figured out how much they thought that RJR was worth, and what the best strategy for buying it would be. By Sunday afternoon, they had agreed on a rough plan. Salomon and Hanson would partner up, each buying 40 to 45 percent of RJR; another investor—they hadn't focused on who—would pick up the remaining 10 percent block. Under the provisions of the Hart-Scott-Rodino antitrust act, a company buying stock in another company had to flag its interest by filing for antitrust clearance as soon as its stake crossed the $15 million mark. Hart-Scott didn't apply to partnerships, so a partnership could keep its interest secret until the holdings totalled 5 percent of the target's shares outstanding, the level at which the Securities and Exchange Commission required a filing.

Clearly buying stock on the open market would be the first step. That was how Sir Gordon usually functioned, and, in this case, that was what made the most sense. The partnership would pick up roughly $1 billion worth of stock early in the week, and then, if the signals were right, launch a bid in the mid-eighties a share. If management or someone else later outbid them, they would be able to cash in on the cheap stock they already owned, reaping enough profit to cover costs. Curiously no one was worried that this strategy, almost identical to the one Shearson had used in the bid for Koppers that spring, would get Salomon into trouble for being party to a hostile raid.

Late Sunday afternoon, Gutfreund, Strong, investment banking chief Jay Higgins, and half a dozen other officials sat amid the French antiques and Impressionist paintings in Gutfreund's living room talking about Hanson and RJR and whether this was the deal Salomon really wanted to do. Gutfreund was frankly wary; buying RJR was no ordinary commitment after all, but a $17 billion undertaking. But he was leaning toward taking the plunge. With a block of stock in his back pocket, Gutfreund would be protected if things went wrong.

Finally, about six, the team called Warren Buffett, Salomon's largest shareholder and a long-time Salomon client. Buffett was renowned for his good business judgment, and since he had once been Reynolds Tobacco's largest shareholder, it was logical that Gutfreund should ask his advice. Buffett was thrilled. He knew that tobacco was an extremely lucrative business; he sensed that the $75-a-share price was low.

Everything seemed to be in place.

Until Monday morning. Gutfreund picked up *The New York Times* on the way to work, as usual, and there on the front page was a teaser on RJR: "KKR expected to bid $90 a share," it read. "See page D1."

Gutfreund's shock at the newspaper headline was nothing compared to Henry Kravis's. Although Kravis had finally decided to go ahead with a $90-a-share bid, he had certainly not authorized anyone to call the *Times*. One of his investment bankers had jumped the gun, probably two: the *Times* usually checked with two sources before running an article.

So, at seven in the morning, as soon as he had seen the paper— the *Wall Street Journal* had a short article too, although it had been called in so late that it didn't even make the entire Manhattan run—Kravis called Jeff Beck to accuse him of making the leak. Beck denied it—the culprit was Wasserstein—but Kravis wasn't sure he believed that.

Then, Kravis got down to business. He needed to talk to four people before he called his formal bid announcement to Dow Jones at 8:00: Peter Cohen, Ross Johnson, Charlie Hugel, and Ira Harris. Although it was only 7:30, he called all four, in that order. Cohen wasn't at home. Johnson wasn't in his Atlanta office. Hugel wasn't in his Stamford, Connecticut, office. At 7:40, 6:40 in Chicago, he finally got through to Harris at home.

"I've been trying to reach Charlie Hugel and Ross Johnson," Kravis said, indicating that neither had yet arrived at his desk. "I'm going to announce a tender for RJR at eight o'clock. I wanted to tell them personally first. Could you pass on the word?"

Harris, only slightly incredulous that anyone was trying to do business at that hour, said he would, although it might not be before Kravis made his offer.

Thirty minutes later, at 8:10, Cohen called Kravis from his car. He hadn't seen the paper, and despite Linda Robinson's call the night before he was still confident that he and Kravis were going to sit down in the afternoon for another talk about RJR.

"I've made a tender offer for RJR at ninety dollars a share," began Kravis. "I just called it in to Dow Jones."

"What?" yelled Cohen. "I thought we were going to talk."

"I know what you were doing over the weekend," said Kravis.

Surely Kravis didn't mean sitting in the football bleachers at Randall's Island in the pouring rain. "What was that?" asked Cohen.

"Trying to lock up the banks," snapped Kravis, irritated that Cohen was pretending not to know. "Setting up a board meeting Tuesday for both Shearson and AmEx to approve a bid."

"Those board meetings were set up a long time ago," said Cohen.

Kravis didn't believe that.

"We're not going away," said Cohen.

Ross Johnson had just finished reading *The New York Times* in his office at 9 West 57th Street when he got a message that Kravis had called him in Atlanta. Johnson called right back. "Jesus, Henry," he said. "I knew you were rich, but I didn't know you were that rich."

Kravis laughed.

They talked for a few minutes. Johnson made it clear that the bidding was out of his range and he was going to drop out, precisely what Eric Gleacher had predicted.

Kravis said that they'd be in touch.

Later that morning, Johnson confirmed that he would drop out to Gleacher as well. It wasn't until the afternoon that anyone suggested that the KKR offer wasn't the best course. Then, Tom Hill called to say that the $90-a-share price was illusory. KKR wasn't bidding for all the stock, only 87 percent; that meant that the average cash price was not $90 a share, but $78 a share. The remainder of the $90 total would be paid later, in "funny money," some yet-unspecified paper. Hill said that he thought the price was closer to $80 a share—and that Shearson could, and should, come back with more.

The article about the KKR bid hadn't made the *Wall Street Journal* in Chicago, but Mel Klein, the deal-maker who had been looking at financing an RJR leveraged buyout by selling trademark participations, saw the news of the bid on the wire just after he arrived at his office.

He'd been surprised, of course, by Johnson's original bid, since both Kravis and Ira Harris had insisted that Johnson had no interest whatsoever in a leveraged buyout. He hadn't intended to do anything about the management offer, though; it was too late to contact Johnson, and Klein, like most leveraged buyout players, never made hostile bids.

And so Klein found the KKR announcement particularly interesting. Six months before, when he and Kravis had talked about RJR over breakfast, Kravis had seemed inclined to do a joint deal if Johnson ever changed his mind. Maybe he still was. Klein dialed New York.

"I don't know," said Kravis when Klein proposed a joint bid by KKR and Harry Gray, Mel Klein & Partners. "I don't know if we're going to need help with the financing. I don't know what we're doing yet."

They talked for a few minutes. Kravis made it clear that if he did take a partner, he wouldn't do it until after the deal closed. At that point, he might be interested in selling Klein 20 to 30 percent of the equity.

Klein was certainly interested in that. "We'll keep in touch," said Klein as he hung up.

Later that afternoon, Klein mentioned the Kravis conversation to Jay Pritzker, his partner. Pritzker liked the idea of getting in on RJR. It seemed to him that it would be the deal of the century.

Even before he headed uptown for the meeting at Hanson Trust, Bill Strong, the Salomon partner who had gotten the ball rolling on the joint RJR deal, knew that he would have to change tactics. Whatever Kravis's offer was really worth, the KKR announcement had kicked up the price of RJR stock by more than $7 a share, pushing it out of the range that Salomon had originally planned to buy at. And since the first step of the Hanson deal had been buying a block on the cheap, Strong knew he would have to come up with something else.

As it turned out, the Hanson meeting was brief. Sir Gordon wasn't up to speed on the company, and he wasn't willing to pay the price. It would take something with a face value of at least $90 a share to top Kravis, and that was no longer a bargain.

Back at Salomon the merger executives talked about what to do next. Unlike Sir Gordon, they weren't so wowed with Kravis's price that they were unwilling to go forward. But they didn't think that Salomon could go it alone. It wasn't just a question of money—unlike Shearson, Salomon with $3 billion of equity could have swung the deal—but management. With Johnson firmly in the Shearson camp, there was no one to run the company in a Salomon deal. What Salomon needed was someone to replace Hanson, a corporate partner, who already owned a food or, more likely, tobacco company, who could take care of the day-to-day operations. There wasn't an obvious candidate. Although Salomon was friendly with a number of food companies, none seemed big enough. If any were interested, they had presumably spent the past five days talking with some other investment banker about a deal.

But there was an alternative: teaming up with Shearson. Cohen clearly needed help. He had been caught with his pants down, so to speak, without bank money or equity when the board had decided to put out the press release. Salomon president Tom Strauss was one of Cohen's closest friends. The two had summer houses next door to each other in East Hampton and often spent weekends together. Cohen had given Strauss a giant gavel when he was promoted to president, and the ticket to a Ruth Westheimer sex-counseling session just for the hell of it.

So late Monday afternoon, Strauss called Cohen.

Cohen was wary. Was Salomon trying to steal Johnson and the management team?

No, Strauss insisted. Salomon wanted to team up.

"We'll get back to you," said Cohen.

Tom Hill was not impressed when Cohen told him about the call from Strauss. He told Cohen point-blank that he thought teaming up with Salomon Brothers was a mistake. Jim Maher of First Boston had called; if they were going to team up with someone, why didn't they choose a partner who had had some experience? Unlike First Boston, which had done dozens of leveraged buyout deals and boasted an established junk bond underwriting and distribution network, Salomon was almost as new to the business as Shearson. The only two deals it had put together on its own, TVX and Revco, were now bankrupt. Salomon, unlike First Boston, wasn't a force to worry about. There was no way that Salomon was going to bring in a competing bidder for RJR; Salomon just didn't have that kind of aggressive drive, or contacts. First Boston was another matter; Maher might well surface with a bidder or form a competing bidding team.

But Cohen had made up his mind. He was teaming up with his friend Strauss and that was that. So in the evening, Hill called Maher back. "Things seem to be under control here," he said. "I don't think we'll be needing your help."

Maher was again free to rustle up another bidder, and he intended to do just that.

CHAPTER 7

White Hat?

October 24 to October 25

The *New York Times* article and the Dow Jones newswire announcing KKR's $90-a-share bid had piqued the interest of another bidder: Theodore Forstmann, the senior partner of Forstmann Little & Co., the world's second-largest buyout group and KKR's arch-rival. Unlike Kravis, Forstmann hadn't previously considered an RJR buyout. When the October 20 Johnson-Shearson announcement had first crossed the tape, apparently with the board's blessing, Forstmann had not looked. However cheap the price seemed, Forstmann never interfered with management deals.

But after KKR made its hostile offer, the situation was rather different. Now RJR, a company that was run by someone he'd played golf with, Ross Johnson, and advised by someone he'd socialized with, Jim Robinson, was under siege, and under siege by Henry Kravis, a man Forstmann believed was destroying the American economy and, in the process, giving buyouts a bad name.

So while Bill Strong and the Salomon team was contemplating what to do without Hanson, Forstmann started to think about getting involved as well. Usually he talked over ideas with his partner, Brian Little, but Little was incommunicado in Thailand on vacation. The other person Forstmann often bounced ideas off of was Geoffrey Boisi, the partner in charge of investment banking at Goldman, Sachs. Although Forstmann didn't trust most investment bankers, he did believe in Boisi, who was a friend as well as a banker and whose firm refused on principle to have anything to do with hostile bids.

Before Forstmann called Boisi, though, Boisi called him. Two Goldman clients, David Murdock, the Los Angeles-based investor who then controlled Castle & Cooke, the parent of, among other things, Dole pineapples and bananas, and Proctor & Gamble, the consumer products company that had conceived the soft cookie but lost the market to Nabisco's Almost Home in the infamous 1983 "Cookie Wars," had a long-standing interest in parts of RJR. Murdock had even asked Boisi to set up a meeting with Johnson two years earlier to see if he could cut a deal to buy Del Monte (he couldn't). "I think we could put together a blue chip consortium," suggested Boisi.

"No," said Forstmann. "I have a better idea. This is a company run by someone I know and advised by someone I know. We'll join management."

"I'm not sure that's the right strategy," said Boisi. After all, Forstmann and Goldman wanted to be on the side of the angels, and given that Johnson had started low and been topped by $3 billion, it wasn't at all clear that Johnson was the angel here. The RJR directors might be looking for someone like Forstmann to come to the rescue.

Forstmann insisted that they should at least talk to management, so later that afternoon, he called Jim Robinson. Robinson said that he was glad that Ted was interested, but he, Robinson, wasn't the person to talk to. Half an hour later Tom Hill called. Forstmann said he was interested in joining the management group. Hill said he'd set up a meeting, and Tuesday afternoon called again to say that he and Johnson would be at Teddy's office at six.

Ted Forstmann makes no pretense of knowing anything about art. Although he is fond of the canvas on the wall of his office, a large bird on a black background, he knows it isn't something a connoisseur would consider collecting, which doesn't bother him one bit. It was painted by a dear friend who lives with the

Indians in Taos, New Mexico, and besides, it covers the wall, which is what paintings are really for.

Indeed, in stark contrast to the headquarters of most financial operators, Forstmann Little's small office suite is decidedly un-luxurious. There's no art, no antiques, no fancy electronics, just some utilitarian desks and half-a-dozen framed World War II posters. The only clue as to just how much money is made there is the French National Lottery poster behind the receptionist, showing a man leaping into the air with a handful of banknotes. According to *BusinessWeek*, the three founding partners are worth well over $200 million; Forstmann alone earned close to $50 million in 1987, something shy of Henry Kravis's take, but plenty by any other measure.

Of course, Forstmann, forty-eight, is a very different character from Henry Kravis. Rumpled, chatty, and charming, Forstmann is a first-class athlete and a supercompetitor. He skis like he was born to it, plays tennis as well as most professionals, and boasted a golf handicap of 5 before he got bored and quit. Although he surely leads a good life, he is discreet by Kravis's standard and certainly not nouvelle. He bought a 6,200-square-foot apartment overlooking the East River in hopes of doing some entertaining, but then discovered it was so big he just "rattled around," and moved instead to a one-bedroom apartment across the street from the Frick Museum. His Colorado house is in old-money Aspen, not glittery Vail; he also has a beach house on the dunes in Southampton. Never married, Forstmann has had plenty of pretty girlfriends but, alas, not yet found the right one (it was Ted's brother Nicholas, who was friendly—he says it was platonic—with Pamella Bordes, the lovely $850-a-night Indian call girl).

Forstmann does have a Gulfstream II airplane, and he travels about town in a chauffeured blue Mercedes sedan, quite a step down from Kravis's stretch limousine. He's positively cheap about staff: his driver doubles as a messenger and Man Friday; his house-keeper also cooks—hopefully well enough to handle a dinner party, but not always—and lives out. When Forstmann Little celebrated its tenth anniversary in 1988, someone suggested that Forstmann hire Walter Cronkite to narrate a videotape. Although Forstmann decided that he liked the idea of a commemorative tape, he opted for comedian Jackie Mason as master of ceremonies instead. Forstmann is contemptuous of charity parties. Instead of putting his name on the Metropolitan Museum, he funds Covenant House, a halfway house that helps teenage prostitutes and drug addicts off the street. With his older brother Anthony, Ted underwrites the "Huggy Bear," a five-day tennis tournament in the backyards of their Southampton houses. Although the game raises $600,000 for three charities, Covenant House, Cities in School, and the Biological Therapy Institute— respectively Ted's, Tony's, and Nick's favorite cause—it remains controversial, even after the Suffolk County district attorney approved the practice of betting on matches.

The only thing Forstmann hates more than conspicuous consuming is "wampum" finance, and needless to say, that means that Kravis, whom Forstmann views as the prime popularizer of the junk bond, and a dissembler at that, is not high on his list. (Kravis thinks that the antipathy had more to do with jealousy, and although Forstmann does think that he deserves some of the recognition Kravis gets, it's clear that there is no one that he would less like to be.) Forstmann sums up the Kravis phenomenon in two words: Gresham's law, or, more wordily, bad money chases out good. Forstmann's money is good. Unlike Kravis, or almost any other leveraged buyout practitioner, Forstmann doesn't use junk bonds in either its plain or more highfalutin payment-in-kind varieties. Whatever issuers say about those notes now, Forstmann insists, they will, in fact, never be repaid, only refinanced, and they are not a safe investment for the mutual funds and bank investment accounts that buy them. Instead of issuing junk, Forstmann gets his mezzanine money from a special-debt partnership pool he pioneered in 1983. Investors, mostly blue chip pension funds, get a guaranteed rate of one percentage point above the five-year Treasury rate plus a 37.5 percent share of the equity of each Forstmann Little deal.

So strongly does Forstmann feel that there's a right and a wrong way to buy companies that he wrote an op-ed article for the *Wall Street Journal*, condemning junk bonds and payment-in-kind securities. "PIK is based on the notion that when a borrower is too broke to pay his interest in cash, he can pay by issuing an additional note which he also can't afford to service," he noted in the article, which, ironically, appeared on October 25, the day after Kravis announced his $90-a-share RJR bid. "This is the intellec-

tual equivalent of doubling your money by folding it in half."
Although in print Forstmann didn't mention Kravis by name, he
nonetheless regards him as the ring leader. His favorite Kravis
characterization: "in another context," wrote syndicated column-
ist R. Emmett Tyrrell after a long talk with Forstmann himself,
"Kravis would be a great promoter of the chain letter."

Of course, Forstmann says that there's a simple reason to pro-
mote chain letters: fees. Forstmann prides himself on receiving
no fees beyond a flat deal fee, nothing for "managing" the company, sitting on its board or handling divestitures, and certainly
nothing for junk financing. With lower costs, Forstmann should
be able to outbid Kravis every time, but he doesn't. Forstmann
also demands higher returns. He regularly passes on a chance to
bid because the asking price is too high; when he does bid, he
doesn't always win. Cooper Industries outbid him for McGraw-
Edison, Ron Perelman for Revlon, KKR for Duracell. Forstmann
Little has bought just fifteen companies since it was founded in
1978 and it boasts a return on equity of more than 80 percent a
year.

Forstmann's grandfather had founded Forstmann Woolens,
once the nation's leading wool fabric maker, and until the company was sold to avoid bankruptcy in 1958, the Forstmanns lived
in splendor in rarefied Greenwich, Connecticut. Although Ted's
childhood wasn't always happy—his father Julius was an alco-
holic—it did instill great sense self-confidence and a determination
to win. The four brothers were encouraged to excel at sports,
playing on their private tennis court and baseball field, and Ted
was the most athletic and competitive of the group. At Andover,
he played on the junior tennis circuit until he quit abruptly at age
sixteen after a bad call. He was a star goalie at Yale, and kept
playing for a year after he graduated in 1961. He almost tried out
for the All-American hockey team, but decided he had to buckle
down. A serious amateur pianist, he was thinking about doing
something related to music, but then changed his mind and went
to Columbia Law School instead: his father, who had always said
he wanted Ted to be a lawyer, had just died, and it seemed like
the right thing to do.

Law wasn't really Ted's calling. Although he did well enough—
and earned his rent betting on his daily bridge game—the only

thing he liked about the profession was the summer he spent investigating homicides in the Manhattan district attorney's office. After a miserable summer at Dewey, Ballantine, Bushby, Palmer & Wood and an unhappy three-year stint at Perkins, Daniels, McCormack, a smaller and supposedly less-bureaucratic firm, Forstmann dropped law for investment banking, working at two small firms and later heading corporate finance at F. S. Moseley Estabrook & Co., which the partners sold to Hallgarten & Co. in 1974. In 1978, after three years of doing his own deals from a desk at Tony's money management firm, Forstmann-Leff Associates, Ted decided to team up with his younger brother Nick who was then working at KKR, to form a buyout firm of his own.

Nick introduced Ted to William Brian Little, an investment banking partner at White Weld, the white-shoe partnership that had just been swallowed by plebeian Merrill Lynch. Little was eager to try his hand at leveraged buyouts, then well outside the mainstream. Unlike Kravis, the three new partners decided to go to their friends for money and quickly rounded up $400,000 from ten investors, including Derald M. Ruttenberg, former chairman of Studebaker-Worthington; race car driver Roger S. Penske, and RiteAid drugstore founder Lewis Lehrman. Unsure that they would be a success, Forstmann promised investors that he wouldn't be paid a cent until the investors collected their first profits (Nick and Little got small salaries). The first deal almost didn't happen. The day after Forstmann shook hands on the $20.5 million purchase of Kincaid Furniture, someone offered the Kincaid family $4 million more. But the Kincaids insisted that they had a deal with "some Yankees." And fortunately, furniture was a winner. Forstmann Little took the company public two years later, giving investors an almost unheard-of 51 percent return on equity. The second buyout, the $25 million purchase of Union Ice, was even more successful, and Forstmann never looked back. Even after subtracting Forstmann's 20 percent carry, Forstmann Little equity investors realized an aggregate return of 49 percent on the first seven deals.

Those acquisitions had been financed with bank debt, but in 1983 Forstmann realized that there was a cheaper source of mezzanine cash: corporate pension funds. Pension money was the patientest of "patient money": by law, pension officers couldn't interfere in the management of the companies they owned. So

Forstmann put together a mezzanine partnership that would combine a decent guaranteed return with plenty of upside. Under the terms of the Forstmann Little Subordinated Debt and Equity Management Buyout Partnership-IV, the most recent investors, including Aetna, Boeing, General Electric, 3M, RJR Nabisco, and American Express, get one percentage point over the five-year Treasury rate plus a 37.5 percent slice of the equity of each deal. That works out to a savings of two to four percentage points over junk bonds—and Forstmann doesn't have to pay an investment banker a fee to find it.

Forstmann's first deal after the 1983 fund closed was the buyout of Dr Pepper, the Dallas-based soft drink company. At $650 million, it was the largest then on record and it used up 60 percent of newly raised mezzanine money. It was also highly controversial. *Forbes* magazine labeled the deal "crazy" and the buyout "least likely to succeed" in an April 1984 cover story. Forstmann disagreed, but he conceded that "my name is Pepper": his reputation stood on the success of that single transaction. As it happened, Forstmann was right. He put the money-losing bottlers on the block, improved management at the core syrup business, and by the time he had sold the last piece to Hicks & Haas for $460 million two-and-a-half years later, equity investors had netted eight times their money, a return of more than 100 percent a year.

One of Forstmann's proudest moments had been his role in the 1985 Revlon take-over, the first mega-junk deal ever. After MacAndrews & Forbes, the holding company controlled by raider Ronald Perelman, launched its lowball $47.50-a-share bid in October, Revlon chairman Michel Bergerac invited Forstmann in as a white knight. The board approved Forstmann's complex $56 a share offer, but Perelman, knowing that Forstmann wasn't interested in cosmetics, offered Forstmann a sweetheart price to buy one of the medical companies and walk away. Although that was financially attractive, Bergerac thought it made him a "loser," and Forstmann, who had promised Bergerac at the beginning that they would work as a team, turned it down. In the end, Perelman convinced a Delaware judge to void the Forstmann deal, largely on the grounds that Bergerac's management contract was not in the best interests of shareholders. Perelman got the company; Forstmann, his honor and a $25 million topping fee.

Forstmann had stayed active, and friendly, since then. He had looked at buying MTV from Warner-AmEx cable, but dropped out after Warner chairman Steve Ross changed the terms for the umpteenth time. He bought Topps Chewing Gum, maker of baseball cards and Bazooka bubble gum; Sybron, a manufacturer of laboratory, dental, and medical products; and the Midland-Ross aerospace and metal fabricating company. In January 1987, he won Lear Siegler at a bargain basement $2.1 billion, after two previous bidders had been unable to raise the junk financing. He was always willing to look at a new opportunity, particularly if it meant playing "white hat" to Kravis's "black hat," as teaming up with Shearson to buy RJR did.

Actually, Forstmann's relationship with Shearson was already a little ragged. Ted had been friendly with Steve Waters before he left for Morgan Stanley; after Waters' departure, no one had picked up the ball. To make matters worse, Shearson had turned down the Topps underwriting in the spring of 1987, a decision that seemed to cast doubt on Peter Cohen's business judgment. (The Alex. Brown & Sons-sponsored offering had been a big success.) But an opportunity was an opportunity and Forstmann was willing to consider working with Shearson if that was the way to be on the side of the angels on RJR. After all, he wouldn't be counting on Shearson to make any decisions, just to deliver Ross Johnson.

While Forstmann and Salomon were deciding whether to get involved in the RJR battle at all, Henry Kravis was trying to reopen negotiations with Shearson. After all, Johnson had told Kravis that $90 a share was out of his price range: surely it made sense to team up. So although his 8:10 call to Cohen had been something of a disaster, Kravis dialed Cohen again. Cohen, outraged that Kravis had accused him of bad faith in the morning, refused the call. Kravis tried to get in the back door by having one of his bankers call Tom Hill, but Hill wouldn't take that call either.

So late in the afternoon, Beattie decided to see if he could establish contact with Cohen. Simpson Thatcher did a lot of merger work for Shearson, and Beattie had plenty of friends in the corporate finance department (Willkie Farr & Gallagher, Jack Nusbaum's firm, only handled Shearson's principal transactions). Beattie called an old friend to find out what was going on. The friend didn't know off the top of his head, but he called back later to suggest that Beattie call Cohen, which he did.

Cohen took the call, and then launched into a diatribe about how Kravis had double-crossed him.

"It might make sense to talk," suggested Beattie after that outburst. "There could be a way that we could get together."

Cohen was very skeptical, but he said he'd call back.

Several hours later, Cohen did, to invite Kravis to breakfast the next morning at the Palm Court, one of the restaurants at the Plaza Hotel just across the street from Kravis's office, on 58th Street.

Agreeing to breakfast, though, apparently hadn't implied a standoff. Someone at Shearson, presumably with Cohen's approval, had been feeding falsehoods to the press. Just before he left for the Plaza meeting Tuesday morning, Kravis had read the Page One story in that morning's *Wall Street Journal* quoting Kravis as having told Cohen at the Friday meeting that KKR was getting into the deal to "protect my franchise." There had been only three people at that meeting, so the story had clearly come from Hill or Cohen. Cohen had certainly talked to the reporter. The article quoted Cohen as saying, "We [Cohen and Kravis] ski together and socialize together, and I thought there was a higher level of conduct called for here." As far as Kravis could recall, he had skied with Cohen only once, at a Shearson client weekend in Vail, and he certainly was not admitting to having talked to Cohen and Hill about a franchise.

After the article, it was perhaps not a surprise that the breakfast didn't go well. Cohen was talking tough. He was sure that Kravis's tender offer was a bluff and that Kravis would drop out as soon as he realized that Johnson wasn't going to jump ship. So Cohen began the meal by announcing that Shearson was pressing ahead with its bid, although, he added, there might be a way to give Kravis a piece of the action, and even a board seat; he couldn't promise.

"What do you have in mind?" asked Kravis.

Cohen said splitting fees and equity fifty-fifty.

Kravis was skeptical. "We've never split a deal," he told Cohen, except for Union Texas Petroleum. "It's not something we're comfortable doing. It's a question of control. If we're going to put money into a company, we have to be in charge."

"Well, it's team up with us or bid against each other," said Cohen.

True, and a bidding war would push up the price. "What's management's deal?" asked Kravis. Maybe there was a way to make this work after all.

"The usual," said Cohen, "the standard deal."

Kravis didn't know what that meant: there was no standard deal. But he let it pass. "What kind of fees are you talking about?" he asked.

"A total of two hundred fifty million," said Cohen. Kravis's share would be $125 million.

"We'll get back to you," said Kravis, although he didn't think it would be to say yes.

Peter Cohen spent most of the day Tuesday in board meetings, first the American Express board meeting on the 51st floor of the World Financial Center, then the Shearson Lehman Hutton meeting downstairs. Not surprisingly, RJR came up at both sessions, but no one said much beyond that the deal was attractive and Shearson hoped to win.

Between meetings, Cohen and Shearson president Jeff Lane broke away to have lunch with Salomon president Tom Strauss. It was a busy day for Strauss too: Tuesday was the first day of the annual Salomon compensation meetings in which Gutfreund, Strauss, and the other members of the executive committee personally approved bonuses and raises for each of Salomon's professionals. With Strauss were two of the Salomon team members, Michael Zimmerman, co-head of merchant banking, and Bill Strong, the corporate finance man who knew the most about RJR because he had been heading the Hanson team. Strauss had wanted to bring Jay Higgins, vice-chairman and head of investment banking, but Higgins was on his way to London to talk to branch executives about proposed bonuses.

Never one for small-talk, Cohen got straight to the point. Shearson would partner up fifty–fifty. Salomon would get half the equity, half the fees, half the decision-making power. Shearson had agreed not to take a carry, Cohen explained, and Johnson had demanded an unusually generous management agreement. Cohen handed Strauss a copy of the contract and Strauss skimmed the terms. "We can't do this," he said.

"I know," said Cohen. Shearson couldn't either. But it was what Shearson had had to agree to to get the deal; Johnson had threatened to take the LBO somewhere else if Cohen didn't agree. The contract would be renegotiated later.

Jim Robinson was troubled at the way things seemed to be headed. Somehow, Cohen and Kravis weren't getting going on a joint deal, which was what Robinson regarded as the only sensible resolution—although Robinson was convinced that Kravis and Johnson would hit it off, if they ever sat down together. That didn't seem to be in the cards. Or maybe it was. Steve Waters of Morgan Stanley had called Robinson on Monday afternoon to say that he thought he could set something up. Robinson was determined to stay behind the scenes while Cohen did the wheeling and dealing, so instead of raising the matter with Cohen directly, he suggested to Johnson that Johnson call Waters himself. Tuesday afternoon, while Cohen and Robinson were at the Shearson board meeting, Johnson did. "I knew you'd take my call," he kidded when Waters got on the line, despite his not having taken Waters's calls earlier in the month.

"I always take your calls," said Waters.

Johnson asked about the possibility of getting together, and Waters repeated what he had said to Robinson: he thought it could work. There might be some ego problems, not the least of which was that both Kravis and Cohen were determined to get the credit for the largest leveraged buyout in history, but Waters was sure that there would be a way to solve that. Johnson and Waters talked about what Johnson wanted to do with the company after he bought it and how far he was willing to bend to work with KKR. Convinced that Johnson, at least, was flexible, Waters called Kravis. Kravis told him to have Johnson call direct.

"Come on down," Kravis told Johnson—Johnson's office was, after all in the same building seven floors up—"I'm happy to talk."

Johnson said he'd be there at four and called Cohen to say that he was on his way. Since Johnson didn't say that he had instigated the meeting, Cohen assumed that it was Kravis's idea, and he took that as further proof that Kravis was desperate to woo Johnson to his team. Johnson's session with Kravis and George Roberts, who had just arrived from California, went well. Johnson rambled on about RJR's food and tobacco operations and why he wanted to do a buyout. There was no question but that Kravis and Roberts were impressed, and the chemistry seemed to work.

The meeting was just winding down when, at 6:15, Johnson got a call from Tom Hill reminding him that they had a meeting with Forstmann at 6:00. "I've got to go," Johnson told Kravis. "I'm supposed to talk to Forstmann."

Kravis was genuinely surprised. He had known that Shearson didn't have the money lined up to do the deal, but it hadn't occurred to him that they were so desperate that they were talking to Forstmann. Kravis didn't think it would work; no deal was big enough to accommodate both Forstmann's ego and Cohen's, if a joint deal could even be financed given Ted's near-religious refusal to issue junk bonds.

Just after Johnson had left, Kravis called Jim Robinson with a proposal for a joint deal. KKR would sell Shearson a 10 percent slice of the equity and pay the firm $125 million, half of what Cohen had told him that morning Shearson planned to collect in fees.

"That sounds a little thin," said Robinson, who was in his car headed toward Rockefeller Center to host a black-tie New York City Partnership dinner at NBC. "But you need to talk to Peter."

As soon as Kravis got off the line, Robinson called Cohen to say that Kravis would be calling. Just as Robinson was repeating what Kravis had offered, Cohen's secretary passed him a note that Kravis was on the other line. "Talk to Henry direct," said Robinson.

Cohen did, and he regarded the KKR proposal as worse than thin: it was so low it was insulting. Although Kravis had put no fuse on the offer, Cohen was angry enough to set his own. "We'll be back by midnight," said Cohen. Presumably to say no.

"We just came from a meeting with your dearest friends," said Johnson, when he arrived at Ted Forstmann's office in the General Motors building at six-thirty.

Forstmann was floored. His dearest friends? "Who's that?" he asked.

"The guys on the forty-second floor," said Johnson.

"What?" asked Forstmann, still puzzled. Then it dawned on

him: they were also negotiating with KKR, whose offices are on the forty-second floor of 9 West 57th Street.

Johnson realized he had made a mistake, and he back-pedaled. "We have to talk to them," he said. "It's pro forma."

Forstmann said that he hoped so. Then he launched into an explanation of how he did deals, and how that was different from how Kravis did deals. Johnson seemed receptive.

Forstmann's secretary interrupted to say that she had a call for Hill, and he went out to take it at her desk. "You won't believe what Kravis just offered," said Hill when he came back. "It's insulting."

Hill didn't volunteer the terms and Forstmann didn't ask.

"We've already made a deal with management," said Hill, after Johnson had given Forstmann an overview of the company. "That can't be reopened."

Clearly something was up. "Well," said Forstmann, "that's okay. But I have my own way of dealing with management, so we might have to come back to it later."

But there was a lot of work to do before Forstmann got to that. He and Hill agreed to meet again at Nabisco's 9 West 57th Street office at eight o'clock. There, Forstmann and Boisi, who hadn't been at the six o'clock meeting, would get more information about the company so that Forstmann could decide if he wanted to buy RJR Nabisco.

CHAPTER 8

Cigar Smoke, Jesse Helms, and Sideline Cheers

October 25

Jim Stern, Shearson's junk bond chief, was home in northern Westchester, an hour outside New York, when he got Peter Cohen's message to head to 9 West 57th, and he wasn't too pleased that he had to go back into the city. He had left work early that night because it was his wife's birthday and he had promised to be home with her and the kids to celebrate. He had already changed into jeans and a sport shirt when the call came through, but he changed back into his suit before he drove in. He even put on the same now-dirty white shirt so that no one would know that he had been home and back.

Stern had been talking to bankers all day about the commercial bank financing, and it wasn't until he arrived at RJR's office at eight that he found out how much was suddenly going on: not only was there a new low-ball offer from Kravis for splitting the deal, there was also the possibility of teaming up with Salomon Brothers or Forstmann Little or both. And Cohen said he wanted to get things sorted out before morning.

That seemed unlikely to Stern, but clearly some decisions could be made. Indeed, even before Stern arrived, Michael Zimmerman, the Salomon team leader, had settled down in "the fishbowl," the large conference room next to Johnson's office with a glass wall facing the corridor and a massive round table that was more than vaguely reminiscent of the Star Trek television set. Zimmerman had gotten his first look at the management contract at that session, and he had repeated what Tom Strauss had told Cohen over lunch: it wasn't going to fly. Salomon was never going to agree to a governance structure in which Ross Johnson, who had put up no money, could overrule Shearson, which had invested $1 billion. Zimmerman was also shocked by the terms of Johnson's money deal. Normally management gets a flat percentage to put them precisely on the same footing as the other investors. The optics of having an increasing scale, albeit tied to performance, and a group of only seven executives were so bad as to be a deal killer.

But Zimmerman saw no point in pressing on the management contract just now. Salomon hadn't yet decided that it was going to team up with Shearson, whatever the management contract said. To make that decision, Salomon needed to know more about RJR, and that was why Zimmerman was at Nabisco's office. Salomon had gotten interested on the basis of public information, but now the firm had signed a confidentiality agreement, which allowed the bankers to look at normally secret internal numbers.

While Zimmerman studied the spreadsheets, Cohen and Hill sat in Johnson's office next door talking about how to respond to Kravis's proposal. Already Cohen had called Dick Beattie to say that the offer was insulting. "It's a starting point," Beattie had said. "Maybe we should talk."

"I don't think there's anything to talk about," said Cohen.

"Think about it," said Beattie. "Call me back."

To Hill, Beattie's words were a clear statement that KKR was willing to give up much more than 10 percent, and he thought that Beattie's invitation was worth pursuing. Like Cohen, Hill wasn't that worried about KKR. Hill was also convinced that Kravis would drop out if Johnson stuck with Shearson; as far as he was concerned, the only advantage to teaming up was that it guaranteed that the deal got done and at the lowest price.

So, at about nine o'clock, Cohen called Beattie back. "I want to talk to Henry tonight," he said. But he didn't know how to reach him; in their last conversation, Kravis had told Cohen that he was going to a dinner party that night but Cohen didn't know where.

Beattie did, but he didn't tell Cohen. Instead he said that he would arrange a call after Kravis got home. "Where are you going to be about eleven-thirty?" he asked.

Cohen gave the number at Johnson's office.

"I'll be back to you," said Beattie.

Ted Forstmann and his team arrived at 9 West 57th as scheduled just after eight o'clock. There were only four of them: Forstmann, his brother Nick, Boisi, and Steve Fraidin, Forstmann's lawyer from Fried, Frank, Harris, Shriver & Jacobson. Someone took them to a small conference room at the opposite side of the building from the fishbowl and they waited a long time for the Shearson people to arrive. Finally Cohen came in with Hill and Jack Nusbaum of Willkie, Farr and what Forstmann describes as "an army" of bankers, lawyers, and technicians. Forstmann took the lawyers' presence as a bad sign. He doesn't like lawyers in any case, and now they were totally superfluous, since he hadn't yet decided that he wanted any part of the Shearson deal.

Hill did the introductions. Forstmann said that he hadn't decided what he was going to do, but he had three options: doing something with Shearson, doing something by himself, or doing nothing. Then he launched into a discussion of how he did deals, including the terms of his mezzanine partnership, and the evils of junk bond finance.

Cohen didn't know anything about Forstmann except that he was a friend of Jim Robinson and he had a lot of mezzanine money. This lecture on how junk was ruining America didn't seem relevant to an RJR buyout, and Cohen shifted impatiently in his seat. To Boisi's amazement, Cohen left before Forstmann had even finished.

Hill introduced Steve Goldstone, Johnson's lawyer, and said that Goldstone would be talking about strategy. Goldstone made a few unmemorable remarks, and then someone stuck his head in the door to say that Hill and Goldstone were needed for a caucus. They disappeared, and after that the more junior Shearson bankers began to disappear as well. Finally, at midnight, there were just six people in the room, Forstmann's team plus two Cohen minions.

Forstmann thought that this was somewhat odd, but the Shearson men professed to be interested in how the nuts and bolts of Forstmann's mezzanine partnership worked, so Forstmann explained that. After a while, there wasn't anything more to say, and they just looked at each other.

It seemed clear that the action was somewhere else.

Jim Robinson had arrived at RJR from the dinner at Rockefeller Center at about ten o'clock, and he got right down to business. The first priority was the management contract. He had known from the time he saw it Friday morning that it was a public relations disaster, but this was the first chance he had had to sit down with Johnson for a one-on-one chat. "This contract," Robinson began, as he closed the door to Johnson's office. "You're getting a big chunk."

"It's a big deal," countered Johnson.

"It's too much," said Robinson. "It's going to be a real problem in terms of pr."

Johnson had heard that before, from Stern, Hill, and Cohen. "Andy negotiated it," he said, implying that he hadn't been aware of the terms.

"Is this all going to seven people?" asked Robinson.

"Oh, no," said Ross. There would be twenty people in the senior management group, and another 156 people in a management sub-group.

"You've got to take a haircut," said Robinson.

"Well," said Johnson. He guessed he could. "But you'd better tell your bandits the same thing. They're going to pay themselves a $170-million fee."

"I guess that's who I talk to next," said Robinson. He left to find Cohen to talk about Shearson's fee, and Steve Goldstone wandered in. Johnson hadn't seen Goldstone since his four o'clock meeting with Kravis, so he briefed Goldstone on that. Although Johnson thought it had gone well, Goldstone was worried that Johnson might have given Kravis the impression that he was willing to dump Shearson to do a KKR deal. Johnson didn't think Kravis had understood that, but nonetheless, Goldstone insisted that he call Kravis to make sure that the point was crystal clear: Johnson was sticking with Shearson. If Kravis wanted Johnson on his team, he would have to join Shearson as well.

Dick Beattie had called Kravis at the dinner party long enough to tell him that they needed to talk as soon as he got home, and at eleven o'clock Kravis called to find out what was up. Beattie briefed Kravis on his earlier conversation with Cohen, and said Cohen would call at midnight.

Midnight came and went.

At quarter after twelve the phone finally rang. It wasn't Cohen, but Johnson. "What you offered them is crazy," he told Kravis, meaning the 10 percent stake plus $125 million. "They aren't going to accept." He hung up.

That seemed rather abrupt, but Kravis didn't have time to think why, when the phone rang again. It was Johnson again. "I'm sticking with Shearson and American Express," he told Kravis this time. "I won't join your group."

Kravis figured that Johnson was calling from a Shearson meeting and that someone had told him he hadn't been tough enough on the first call. "That was never an issue," said Kravis. "I assume you're stuck together like glue."

Johnson didn't have a response to that, but five minutes later, Kravis's phone rang yet again. This time it was Cohen. "Why don't we get together to talk," he said.

"Okay," said Kravis. "I'll call you in the morning."

"Now," said Cohen.

"Now?" said Kravis. "It's the middle of the night."

"If we're going to talk, it has to be now," said Cohen.

Kravis thought that that was preposterous, but he didn't have much choice. If it was now or never, he was talking now. "Okay," he said. He phoned Roberts at the Carlyle to say he was on his way. Then he called Beattie. "Are you dressed?" he asked.

Beattie was, but in jeans and a sport shirt. There wasn't time to change. Beattie grabbed his parka and hurried downstairs to flag a cab to Nabisco. He'd pick up Kravis and Roberts on the way.

While they waited for Kravis to arrive, Cohen, Hill, Johnson, and Robinson held a quick strategy session. The four team members agreed that they would all sit down with Kravis and Roberts when the KKR people first arrived—both Jack Nusbaum and Steve Goldstone would be there too—but that Robinson and Johnson would leave before any serious negotiating got underway. Hill thought it made more sense for the financial partners to hammer out their deal by themselves. Cohen would play nice guy and chairman, Hill would be the heavy. After he left the meeting, Robinson would break the news to his friend Teddy Forstmann that Kravis had come for a final round of talks.

Kravis, Roberts, and Beattie showed up at about 1:00 A.M. After a few minutes of small talk, Johnson and Robinson excused themselves. "We'll be down the hall if you need us," said Johnson.

Roberts sniffed. Apparently the Shearson crew had been chain-smoking cigars for hours; the air in the office was so thick that it was hard to breathe. "Do you make cigars too?" he joked. He gestured at the air. "Is there somewhere else that we can talk?"

There wasn't. All the other conference rooms were occupied, by Salomon and Forstmann.

"Do you want me to stop?" asked Cohen, who was smoking a cigar.

Given the amount of smoke in the air, it didn't really matter. Still, Cohen, who had been sitting in front of Johnson's desk, got up and walked around to the back. When he finished that cigar, he put a fresh one in his mouth, but he didn't light it. The others sat in the circle of white upholstered chairs around the coffee table.

"Why don't you begin, Tom," said Cohen.

"Let's get something straight," began Hill. "As we see it, you've made a bad misjudgment here. You've made a hostile offer, and we're not going to let you get away with it. We're going to get Jesse Helms after you." Helms, the senator from North Carolina, did have more than a passing interest in the fate of RJR, the state's largest employer. "We're going to get your investors after you. We're going to tell the press that you are hostile."

Roberts shook his head. "That's very interesting," he said, "but we haven't made a hostile offer."

"Tom," said Kravis. "Remember, this is something new for you. You're not on the defense. You're a bidder. We're a competing bidder. If you want to talk about a deal, fine. If that's all you have to say, we'll go home."

There was a long silence.

"Maybe we can work something out," said Cohen. "You have three choices. You can join us. You can buy part of RJR from us. Or you can go ahead on your own." But the proposal Kravis had made at six-thirty was clearly out. The only split Cohen was willing to consider was fifty–fifty.

Kravis was dubious, but it was worth exploring, as long as

Cohen was willing to cede control of the board to KKR. "What's the deal with management?" he asked.

"We can't talk about that," said Cohen.

Kravis didn't press, but he knew something was up. If management was getting the "standard" deal, Cohen wouldn't be so evasive about it. Perhaps Cohen's second alternative, buying part of RJR from Shearson, was workable. Johnson had already been quoted in the newspaper as saying that he intended to sell all the food businesses; now Roberts suggested that KKR might be interested in buying them with an installment note, the tax deferral trick that Campeau had used to save $200 million in taxes when it busted up Federated Department Stores in the spring.

Cohen didn't seem to understand how that would work.

"How much do you think the company is worth?" asked Roberts.

There was another long pause. "Fifteen-and-a-half billion," said Hill.

Roberts thought it was worth more like twelve, but he walked through the installment payment system at a price of $15 billion. KKR would pay with a ten-year note, which, because RJR would be liable for capital gains tax only as the cash came in, would save the company roughly $4 billion in capital gains taxes. But although RJR wouldn't get the cash immediately, the shareholders would, since the company would "monetize" the note by borrowing against it at the bank to fund a special cash dividend.

The idea was a nonstarter. Cohen clearly wasn't interested in preselling assets to KKR, particularly not at Roberts's $12 billion price. There was nothing more to talk about. Kravis, Roberts, and Beattie went back downstairs to flag a cab. Although it was one-thirty in the morning, there were half-a-dozen limousines parked outside the building. Kravis looked at Roberts. Who else was talking to RJR in the middle of the night?

Robinson and Johnson had gone straight from the Kravis-Cohen meeting in Johnson's office to Ed Horrigan's office on the other side of the building. After they had settled down in the armchairs, Robinson sent one of the Shearson people to summon Forstmann over. Forstmann was a little surprised to see Robinson—he hadn't been at the earlier meeting—but he figured that the tuxedo and loose tie was part of the titan of industry image. "Do you want a drink?" asked Robinson, looking at the bar.

Forstmann didn't. "We're not getting anything done," he complained to Johnson. "It's late. We need to get started figuring out what RJR is all about. Maybe we could have a talk with management."

"Kravis didn't need to talk to the management before he bid," said Johnson.

"We're very different from Kravis," said Forstmann. "We don't do hostile deals." Among other reasons, because bidding without information didn't make a lot of investment sense.

"Kravis doesn't think he needs management," said Johnson.

Forstmann was getting irritated: why did Johnson keep bringing up Kravis? "Who cares what Kravis thinks," said Forstmann. "You won't have a deal unless you get things moving with us."

Robinson put his hand up. "Teddy," he said. "I have to tell you something. Down the hall, we're meeting with Kravis."

"You're what?" said Forstmann. He couldn't believe it. Six hours ago, Hill had told him that what Kravis had offered was insulting and Johnson had said that his four o'clock meeting with Kravis was "pro forma." How could they now be negotiating? And why hadn't he been told? Was Shearson playing games? "What do you think you're doing?" he asked.

"It's not going to go anywhere," said Johnson.

"Then why are you wasting your time?" asked Forstmann.

"Teddy," said Robinson. "I agree with Ross. It's very unlikely that it will go anywhere."

"If you're negotiating with us, it's wrong to talk to them," said Forstmann.

"What we are doing is the best thing," said Robinson, "not the right thing."

"Oh," said Forstmann. He thought Robinson looked pained. "I see."

There was a long silence.

"Don't you understand that we're different from Kravis," said Forstmann. "If I had read about your deal"—which of course he had—"I would not have jumped in"—which he hadn't. "I would have cheered management from the sidelines." But now that KKR had made an offer, effectively starting an auction, it was open bidding, and Forstmann was looking to get involved on the side of the board.

"We'd like to be able to call you when this is over," said Robinson.

"You have my phone number," said Forstmann.

And Robinson would have to call, because Forstmann had already decided that he wasn't sticking around. He marched back to his conference room and told his team what had just happened.

That was it. As far as Boisi was concerned they were leaving, but he was so mad at the way that Forstmann had been treated that he strode into the hallway to give the Shearson people a piece of his mind. When Boisi came back, Ted and Nick Forstmann and Fraidin had gathered up their papers. The four put on their jackets and headed for the door. Or one of the doors. The conference room had two exits, one directly into the executive reception area, one past the kitchen into the back corridor. For no reason in particular, they chose the door to the corridor.

And when Boisi opened it, who should be striding toward them but Peter Cohen.

"Let's get going," he said.

Apparently Boisi's complaining to the Shearson executives had gotten Cohen worried. The Forstmann team caucused. "Do we stay or go?" asked Boisi. If Ted had truly had it, they might as well go, since there was no point in talking about anything. If Ted thought there was still a chance of doing something, then they should stay. They had nothing to lose, and perhaps something to gain. Surely Cohen would be so embarrassed by the way he had treated Ted thus far that Ted would have some extra bargaining leverage.

"We've just been talking to Kravis," said Tom Hill, when everyone had settled at the table. "It didn't work out."

"Are you going to be taking any more calls from them?" asked Boisi.

"I think we're obligated to take one more call," said Hill.

"Then what?" asked Boisi. "Do you think that's the last time he is going to call? Will you tell me that if they call again, you won't call back?"

"You should answer that," one of the bankers said to Johnson. Johnson didn't, but Forstmann had made his point. There would be no more discussions with Kravis as long as Forstmann was on the team.

Finally, they began to talk about RJR and the Shearson bid. Boisi explained that what Forstmann and Goldman had in mind was a blue chip consortium, fully financed, and "wrapped in the American flag." He thought that the best way to raise the bank money was to presell assets and said that he had talked to both Proctor & Gamble and Castle & Cooke, who were interested in pieces.

Johnson interjected that he didn't want to do any presales. Surely they would get the best prices selling the food companies in small pieces.

"That's true as a matter of value," said Boisi, "but you'll never get there because you won't be able to get bank finance to buy the company in the first place."

As they were arguing about that, Cohen suddenly mentioned that Shearson was also talking to Salomon. It wasn't clear in what context, but it didn't really matter. Forstmann still wasn't sure what he wanted to do and Salomon's presence didn't affect that decision one way or the other.

CHAPTER 9

Kangaroo Court

October 26 to October 28

While Peter Cohen, Henry Kravis, John Gutfreund, and Ted Forstmann were maneuvering behind the scenes, Marty Davis was focused on Gulf + Western, the company he was paid to run. Like the other members of the Special Committee, Davis had left Atlanta on October 20, after the morning meeting to hire Dillon and Lazard, and he had no more RJR business to attend to until Wednesday, October 26, when the committee was scheduled to meet again in New York. As a committee member and director, he was naturally interested in the voluminous press coverage that had followed the Thursday morning press release. Davis had been surprised, if delighted, by Kravis's $90-a-share bid on Monday, and bemused by the Tuesday report that he had told Cohen he would bid to protect his franchise. Although Davis could imagine someone thinking that, it seemed a singularly stupid thing to say.

Actually, what was most on Davis's mind as he left his office on Columbus Circle for the Wednesday meeting was not Kravis but Johnson. Johnson's behavior since October 19 seemed to Davis beyond the pale. The dinner in Atlanta had been bad enough; now it seemed clear that Johnson looked at the Special Committee as a kangaroo court rather than a decision-making body. It wasn't just that KKR had "bumped" the price up by $3 billion, an amount that Ira Harris, Davis's friend and the committee's banker, noted was large enough to make the list of ten largest deals ever.

Worse, Harris and his team had learned over the weekend that Johnson had apparently known that at $75 a share he was scalping the shareholders. In accordance with Davis's insistence that the bankers get cracking on their own evaluation of RJR, Hugel had reluctantly combed through Johnson's files and sent several cartons of documents to Lazard headquarters at One Rockefeller Plaza in New York on Thursday afternoon. Those papers certainly suggested that $90 a share was a more appropriate opening price; indeed there was hardly a study in the box that put the value of RJR at less than $85 a share and one, by former Standard Brands president Reuben Gutoff, even stated that the company could go for $100 a share in an auction.

The conclusion was obvious. Johnson had expected the committee to rubber-stamp his lowball bid without so much as looking at it. Davis wasn't about to do that, even if he did consider Johnson a personal friend. Ethics came first.

So when Davis arrived at the meeting, he was determined to disabuse the other committee members of any notion that they might have about doing Johnson a favor. To that end, the first thing Davis wanted to know was whether Charlie Hugel had contacted Kravis to welcome him as a bidder, and if not, why not.

Hugel hadn't, for no reason that he was willing to admit to Davis, but he promised that he would. Nor had Hugel given any more thought to how the company should be sold. Davis assumed that that meant that he thought he was going to sign on Johnson's dotted line at the end of the week, and Davis made it clear that that was not to be. They were going to have an auction and they were going to look at a restructuring as an alternative if none of the bids were high enough to be considered fair. That statement produced a heated debate. Hugel insisted that the company couldn't restructure. If Johnson and his team left, there would be no management.

"So what?" said Davis. They would find someone else. It might not be easy, but if that was what was in the best interests of the shareholders, that was what they were going to do. By the time the meeting broke up at five-thirty, Davis and Hugel were hardly on speaking terms.

Ironically, they had to spend the evening being civil to each other. That night, Hugel was the honoree at a New York City Boys Club dinner at the Waldorf-Astoria. Hugel hadn't ever done much for the Boys Club—his charitable activity is heading the board of trustees at Lafayette College, his alma mater—but Johnson, the dinner chairman, had pulled strings to get Hugel the honor.

If Johnson had hoped that the dinner would be a reminder to Hugel that he owed his friend a favor, it didn't work. Davis and his wife were seated at Johnson's table, and Hugel, at the next table, didn't so much as come over to say hello.

Honored and chastised, Hugel finally called Kravis on Thursday morning with his welcome message. It was clear from Kravis's tone that he was greatly relieved. Given the horrendous press he had already gotten about the protecting-the-franchise remark and the unsolicited bid, Kravis had been worried that Hugel would remain silent, or, worse, criticize KKR as Kroger had done, forever tarring the firm as a raider. Hugel's call was a clear signal that that wasn't going to happen. Even if the committee didn't actually give KKR any help, the firm would now at least be perceived as friendly. Phone call notwithstanding, Kravis didn't expect much help. He was so sure that Hugel was in Johnson's back pocket that when he had gotten wind of the Special Committee meeting on Wednesday afternoon, the day before Hugel's call, he assumed that the reason it had been called was to approve Johnson's contract to buy RJR. Bruce Wasserstein had even panicked and insisted that Dick Beattie call first Peter Atkins, and, when he couldn't get through to him, Atkins's boss Joe Flom, to insist that RJR not sign the Shearson agreement until they had talked to KKR. Beattie had left the room, but not called. Going over Atkins's head had seemed like the best way to set him against KKR, and Beattie knew that Atkins was too good a lawyer to contemplate signing a sweetheart deal with management two days after a competing bidder announced a tender offer. After standing in the hallway for a few minutes with his partner Casey Cogut, Beattie had gone back into the conference room, and assured Wasserstein—and Kravis—that "everything is going to be okay," without volunteering how he knew.

With Hugel apparently firmly in Johnson's camp, and the RJR

books closed, Kravis had begun to investigate other sources of information about the company as soon as he got to the office Wednesday morning. One of the first calls was to Tylee Wilson, Johnson's predecessor; Wilson had been trying to get in touch with Kravis for two days now. As soon as he saw the KKR bid on the wire, Wilson had called his old friend Jim Walter, chairman of Jim Walter Corp., the Florida-based building company that KKR had bought in the summer of 1987, to offer to help.

After some back and forth, Wilson agreed to come to New York for a meeting Friday morning. As it happened, before he showed up, Hugel called Kravis to set up a meeting Friday afternoon, but Kravis decided not to cancel the session with Wilson. He was sure that Wilson would be helpful; he might even be the man to bring in as chairman if KKR won RJR. So, Thursday afternoon, Kravis sent his G-III plane to Atlanta to pick up Wilson.

Curiously, even before Wilson arrived, people seemed to know he was coming. Reynolds Tobacco executives began to call to volunteer their mostly negative opinions. Reporters began to call Kravis's office to ask if he had already hired Wilson, and Steve Waters reported that Johnson himself was agitated by the news. For days, Kravis worried that his phone had been tapped. In fact, the explanation was much simpler. When Kravis had called Wilson's office in Jacksonville, Wilson had been in Atlanta at a BellSouth board meeting. Wilson's secretary had pulled him out of the session to give him Kravis's message, and although Kravis had specifically told Wilson to keep the trip a secret, Wilson had immediately announced to the directors that Kravis was bringing him to New York to become chairman of RJR.

For all the trouble, the Friday morning meeting with Wilson was a washout. Wilson was trying to be helpful, but he had been away from the company so long that his information was no longer current. Although Wilson had gotten high marks from stock market analysts back in the days that he had been chairman, he didn't impress Kravis. He was a management consultant type, not a hands-on manager.

Fortunately, the meeting with Hugel that afternoon went reasonably well. Hugel insisted that the committee intended to fully cooperate with KKR and he told Kravis that he could look at the books as soon as he signed a confidentiality agreement.

"Is this really going to be a level auction?" asked Kravis. "Or does management have an understanding?"

"It's going to be a level auction," said Hugel.

By this time, Kravis's investment bankers had picked up the word that Shearson was talking to at least half a dozen companies about buying various RJR assets. It wasn't clear how serious those discussions were, but Kravis now told Hugel that he wanted them stopped. Shopping pieces of the company could damage RJR's competitive position, Kravis explained, and as a possible future owner, he was very worried about that.

Cynics said that there was a second, more important, reason to put a ban on presales. Kravis knew that KKR didn't have to do any preselling to line up its bank money; given KKR's record, the banks would tend to believe what Kravis and Roberts said they could realize from a bust-up. Johnson and Cohen didn't have the same credibility. It was even possible that without preselling, they would not be able to put together the money at all.

Whatever Kravis's real motivation, his charge that Johnson was preselling gave Hugel an excuse to call Johnson. After Johnson had denied any intention of preselling assets, Hugel asked again when he planned to bid.

Johnson didn't know.

CHAPTER 10

Mad Enough to Punch the Wall

October 26 to October 30

While Kravis was talking to Wilson and Hugel, Ted Forstmann was cutting a deal with Peter Cohen, or trying to. It wasn't going very well.

Cohen's poor form in talking to both Kravis and Forstmann Tuesday night notwithstanding, Forstmann did want to be on the side of the angels and he still thought that that was Shearson. So he was willing to keep discussions going. Wednesday morning, things seemed to be back on track. Cohen asked Forstmann to sign a confidentiality agreement, normally a prelude to producing some useful information about a company's functions.

Steve Fraidin, Forstmann's lawyer, spent most of the day trying to work out the details. Fraidin had opened negotiations with Jack Nusbaum, Peter Cohen's lawyer, whom Fraidin took to be representing the Shearson group, since he had sent the draft over. But after Fraidin and Nusbaum had ironed out their problems, Nusbaum said he was only representing Shearson, and Fraidin would have to talk to Steve Goldstone's partner George A. "Gar" Basin at Davis Polk, and Peter Atkins at Skadden as well. Fraidin did, but the fact of the triple negotiation was worrisome: just who was in charge here? Fraidin wondered. And, given the disorganization, was it really going to be possible to agree to anything?

Once the confidentiality papers were signed, Cohen invited

125

Forstmann to a meeting with Tom Strauss at Shearson head-quarters. Forstmann had assumed that they were going to talk about RJR operations, and brought Geoff Boisi along to help. But the company didn't come up; instead, the discussion focused on finance. Talking about how to raise money before you figured out how much the company was worth was doing the deal ass-backwards as far as Forstmann was concerned. But it didn't seem appropriate to complain; surely they would get to the company eventually.

"I don't think that's going to work," said Boisi after Cohen had outlined how he thought the layers of money could be put together. When Boisi tried to explain why, Cohen wasn't able to respond. This wasn't his area of expertise. "Why don't we get you together with the LBO guys," he suggested, at a meeting at 9 West 57th Street that night.

Boisi agreed, but there was one item he wanted to settle right now: presales. This time Hill conceded that preselling assets would make it easier to line up bank money. However, Hill said, under the terms of the management agreement that wasn't pos-sible: Johnson was to do all the selling.

Boisi was startled. That wasn't the sort of thing that went into management contracts. "What else does this contract say?" he asked.

Hill didn't answer directly, but as Boisi pressed, the outlines emerged: if certain "bogies" were met, to use Hill's term, man-agement would get a percentage of the equity, although what percentage was left unsaid. Management would control both the board and corporate governance; Forstmann could make sugges-tions, but Johnson had the final say.

"How much money is Johnson putting in?" asked Forstmann, incredulous that Shearson had surrendered control.

None, said Hill. Johnson's only contribution came from cashing in his options.

"That doesn't make any sense," said Forstmann.

Hill said that it was non-negotiable.

"Can I have a copy of this?" asked Fraidin, Forstmann's lawyer.

"We'll see," said Nusbaum.

"Look," said Forstmann. "You can't have an agreement like that. It's going to kill the deal."

Forstmann knew whereof he spoke. He had had a signed agreement to buy Revlon, and a Delaware judge had thrown it out primarily because of the management contract that he said tainted the deal. The Revlon contract had been miserly compared to what Johnson was apparently getting, and it had certainly not included any corporate governance power.

Cohen and Hill seemed disinclined to tinker with the contract until Boisi volunteered that it was a deal-breaker. That got Cohen's attention, and as the meeting broke up, he said that he would talk to Johnson immediately.

He didn't. When Boisi and Nick Forstmann arrived at 9 West 57th that night, Hill confessed that no one had raised the contract with Johnson yet. Actually the session got off to a bad start. Hill made a joke that Boisi thought was insulting to Nick, and Boisi told him to be more respectful if he wanted Forstmann's money. By that time, it seemed clear that nothing serious was going to be discussed at the meeting. There were so many Shearson and Salomon guys in the room that they had to sit in a double row around the table. Boisi knew that decisions never got made at a mob session.

Eventually Jim Stern passed out a financing plan.

Boisi was aghast. There was no way that this was going to work. But before he could say anything, Chas Phillips, the junk bond man from Salomon, jumped in. Although Salomon itself didn't have much experience with junk, Phillips did, having just defected from the large merchant banking department at Morgan Stanley. This was the first time Phillips had seen Stern's plan, and he said flatly that it wouldn't work. There was too much debt and not enough equity; the maturities were too short and badly distributed, the interest rates were ridiculously low.

Boisi elaborated on those problems, and he pointed out that in addition to its obvious conceptual flaws, the plan was also structurally impossible since it didn't include the Forstmann equity partners. Boisi remembered quite clearly telling the Shearson people the night before that the equity partners had to be included along with the mezzanine partners. Forstmann didn't do deals for just half his investors. Forstmann would need at least 60 percent of the stock, 37.5 percent for the mezzanine partners and another 23 percent for his equity investors.

"We can't give you that much equity," said Stern.

Boisi outlined how they thought the deal could work, but Stern didn't make any commitments. Instead, he turned the meeting back over to Hill to discuss bidding strategy. Boisi suggested that Shearson make part of its payment to shareholders in the form of a "stub," and residual stock interest in the leveraged company. He also thought that when the group got around to bidding, and the Shearson guys had made it clear that they didn't intend to do that any time soon, they needed to put more cash on the table than Kravis had. Boisi was convinced that whoever offered the most cash would win.

Hill made it clear that he had no interest in giving away equity and he intended to bid cash, but he didn't focus on either point. Instead he seemed mostly concerned about whether Kravis would go ahead with what he regarded as a hostile bid. One of the Salomon people had suggested countering the KKR offer with an offer of their own since all that Shearson currently had on the table was an informal indication at $75 a share, but that idea didn't seem to be popular. Salomon was also pushing something called "the ups," a proportionate interest in the total proceeds of the sale of the food companies. To be sure, giving shareholders the ups meant less profits for the buyout group, but short of true stub, it seemed like the best way to get the deal done. Hill didn't dignify that with a response.

By the time the meeting broke up near midnight, Boisi was convinced that the Shearson guys didn't have a clue as to what they were doing and he was worried that Forstmann and Cohen weren't understanding each other. Forstmann's position was that this was his deal and Cohen would just be an investor. Cohen clearly didn't grasp that, and Boisi wasn't sure that Forstmann understood that Cohen, despite his words to the contrary, regarded Forstmann not as a partner, but simply as an investor in his deal.

Cohen, too, was beginning to wonder if Forstmann was the ideal partner, or indeed if he even intended to be a partner. Forstmann himself seemed to be trustworthy, but Cohen was sure that Boisi was up to no good. Boisi seemed more interested in his idea of a blue chip consortium than in making Shearson's bid work, and Cohen was convinced that instead of getting Forstmann to focus on the Shearson deal he was just poisoning him against it. At the same time, Johnson was grumbling that he didn't want to do a deal with Forstmann because it meant giving up the carry. Cohen would have dropped Forstmann immediately, except that he needed him. Shearson didn't have equity. It didn't have debt. It didn't have mezzanine money. It didn't even have a financial structure. And Forstmann could help on all those fronts.

So despite his misgivings, Cohen decided to keep stringing Forstmann along. When Boisi called Thursday afternoon to complain that Cohen wasn't treating Forstmann properly, Cohen tried to be accommodating. "We'll come up and talk," he suggested, meaning him and Strauss. Whatever Boisi had intended the six o'clock session at Forstmann Little's office to accomplish, it was pretty much a wash-out. Cohen still hadn't cleared up the question of the management contract with Johnson, and Stern still hadn't come up with a financing plan that either met Forstmann's stated investment criteria or seemed likely to work. Neither Cohen nor Strauss was qualified to answer questions about operations.

At one point, Forstmann left the office, and Boisi tried to smooth over the Goldman problem. "We're all going to be on Wall Street for a long time," he said. "We've got to be able to work together. Goldman is working for Forstmann Little. We're just an adviser. If you need capital, if you want us to do something more, we're willing to think about that."

The last thing that Cohen wanted was a bigger role for Goldman, and whatever good that speech did was quickly undone several hours later when Boisi called Cohen at home to complain that Shearson was talking to Philip Morris despite Cohen's promise to deal with Forstmann Little exclusively. Shearson wasn't in fact dealing with Forstmann exclusively; that very afternoon there had been a meeting with two of the top advisers to Robert Bass about getting the Bass Group involved. Fortunately Philip Morris was not among the companies that Shearson had approached—Cohen didn't know that Johnson had talked to Philip Morris on his own—and he could, in good conscience, deny that rumor with vehemence.

"Can you give me your word?" asked Boisi.

"Yes," said Cohen.

Unfortunately, Boisi soon learned that Cohen hadn't been quite honest. When he opened his *Wall Street Journal* on the way into Manhattan from Locust Valley Friday morning, he read that Shearson was talking to the Bass Group, First Boston, Paine

Webber, and Mitsubishi. It was only six-thirty, but Boisi picked up the car phone and called Ted Forstmann at home. Forstmann groggily suggested that Boisi call Cohen, so as soon as he got to his office, Boisi did. "We need to figure out whether we can work something out with Shearson or go our own way," he said.

"What do you mean, go your own way?" Cohen asked.

Boisi wasn't precise, so Cohen called Forstmann. "That guy Boisi called me this morning," said Cohen. "I got so mad I punched the wall."

Punched the wall? Forstmann wasn't sure how to respond.

But Cohen pressed on. His people had done a lot of work on the capital structure. He wanted to meet that afternoon to talk it through. "Just a small group," he said. "I don't want a lot of advisers."

Forstmann laughed. Cohen himself always seemed to travel with an army, and there were only four people on Forstmann's team: Nick, Boisi, Fraidin, and Forstmann himself. In the middle of the afternoon those four arrived at World Financial Center. They waited for a while in Cohen's office with Shearson vice-chairman George Scheinberg, who was in charge of Shearson's capital commitments committee. Finally, Cohen came in.

"What's Boisi's role here?" he began. "Is he bound by the same confidentiality agreement that Forstmann is?"

Boisi said yes, he was.

"That call this morning," said Cohen, "was that legal what he was talking about?"

No one answered.

"You, lawyer," snapped Cohen.

Fraidin looked up. He'd been making a note on his pad. "Were you talking to me?" he asked.

"Yes," said Cohen. "Can you make an offer without violating the confidentiality agreement?"

"I think you're asking the wrong person," said Fraidin. "I'm Forstmann Little's lawyer. You have a perfectly fine lawyer of your own and I suggest that you consult him. I will tell you, though, that I am obviously advising my client that he can."

Cohen left the room. Forstmann assumed that he wanted to call Jack Nusbaum, but Cohen says that that's not the case. Indeed, Cohen insists that had he understood that Forstmann really thought he was legally free to do his own deal if the Shearson partnership collapsed, he would not have kept talking.

And they did keep talking. There were several issues that Cohen wanted to iron out. The first was fees. Forstmann was adamant that the buying group should earn no fees for assembling the financing or overseeing the company. According to Forstmann, the group should make its profits only when the businesses were resold and the investors cashed in. Cohen was in this deal for fees; Shearson stood to make $300 million for "negotiating" the transaction and raising the money, and even more for negotiating the divestitures necessary to pay down debt. Cohen wasn't ready to kiss that money goodbye.

Another open point was how the equity was going to be split. Although Cohen had suggested at the meeting in Forstmann's office the night before that Forstmann get 50 percent of the equity to be shared equally between his two partnerships, Cohen now thought that 33 percent was more like it; that way each of the three partners, Shearson, Salomon, and Forstmann, would have an equal piece. Of course, Johnson's share would have to come from somewhere too.

Forstmann had said that he wouldn't be part of an offer that included junk bonds or PIK securities; Cohen was sure that that was only a negotiating position, and he told Forstmann that there was no choice. The banks had insisted that because of the high interest rates on the loans, Shearson would have to conserve cash and cut the tax bill by using PIK. The tax kick was critical; according to Cohen, the banks wouldn't put up the money without a substantial dose of PIK for investors. That statement went over like a lead balloon. No banker had ever suggested to Forstmann that he use PIK paper instead of cash to make a bid; as he saw it, if you were paying so much interest on your bank debt that you couldn't pay interest on your cram-down paper, you couldn't afford the company in the first place.

Since none of those points seemed close to being resolved, Cohen turned the talk to bidding strategy. The Shearson group had to outfox Kravis, and Cohen was hoping that Forstmann could given him some insight into how Kravis's mind worked. That question was a nonstarter. Forstmann firmly believed that the only way to win an auction was to bid your best price, and given how he felt about Kravis, he didn't want to spend any time guessing what that so-and-so was thinking. Indeed, Forstmann found most of what Cohen wanted to talk about irrelevant. Forstmann wasn't interested in tactics just now. He wanted to get some information about the company so that he could decide if he was going to bid.

An associate came in with a piece of paper. Cohen handed it to Forstmann. It was a proposed deal structure, but as far as Forstmann was concerned, it was Greek. There were so many layers of wampum securities that he couldn't even read it. There was junk. There were PIKs. There were deferred payment PIKs. It seemed clear that there was no way the thing could possibly fly.

"We can't do this," said Forstmann. He started to explain how he thought a plan could be put together.

Cohen cut him off. "Work on it," he barked at the associate.

The associate left, and then Cohen got up and chased after him.

Once again, the Forstmann team was alone in a meeting. "This is ridiculous," said Forstmann, clearly warming up for a tirade on how impossible Cohen was to work with.

Fraidin put his finger to his lips to tell Forstmann to be quiet. After all, Scheinberg was still there, although he hadn't yet said a word.

Forstmann shook his head. "The only way to make this work is for us to design a deal structure. I'm going to find Peter."

A few minutes later he located Cohen in a "roomful of eighty people." "We need to talk," he said.

The two walked back to Cohen's office. When they sat down, Forstmann put his hand on Boisi's knee. "I don't know exactly what happened on the phone this morning," he said. "But Boisi is on my team. I knew what he was going to say to you and I agree with what he said completely."

What Cohen got out of that, aside from a conviction that Boisi was impossible to work with, was that he needed to dream up a better financial structure, and by early Saturday afternoon Jim Stern had worked something up. Cohen called Forstmann at home to see what he thought. The housekeeper said that Forstmann was out; Cohen left a message. Cohen still hadn't talked to Ted by late afternoon, so he called again. Because Cohen's secretary wasn't in, the phone would have gone unanswered if Forstmann had called while Cohen was in one of the long meetings in the boardroom. But the housekeeper said that Forstmann was still out. Cohen figured he was enjoying the sunshine, and would call back when he finally got home.

Cohen went to one final meeting and then, at five o'clock, he and Tom Strauss rushed out to catch the helicopter to East Hampton. Long before the bidding for RJR had broken out, the Strausses had invited the Cohens to a dinner party this Saturday night, and both Strauss and Cohen planned to be there even though it meant that they would have to leave at the crack of dawn Sunday morning to get back to Shearson in time for the ten o'clock meeting Cohen had scheduled.

As they hurried out the door, Cohen realized that Forstmann hadn't yet returned his call. He would call from East Hampton that night.

Brian Little, Forstmann's partner, got to San Francisco on his way home from Thailand on Saturday morning, and he was so puzzled by what he read in the newspaper that he called Ted to find out what was going on. "Is this true what I'm reading?" he asked. "Are we trying to do a deal with Peter Cohen?"

"No," said Forstmann. "We're trying to do a deal with management." It had been clear from Little's tone that he didn't like the idea of Forstmann talking to Cohen. "I thought you liked Peter Cohen," Forstmann added. "He told me he lived next door to you. He said to tell you hello."

"Peter Cohen?" Little sputtered. "I'd rather be in business with Kravis."

Forstmann was beginning to feel the same way. Indeed, that was why he was in his office at all that afternoon, and why he hadn't returned either of Cohen's calls. The last thing Forstmann wanted to do right now was to talk about what Kravis might or might not be thinking or to hear the terms of yet another preposterous capital structure. Forstmann had to decide whether he really wanted to buy RJR. Although he was supposedly on the management team, he didn't seem to have access to any information about the company; he hadn't actually met anyone from the company except Johnson, and he had seen him only on the night of the Kravis fiasco. Even if he had had the right kind of information, Forstmann was beginning to wonder whether he could tolerate a long-term relationship with Cohen. So far Cohen had been rude, condescending, and perhaps dishonest. So Forstmann was looking at the numbers and thinking. Of the three alternatives that Boisi had reminded Cohen that he had, doing a deal with Shearson, doing a deal without Shearson, and doing nothing, Forstmann was leaning strongly toward doing nothing.

And he was still leaning toward doing nothing when Peter Cohen called him at home at ten-thirty that night. "I'm at Tom Strauss's house in the country," said Cohen. Forstmann could hear the dogs barking and children yelling in the background. "We've got a new capital structure." He listed the terms.

To Forstmann's utter astonishment, it sounded like it might work.

"Are you talking about junior debt or senior debt?" he asked. Cohen had not specified when he had explained what the mezzanine partners would get, and there were billions of dollars between them. In a bankruptcy, something that you had to think about whenever you did a leveraged buyout, senior creditors get paid off in full before junior creditors get a cent.

"Senior debt," said Cohen. Or he thought so. Actually he wasn't sure.

"If we're going to do this," said Forstmann, still incredulous, "I need to know what Ross's deal with you is, and I need to start finding out about the company."

"That's what we're going to do tomorrow," said Cohen, at Shearson at ten o'clock.

"Okay," said Forstmann, although he couldn't be there at ten because he was being interviewed by ABC's David Brinkley for his Sunday morning talk show. Forstmann was rather proud to have been invited. Brinkley didn't usually cover business at all; his show was really dedicated to political analysis, but although tomorrow was the next to last Sunday before the 1988 presidential election, Brinkley had decided to devote his program not to the race but to leveraged buyouts. The controversy over RJR had almost pushed the campaign off of the front page.

Cohen insisted that it be a small meeting, and since Forstmann thought that going over the new structure and the management contract would be simple, he agreed. Instead of bringing three advisers, he would bring two, Nick and Fraidin. Geoff Boisi, whom Cohen didn't like anyway, would stay home.

It was almost midnight by the time Forstmann finished talking to Cohen and that was too late to call Salomon chairman John Gutfreund. But Forstmann did call Sunday morning, before he left for ABC. Thus far, Gutfreund hadn't appeared at any meeting that Ted had been at, but Forstmann knew that he was involved, and he hoped he could win Gutfreund's support for the kind of deal he wanted. "I wouldn't try to run Salomon Brothers for a day," he said. "I don't know anything about investment banks. On this deal, you don't have the skills that I do and you should listen."

"I'm listening," said Gutfreund.

Cohen and Strauss had taken the helicopter back from East Hampton to New York early Sunday morning, and they had spent the first few hours at Shearson reviewing the numbers and looking at the structure they planned to show Forstmann in the afternoon. When he had checked with Jim Stern about the financing, Cohen discovered that he had been wrong when he answered Forstmann about the debt the night before; Forstmann's mezzanine partners were getting junior debt, not senior. Given the fuss that Forstmann had made about that already, Cohen knew that that could cause problems.

Stern also said that some of the numbers had changed. Forstmann's equity stake had dropped from 50 percent, a quarter for each of his two partnerships, to 33 percent, a third of the deal.

At half-past eleven, Cohen settled down in the conference room next to his office to watch David Brinkley.

Predictably, Forstmann blasted junk bonds. "What has gone wrong here is that people have created a new source of money which is commonly called junk bonds," he said. "Even that was okay in the beginning, but then they created new securities where interest isn't paid currently and all that kind of thing. I have a hard time understanding how certain kinds of financial institutions with fiduciary responsibilities can be allowed to purchase securities that have such high risk attached to them."

To Cohen's amazement, Forstmann also roundly criticized leveraged buyouts like the one he was apparently planning to invest in. "Investment discipline is the phrase that's going to come back and be talked about," he told Brinkley. "In the beginning, the innovators of this idea, of whom I was one, paid a great deal of attention to the type of company we were buying and the cost of the money we were using. At Forstmann Little, we still do that. We've bought seven billion dollars worth of businesses and every one of them has been a success. What has happened is that imitators by the hundreds have gotten into this business, and as imitators have flocked in, discipline has eroded and, as a result, breakups that didn't make sense have occurred."

Ted's Mercedes had gotten a bad dent in the side on the way back from Shearson Friday afternoon when another car had smashed into it in the rain, and Ted had had to borrow Nick's car to get to the ABC studio at Lincoln Square for the taping. After watching himself on television at eleven-thirty, Ted picked Nick up and started downtown to Fraidin's office. Traffic on the FDR Drive was backed up for miles; according to the radio there was some kind of parade at the South Street Seaport. When the Forstmanns finally got to Water Street, they caucused in Fraidin's office and then drove on to Shearson.

Cohen's insistence that Forstmann keep his team small by not bringing Boisi, turned out to be preposterous. Amid the teeming masses of Shearson and Salomon bankers there, Boisi would surely not have been noticed. There were so many people milling around that Forstmann never even saw Ron Freeman, the Salomon Brothers official who had been on the ABC panel with him. At the studio Forstmann had joked that Freeman was good enough for Brinkley but not for negotiating; apparently that was true.

This time the Forstmann team was ushered into the boardroom which, Forstmann estimated, was roughly the size of his entire office suite. It was filled with people whom Forstmann hadn't met and who seemed uninterested in why he too was there. After the by-now predictable unexplained wait that preceded every Shearson session, Cohen, Gutfreund, Strauss, and Nusbaum finally came in. They sat down at a small table in the middle of the chaos and began.

"I misspoke on the telephone last night," began Cohen. "It's junior debt, not senior."

Forstmann shook his head. That the debt was senior was what

had made the proposal workable in the first place. Still, he had to give Cohen credit for being honest.

"And there are some other changes," said Cohen, "technical things." He passed out copies of the proposed capital structure.

Forstmann looked at the numbers. It was about as similar to what Cohen had described on the telephone as abc is to xyz. Not only had his mezzanine partnership gone from senior to junior, the other numbers were also radically different. The total equity slice to be shared by his two partnerships had shrunk to 33 percent, and the projected return was the lowest Shearson had estimated yet. Forstmann was disappointed: this new version was completely unacceptable.

Nick nudged Ted. He'd added up the numbers and they totalled $7 billion more than Cohen would need for an offer of $90 a share. "Ask him what the price is," whispered Nick.

"What's the price?" asked Ted.

"The price?" repeated Cohen. He didn't know. But Jim Stern would. Cohen yelled across the room to Stern. Stern started in their direction; on the way, he paused to snap at a Shearson banker. Cohen saw Ted's eyebrow go up. "Should I fire him?" Cohen asked.

Stern explained that the price was $92 a share, and that the extra financing had been for refinancing the Shearson bridge loan plus some of the existing debt.

That made sense but it didn't make the structure more palatable. Still, as long as he was here, Forstmann might as well have some fun. "Let's talk about the management agreement," he said.

The room was silent for a minute. "I knew he would ask that," Gutfreund finally said.

Not surprisingly, Cohen wouldn't let Forstmann see the contract, but he did ask Nusbaum to read through the terms; Fraidin took copious notes, much to Cohen's irritation.

It was worse than Forstmann had imagined, although certain items had apparently been renegotiated as a result of his earlier complaints. Now Johnson was putting up $20 million for his still-unspecified stake. Whatever that starting point was, Johnson could earn another 11.5 percent if he managed a 50 percent return on equity, something that Forstmann thought was conceivable at the original $75 a share but surely impossible at the current price of $92. That was egregious but perhaps doable. What was totally impossible was the corporate governance system. According to Nusbaum, no one person was responsible for decisions. In effect, there was no buyer. Under a complicated system of checks and balances, neither Shearson nor Forstmann was in the driver's seat; nor was Johnson, although he had veto power over major corporate actions. "You mean for my $3 billion, I don't have control over anything?" asked Forstmann.

"You have board seats," said Nusbaum.

"But Johnson can overrule me," said Forstmann. "What if Johnson gets fired?"

Johnson couldn't get fired, explained Nusbaum, not without paying him an amount that even Shearson wasn't willing to contemplate.

Clearly, they were expecting him to object, but Forstmann didn't give them that pleasure. "Okay," he said. "What about the fees?"

The mood lightened. Cohen handed Ted a fee schedule. It was complicated. Forstmann wasn't sure what most of the fees were for. So he asked. There was one fee for negotiating the deal, another for placing the bonds, another for some oblique purpose that turned out to be Forstmann Little's.

Finally Forstmann was finished. "I'm gone," he said.

Cohen looked like he was about to faint. "You're gone?" he said.

"I'm going to my office to think about this," said Forstmann.

CHAPTER 11

Waiting for Shearson and Godot

October 26 to November 2

Ross Johnson had not been involved in the talks with Ted Forst-mann, John Gutfreund, Bob Bass, or anyone else. Indeed, since the meeting with Kravis on Tuesday night, Johnson had been left pretty much in the dark as to precisely what was being discussed with whom. With Cohen tied up and uncooperative, Johnson, like Boisi, was left with the newspaper as his best source of in-formation. Every morning Linda Robinson's office sent over a large stack of newspaper clips—RJR was, after all, front-page news all across the country—and Johnson read the articles care-fully. He was particularly amused by the *Wall Street Journal's* account of the Tuesday night meeting with KKR. According to the article, the reason that the talks had collapsed was that George Roberts had made an antismoking remark! Johnson had been in Horrigan's office talking to Forstmann at the time, but although he had heard later that Roberts had said something of the sort, no one had made much of a fuss.

By the time he read that article, though, Johnson was getting worried. Beyond knowing that Cohen was talking to Salomon Brothers and Forstmann Little, Johnson didn't have a clue as to where things stood. He didn't know what the financial architecture was, if there even was one. He didn't know what banks had been contacted, if any. He didn't know how much equity Shearson planned to commit or how much Shearson ultimately planned to bid.

What he did know was that Charlie Hugel kept hassling him to make an offer and that Shearson didn't have the money to make one. Johnson found that puzzling. Surely, it couldn't be that hard to put the money together. As far as Johnson could tell, investors were panting to get in on the deal: Giovanni Angelli, chairman of Fiat SpA, had gotten a message to Andy Sage saying that he was interested in putting up a substantial equity stake; Saul Steinberg, the fabled raider, had called to offer $300 million.

Shearson's ineptness would not have been so frustrating except that Johnson and his team members didn't have much else to do. They spent their days wandering from one Nabisco office to another, gossiping and speculating as to how one might put together the money to finance the deal. No one wanted to get too far away for fear something would finally happen. Sage even bought a television set to while away the hours in his office, only to discover that reception is so bad in midtown Manhattan that all he could get without a cable were cartoons.

So it wasn't long before the RJR people began to hassle Shearson. First, Johnson called "Jimmy Deep-pockets," as he referred to Jim Robinson behind his back. He expected that Robinson would ultimately write a check for any money that Cohen couldn't raise. Robinson vaguely assured Johnson that everything was under control. Then Sage called Cohen and Stern separately, but didn't succeed in extracting much information. Finally, Frank Benevento called Tom Strauss, who was quite helpful, if quite discouraging, outlining precisely what little progress had been made.

By Thursday morning, October 27, Johnson was fairly seething about Shearson's lack of imagination. Why was Cohen wasting time talking to Forstmann, who was going to take a carry in exchange for his mezzanine money? Why didn't Shearson just create some mezzanine paper and sell it to institutional clients? Wasn't that what Johnson had hired Shearson for? Jim Stern was very cool when Sage called to suggest that. "We can't possibly raise enough mezzanine money before the deal closes," he said, and although Cohen suggested that Shearson could make a mezzanine bridge, he refused to cut off talks with Forstmann until

Stern had come up with a workable structure for the mezzanine paper that Stern mysteriously failed to produce.

While Johnson was "waiting for Shearson and Godot," he suddenly picked up the word that KKR was so desperate for money that Kravis was considering teaming up with cash-rich Philip Morris, presumably as a buyer for Nabisco after the KKR purchase closed. Johnson knew that Philip Morris was interested in Nabisco; he had talked to Hamish Maxwell about a joint venture as recently as August. He also knew that Maxwell's plan to buy Kraft wasn't going smoothly. Kraft had rejected Philip Morris's original offer, high as it was, and had suggested that it wouldn't agree to a merger unless Maxwell hiked his price by $20 a share, a total of $2.6 billion. Johnson thought that Nabisco was a more attractive food company than Kraft, and he was sure that Maxwell would be interested in buying it as an alternative.

But there was no reason for Maxwell to be thinking about buying it from Kravis. If he wanted Nabisco, surely it was more logical for him to talk to his friend Johnson. So while Stern and Hill talked to Forstmann and others, Johnson began to think about how a Philip Morris deal could work; he quickly stumbled onto something interesting. Under IRS rules, two companies could contribute assets to a partnership without triggering capital gains taxes, and they could also dissolve the partnership without paying taxes as long as it had lasted for two years. That seemed to mean that if RJR and Philip Morris each contributed their food subsidiaries plus some cash to a joint venture and stuck together long enough, they could arrange a divorce in which Philip Morris got the companies and RJR got the cash and no one paid any tax. By contrast, if RJR sold the food business to Philip Morris direct, RJR would pay a capital gains tax of $4 billion.

Thursday afternoon, Johnson called a top secret meeting at his apartment at 800 Fifth Avenue to brainstorm. The advisers agreed that the plan was worth pursuing, so after the meeting broke up, Johnson called Goldstone to get a Davis Polk lawyer cracking on the tax question. Johnson also wanted to revive the idea of a tobacco joint venture in Europe, the scheme he had floated to Maxwell in the spring, and the lawyers dusted off the work that they had done on European antitrust. Then Johnson called Maxwell to set up a meeting Friday with Horrigan and a junior Shearson M&A expert to go over both ideas. Unfortunately, the Philip

Morris partnership quickly fizzled. Maxwell's estimate of what he was willing to pay was well below Johnson's values. Friday night, Maxwell reopened talks with Kraft, and signed a deal in the wee hours of Saturday morning at $13.1 billion.

After the meeting at his apartment about Philip Morris, Johnson headed over to 9 West 57th Street for a meeting that Cohen had set up with David Bonderman and Peter Joseph, two top advisers to Robert Bass. As Johnson understood it, Cohen had proposed that Bass join Shearson and Salomon as an equal equity partner. The one-third stake, less if Forstmann decided to do a deal after all, would cost roughly $400 million.

Certainly Bass had plenty of money to do a deal. His personal net worth was well over $1 billion, and he also controlled Acadia Partners, a joint venture with Shearson and Equitable Life that boasted $1.4 billion in assets, mostly invested in leveraged buyouts. That summer, Bass had opened negotiations with the federal government to buy American Savings & Loan, a bankrupt California thrift. Although that transaction had by no means closed, it then included a controversial provision, later dropped, that would allow Bass to use a portion of American Savings's assets to fund a $1.5 billion merchant bank.

Joining an RJR bid at this point wasn't really Bass's kind of deal. To be sure, RJR was an attractive and highly profitable company, but Bass had typically accumulated a toehold, bid low, and dropped out the moment competition appeared. It turned out that strategy wasn't even an issue. Friday morning, Bonderman called back to say that Bass wasn't interested. Bonderman had set up the Johnson meeting without checking with Bass first, and Bass had a firm policy against investing in a tobacco company.

Three days later, on Monday, October 31, Forstmann dropped out too. As he put it, first to John Gutfreund and then to Cohen at nine o'clock that morning, Forstmann couldn't live with Johnson's contract, the junk-heavy structure, the fees that Shearson would collect, and the fuzzy corporate governance system.

Cohen had tried to coax Forstmann back with a promise to rework the structure once again, but Forstmann wasn't biting. "We've been at this five days," he told Cohen, "and I still don't know anything more about the company than when I started."

That left Shearson and Johnson back at square one. Johnson wasn't pleased.

* * *

Although Johnson was blaming Cohen for the fact that the money wasn't yet in place, Cohen thought that the problem was Gutfreund, who was taking such a very long time to make up his mind. By the time of the Bass meeting, Cohen was so frustrated that he promised Lee Kimmell, Salomon's financial institutions chief and his closest friend at Salomon after Tom Strauss, that he would buy him a giant cigar humidor if Kimmell could deliver Gutfreund. Kimmell had been trying mightily for days now, without success. "We're making 6 percent in our basic business," Kimmell told Gutfreund again and again. "Now you have a chance to invest $750 million and make 40 percent. What are you waiting for?"

Gutfreund's answer was an assurance that the financing was there. Having grown up as a trader, Gutfreund was far more attuned than Cohen to how difficult it would be to put together the bank and mezzanine money Shearson needed to make the deal work. By this time, it was clear that getting the $16 billion of bank money that they would need—the number had jumped from $14 billion now that Kravis had come in with a $90-a-share offer—would strain the banking system. Even if every bank in the world put up its legal maximum—New York banks, for example, are only allowed to lend 15 percent of their capital surplus to a single borrower—the total would barely be enough.

Unlike Cohen, Gutfreund had never thought that a partnership with Forstmann would work. According to Chas Phillips, sparks had flown at the Wednesday night meeting on finance, and Cohen had carped endlessly that Goldman wasn't playing fair. Salomon, which had its own problems with Goldman, was inclined to believe that.

Nor was Gutfreund taken by Cohen's assurance that American Express and Mitsubishi would put up the necessary mezzanine money. However interested those two institutions were in the deal, it was inconceivable that they would be willing to put up enough mezzanine money to fill the gap that Forstmann was supposed to be filling. In addition, there needed to be a colossal amount of junk bond financing, well over $3 billion, and Gutfreund wasn't at all sure that the Shearson group could sell it. Certainly Shearson couldn't. Shearson was, at heart, a wire house; it did not have much of a syndication department; it had *never* handled a major junk underwriting before. Gutfreund assumed that when push came to shove, Salomon, with its well-developed underwriting and sales network would be the firm that actually placed the paper. So while Cohen talked to Forstmann, Gutfreund talked to his bond sales team. Over the weekend, a team of bond salesmen from Salomon called each of the firm's bond-buying clients to gauge interest in an RJR issue on various terms.

Already other frictions had begun to develop. One was Gutfreund's cautious, plodding approach. Gutfreund was not as concerned as Cohen about intangibles; having watched two Salomon deals go belly-up, Gutfreund was determined not to overpay. For Cohen, who had started the fight, what mattered was winning—and polishing up the tarnished Shearson name. Another problem was Gutfreund's total inexperience as a deal-maker. Gutfreund frequently remarked that this was all new to him and he groused that the process was "like being in the army: hurry up and wait." Tom Strauss even amused his own bankers by complaining that the long hours were putting a strain on his marriage. Cohen hadn't done very many deals either, but he was determined not to let it show.

Finally there was the size of Gutfreund's team. Gutfreund and Strauss usually showed up at meetings with a crew of a dozen or more advisers, including vice-chairman Jay Higgins, Salomon's senior banker; Michael Zimmerman and Ronald Freeman of merchant banking; Chas Phillips from capital markets; Charles Nathan of M&A; and Kimmell, head of the financial institutions group. Cohen came alone, or with Jim Stern and Tom Hill, and he rolled his eyes whenever he saw the Salomon team. He was forever suggesting that Gutfreund leave his advisers behind.

Finally, Tuesday afternoon, November 1, Gutfreund made up his mind. He would go ahead if the Salomon directors approved. They did, although Warren Buffett had made quite a fuss about Johnson's management contract. Gutfreund had already termed it "unseemly" and agreed that it would be renegotiated when the time was right. The banking team had already decided that the time would be right just before Salomon got around to writing its $1 billion check.

After the board meeting, Gutfreund, Strauss, and the rest of the Salomon team went to Shearson for dinner with Johnson and Cohen in the Shearson boardroom. Although the meal had been

intended as mainly ceremonial, the talk quickly turned to strategy.
Steve Goldstone, Johnson's lawyer, believed that an auction was
the single worst thing that could happen. Like Atkins, Goldstone
had been involved in the Fort Howard case, and he was certain
that having been criticized once for allowing the board to do favors
for management, Atkins would not let that happen again. In an
auction the board would bend over backward to appear independent of Johnson. Hence Goldstone didn't want Shearson to have
to compete. He had been in the room during the Kravis-Cohen
meeting the night of October 25 and he didn't think that there
was any chance that KKR and Shearson would team up, so he
proposed that Shearson try to scare KKR out of the bidding by
making an offer so high it couldn't be topped. Goldstone thought
that $100 a share would be enough to do that.

"It's easy for you to spend my money," snapped Gutfreund.

"I'm not spending your money," said Goldstone. "I'm just
saying that I think you should put your highest number on the
table now."

Gutfreund shook his head in disgust. He was comfortable with
auctions; he had gotten to the top of Salomon—and Wall Street—
by bidding right in auctions.

Goldstone was way off of his turf. Price and bidding strategy
were really questions for bankers, not lawyers, but fortunately
Tom Hill jumped to his defense. "Steve is right," he said. "We
need to conquer the space. That's the only way to regain momentum."

After a long discussion, Gutfreund conceded that he might be
willing to pay $100 a share, but he remained unconvinced that
that was the number to choose now.

Ironically, the only person in the room who seemed unwilling
to go so high was Johnson, the man Goldstone was supposed to
be representing. He shocked everyone by insisting that RJR
wasn't worth anything close to $100 a share and that he couldn't
run a company with the leverage it implied. "I'll have to have
my people look at the numbers," he muttered as he left at
midnight.

Goldstone's theory that Johnson might be able to preempt an
auction was not totally off the wall. By the time he raised the
question over dinner, Goldstone had already fielded several

phone calls from Peter Atkins asking for a bid from Shearson. That suggested to Goldstone that the committee was desperate for a second offer, and that Shearson might be able to extract a concession in return for making one. So when Atkins called again on Wednesday morning to ask, "Where's your bid? There's a Special Committee meeting tomorrow, and we really want to have your bid," Goldstone decided to try.

"What is the point of my giving you a bid?" said Goldstone. "What is the quid pro quo?"

There was a long silence.

"You've seen the press reports," said Goldstone. "You know that we've been talking to KKR. Maybe we will get together with KKR. Then there will be no auction and you'll get a price that you'll find disappointing." Of course, Goldstone himself thought that there was zero chance of teaming up, but there was no need to tell Atkins that. "If you sign us up, you guarantee that there is an auction and you put a floor on the price. I can assure you that we'll give you a very full price."

Atkins laughed. "Now you've given us something to think about," he said. "Do you have a form of merger agreement?"

"Yes," said Goldstone. "I'll send it up."

Atkins hadn't made any promises, but Goldstone was nonetheless optimistic that they would be able to work something out, and Goldstone told the other Shearson advisers just that at the strategy lunch at Shearson at twelve-thirty Wednesday.

Again Gutfreund was very skeptical. "It's pretty easy to spend my money," he repeated. "Can you guarantee us that if we make that kind of bid, we will get a merger agreement."

"No," said Goldstone.

"Can you say it's likely?"

"No," said Goldstone.

"What are the odds?" asked Gutfreund.

"Low," said Goldstone. "But you have to make a judgment. If you're willing to bid one hundred dollars a share in any case, and you conceded that yesterday, then you should do it now."

Gutfreund made a speech about what a strong bid $92 was.

Goldstone said he was wrong.

Hill talked about conquering the space.

"There's no way we should bid a soft ninety-two dollars," said

Goldstone, making his final pitch. "We should bid one hundred dollars a share. That's a classic bidding strategy."

What Goldstone thought didn't really matter since, as Gutfreund noted, it wasn't his money, and although Hill thought Goldstone was right, Cohen didn't come to his defense. After an hour, Gutfreund seemed to have won. The bid would be $92 a share.

"This is the worst mistake in M&A history," said Hill as the lunch broke up.

CHAPTER 12

High Stakes, High Fashion

Henry Kravis hadn't had any contact with Cohen or Johnson or indeed anyone from the Shearson side since the October 25 meeting at RJR. What he knew about the goings on with Forstmann, Bass, and Hugel, he had picked up on the grapevine and in the newspaper. Actually, the newspapers were a fertile, if not always accurate, source of information. The RJR takeover was the biggest story to hit the financial pages in years, and it was covered with zeal and imagination. When there wasn't hard news—and there rarely was—reporters scrambled for anything they could get. The result was headline articles about such side issues as employee morale, company politics, and income tax policy.

Reporters had canvassed the business community for opinions on buyouts, hostile takeovers, and corporate debt. There had been articles suggesting that lending to buyouts would trigger a 1930s-style depression or at least cause a collapse of several major banks. Other articles had suggested that the RJR deal alone would cost Uncle Sam $5 billion in lost tax revenues because of high interest payment deductions; according to one frequently printed theory, the deal would be financed by increased food prices. However true, false or misguided the articles were, they were surely bad for buyouts.

Needless to say, a piece of real news, like Federal Reserve

Bank chairman Alan Greenspan's statement in Senate testimony that Congress might want to look at changing the tax laws to discourage buyouts got headline coverage.

The papers had been silent on what the Shearson team was up to after the KKR talks broke down, but Kravis knew that they had been working hard. He could see the top of 9 West 57th Street from his apartment fifteen blocks away, and every night when he went to bed he noticed that the lights were still on on the Nabisco floor. Indeed they were on so late so many nights that he was beginning to think that Johnson kept the office lit twenty-four hours a day. Because KKR not only shared the same building with Nabisco but also the same elevator bank, Kravis was forever bumping into the Shearson team members, and he checked the building sign-out list when he left for the day to see who from Shearson had been there. Kravis had passed Nick Forstmann in the lobby one evening—Nick was going to the Wednesday night meeting on finance with Jim Stern, Chas Phillips, and Tom Hill—and to Kravis's surprise, Nick's partner Steve Klinsky had gone out of his way to introduce himself.

Whatever else they were doing upstairs, the Shearson people were certainly talking to the press. Kravis was sure Cohen and Hill were responsible for the disastrous publicity he had gotten since the first protect-the-franchise meeting. Since then he had been described as everything from megalomanic to hostile to just plain dumb. There had even been a Shearson-planted article in the *Journal* attributing the breakdown of negotiations October 25 to Roberts's having asked Cohen to put out his cigar. Any hopes that Kravis had that Shearson would cool it were dashed on Monday, October 31, when he picked up his *New York Times*. Right on the front page was a headline: "Several Giant Pension Funds Investing in Offer for Nabisco." In addition to the now predictable anti-buyout quotes, the article included a list of all of KKR's seventy-six investors, apparently cribbed from a bank telex on an earlier KKR deal. Surely the publication of the list meant that investors would soon be inundated with calls from reporters, buyout-hating corporate executives, and concerned shareholders. In frustration, Kravis called Hugel. Hugel offered to call Anise Wallace, the author of the *Times* piece, as well as all of the KKR investors to assure them that KKR wasn't hostile.

Like Cohen and Johnson, Kravis and Roberts were spending

most of their time putting together financing, but they were having a much easier time of it. To be sure, a $20 billion deal was new turf for KKR too, but having successfully financed many smaller deals, they had a good sense of what worked and what didn't, and how to get the banks on board. So the terms got nailed down relatively quickly. The biggest worry was the insider trading investigation. Rumors that a Drexel indictment was imminent seemed to get louder every day. Kravis and Roberts didn't doubt that in the absence of an indictment, Drexel could sell the $5 billion worth of junk bonds they needed; it wasn't clear what would happen if an indictment came down. Peter Ackerman kept insisting that formal charges would not affect Drexel's ability to raise money, and Merrill said it was standing by, but Kravis and Roberts remained worried that there would be trouble if the charges came at the wrong moment.

They were also worried about the due diligence process. Although getting information from the company to confirm value estimates and line up bank loans is usually a straightforward task, Johnson, or at least someone on his team, seemed to have thrown a monkey wrench into the works. When Kravis arrived at the Plaza Monday afternoon to meet the operating team and go over questions about profits and operating minutiae, he quickly concluded that everyone had been bludgeoned into silence. At the beginning of Nabisco chief John Greeniaus's presentation, one of the Lazard bankers not so subtly announced that "when you're finished with this meeting, you're expected across the street," apparently to tell Johnson what he had said. Some staff members, like Dean Posvar, the head of strategic planning, seemed to remember nothing more than their names. A handful were worried about their futures; Dolph von Arx, head of international tobacco, volunteered that he had been misquoted in Monday's *Journal* as saying that he and his eight top associates would leave if KKR won the bidding.

It wasn't clear whether the bad attitude affected the numbers that KKR was getting. Although it was easy to imagine that it did, fudging or lying in the session was all but impossible, since a banker from Dillon and a banker from Lazard were always there. Still, there was no question but that Johnson was trying to scare Kravis away. Monday night, as Kravis and Dick Beattie were walking down the Plaza's fourteenth-floor hallway to a six o'clock session on tobacco liability, Harold Henderson, the general counsel, stopped to introduce himself. "Can I see you for a minute?" he asked Kravis. "Alone."

Kravis and Henderson stepped into Kravis's private suite. "I'm with Ross Johnson, do or die," said Henderson. "I won't work for you."

"You don't have to say that," said Kravis. "I'm not making any decisions yet. Why don't you wait and see what happens?"

"No," said Henderson. "If Ross goes, I go."

That bothered Kravis until Tuesday, when he heard the same words from half a dozen other senior executives.

Kravis was still interested in a Shearson deal on the right terms, partly to make sure that management was on his team, partly to forestall a bidding war that might push the price as high as $100 a share. Kravis knew that his own relations with Cohen were pretty frayed, but he thought that Beattie might have better luck, so just before the two left for the Henderson meeting Beattie had called Cohen to see how the land lay. The prognosis wasn't good. Cohen was still furious about the 10 percent proposal Kravis had made the week before. "Well, I'm sorry you feel that way," said Beattie, "but I think there's still some reason to talk."

"After Henry's proposal?" snapped Cohen. "After offering us 10 percent?"

"That was just a starting point," said Beattie, trying to put things into perspective, "part of the bid and ask."

Cohen wasn't impressed.

"Look," said Beattie. "We're willing to talk. Why don't you think about it."

"We need at least fifty percent," said Cohen.

"We can't give up more than fifty percent," said Beattie. "Under the terms of our partnership agreement with investors we have to control the board. Maybe we could work something out with a sixty–forty board."

"I don't know," said Cohen. Sixty–forty was definitely not what he had in mind. "I'll get back to you."

Cohen didn't, and so Kravis began to think again about finding an alternative management team. Ty Wilson hadn't had much to contribute. Maybe Paul Sticht would. Kravis put Paul Raether on the case; Raether had met Sticht several years back through his father-in-law, who happened to own a condominium at Lost Tree Village, the same West Palm Beach complex where Sticht had a place. Raether got his father-in-law to look up Sticht's number in the Lost Tree Village directory, and Raether called. No one answered any of Sticht's three home numbers: in Winston-Salem, New Hampshire, or Lost Tree Village. Raether tried in the afternoon. He tried several times Tuesday. Still no response. Raether didn't want to leave a message with Sticht's secretary for fear that Johnson would get word that he had called.

Then, Wednesday, as Raether was sitting in his office wondering what to do, a friend called to say that one Robert van Kamp, a former RJR executive and tobacco industry consultant, happened to be in his office just around the corner. "I think you ought to talk to him," said the friend.

Why not? "Send him over," said Raether.

Van Kamp arrived a few minutes later, and Raether began peppering him with questions about tobacco.

"You know, the person you really should be talking to is Paul Sticht," said van Kamp.

"I've been trying," said Raether. "I can't get a hold of him."

"He's in West Palm Beach," said van Kamp. "I talked to him last night."

Raether had already tried Sticht's three numbers that morning, without success, but when van Kamp dialed Lost Tree Village, Sticht answered. Raether and Sticht talked for a few minutes. Sticht said that he wanted to be helpful and that he would stop at KKR on Monday afternoon, November 7, when he had to be in New York for another meeting.

About the time Raether finally reached Sticht, Kravis left the office for the Grand Ballroom of the Plaza Hotel where his wife, Carolyne Roehm, the fashion designer, would be unveiling her spring collection. Attending a fashion show was a slightly unusual thing to do in the heat of a takeover battle, but Kravis had always supported Roehm's career and he wasn't about to change that for a cookie company.

One of the first people he saw by the runway was Linda Robinson. "It's really too bad that you and Ross can't get together," she said.

Kravis agreed that it was too bad. It was even more too bad

that one of them might end up paying an extra $3 billion just because of the competition.

"I think if you and Ross could just sit down together without all this emotion, you could work something out," said Robinson. "Ross is really the quintessential KKR executive."

"I'm happy to meet," said Kravis.

Robinson wasn't a banker and she didn't want to overstep, but she thought that this was worth pursuing. "Look," she said. "I can't negotiate for Ross, but if you're serious, I think I can set up a meeting."

"I'm serious," said Kravis.

"Will you promise that there's going to be no game-playing between us?" asked Robinson. "What we say to each other is absolutely straight?"

Kravis promised.

"Well," said Robinson. She knew that Beattie had suggested a sixty–forty split to Peter Cohen earlier in the week; Cohen wasn't going to sit down unless Kravis first agreed to fifty–fifty. "We need to work a few things out before a meeting. I'll call you later this afternoon."

Kravis chatted with several other guests. Then he took his place between Oscar de la Renta, the fashion designer who had been Roehm's mentor, and Barbara Walters, the ABC talk show host.

The lights dimmed, the music started—"Hit the Road, Jack," "Georgia" and "They Can't Take That Away from Me"—and the models bounced down the runway.

When it was over, Roehm came out for her bow. Kravis waved and headed backstage to congratulate her. Then he walked back to his office to wait for Robinson's call.

Robinson had to go to a meeting when she first got back from the fashion show, but as soon as that was over she called Kravis. They agreed that the board would be split fifty–fifty, not sixty–forty. They agreed that the equity would also be split fifty–fifty. They agreed that Drexel would not necessarily be sole manager in the junk bond financing. They agreed that Johnson would be chief executive.

"Okay," said Robinson, "where should we meet?"

It seemed clear that neither KKR's office nor Nabisco's was ideal; surely they should choose neutral territory. Kravis suggested the Plaza, right across the street, and he said he'd have his secretary, Leslie, make the arrangements.

There was just one more thing: Kravis had to tell Johnson exactly what he had just promised Robinson. It wasn't that Robinson didn't believe Kravis, but she knew that she and her husband were the only ones in the Shearson camp who thought that there was any hope of getting Kravis and Cohen together, and her credibility was particularly weak since she was a lowly pr consultant, and a personal friend of Kravis's at that. The last thing she wanted was to have Kravis show up at a meeting and promptly back off from what he had promised her. So Robinson walked down the hall to Johnson's office, and together they called Kravis. He confirmed the agreement.

Then Johnson called Peter Cohen. "I've just talked to Henry Kravis," he said. Johnson didn't explain under what circumstances, and Cohen took that to mean that Kravis had been hassling Johnson, and probably also trying to woo him away. "We've agreed to a fifty–fifty split of the equity and the board," said Johnson. "I'll be chief executive."

Cohen was a little surprised that Johnson had gotten that agreement, since the last thing he had heard from the KKR camp was Beattie's sixty–forty. "You need to call Henry," said Johnson, to work out the details. So Cohen did. Again, Kravis confirmed the fifty–fifty split. "Let's meet at six," he said. It was already five-thirty. "Keep the team small."

Cohen took that to mean, come alone. He called Tom Strauss to say he was heading to a meeting with Kravis. Then he hurried uptown.

It was, indeed, a small and high-powered group that met at the Plaza half an hour later, just Kravis, Roberts, Cohen, Johnson, and Jim Robinson. Unlike the meeting a week before, this one started off on the right foot. Roberts had brought a box of cigars for Cohen, but given the upset over smoke at the last meeting, Cohen didn't want to set the talks off course, so he didn't light up. The obvious starting point was to confirm again the fifty–fifty split, for everything, although Kravis insisted that he wanted Drexel to have a leading role. "How much equity does management get?" asked Kravis. "What's the deal?"

"They're putting in twenty million," said Cohen.

"Who's they?" asked Kravis.

"The management group," said Cohen. He named half a dozen people: Johnson, Sage, Horrigan, and Welch among them.

"For what?"

"Eight-and-one-half percent," said Cohen. "If they meet certain performance targets, they get more." The scale ratcheted up: for a 50 percent rate of return, management got 19.5 percent.

Something didn't compute. "What happens if you just get your money back?" asked Kravis.

"Then they get eight-and-a-half percent."

"How much are you putting into this?"

"One and a half billion." At least at $75 a share that was what Shearson had planned to contribute. Now that the price had jumped by $15 a share, that total would surely jump.

"You mean if the deal is a flop and all you get back is your one and a half billion, they still get eight-and-a-half percent?" asked Kravis. "That's one hundred twenty-seven million, six times what they put in. That's a dumb deal."

"Well, we haven't finished negotiating it," said Jim Robinson.

"Where does this equity come from?" asked Kravis.

"Out of our pocket," said Cohen.

Kravis pondered that. "Okay," he said. "Whatever management gets comes out of your pocket."

"No," said Robinson. "The first eight-and-a-half comes out of our pocket. After that it's fifty–fifty."

Kravis shook his head. Under Robinson's plan the Johnson-Shearson group would end up having more equity than KKR.

They agreed to break and reconvene two hours later, at nine o'clock, with lawyers. Cohen, Johnson, and Robinson went back to the Cookie Palace to caucus. By coincidence, Stern had scheduled a finance meeting at Shearson that night, so all the junk bond people were downtown, but Gutfreund and Strauss and their entourage were waiting, along with George Scheinfeld from Shearson, Sage, Horrigan, and Linda Robinson. Although Hill had offered to come to the Cookie Palace—or the Plaza—Cohen had told him not to bother. If he needed Hill, Cohen said, he would call.

Cohen briefed everyone who was there on the Plaza meeting. Although Cohen and Strauss were still somewhat bewildered that Kravis had changed his position and was willing to compromise, they agreed that teaming up was the best course. The only hint that there might be a problem was Kravis's statement that Drexel had to be involved. In the ego-driven banking world, appearances matter, and deals have been known to collapse over such seemingly meaningless details as which firm's name goes on the left side of the tombstone announcement as the lead underwriter. Strauss had conceded on the first day that Shearson would get that position over Salomon on the RJR junk financing, and now Gutfreund volunteered that Drexel was not going to usurp Shearson's place.

It was clear from the way he said it, though, that Gutfreund really didn't want Drexel involved at all. As a negotiating position, that was hardly a surprise. Salomon and Drexel were long-standing enemies. Salomon claimed that Drexel had poached clients with underhanded tactics like telling a Salomon salesman to show up in the wrong hotel for a road show presentation to investors. Many Streeters, including some of Salomon's own banking partners, thought that Gutfreund's hatred of Drexel was irrational, but no one doubted that it was real.

Meanwhile, Kravis and Roberts were having dinner at the Oak Room, the swanky restaurant on the ground floor of the Plaza. They had called Beattie from the suite, and he arrived from his office at about seven with Casey Cogut, the other Simpson Thatcher corporate partner working on the RJR deal. Kravis explained what had happened so far and they all talked about that and about what to do next.

Just before nine, they went upstairs to the suite to wait for Peter Cohen and his lawyers. While they were sitting in the living room, waiting for Cohen to arrive, Cohen called to ask if he could bring Tom Strauss, his partner. Although Kravis had been dimly aware that Salomon was involved, he had not focused on what Solly's role was. Cohen seemed to be the decision-maker, but if he wanted to bring Strauss, that was okay with KKR. At least on a business level. Kravis was irritated that Strauss, who, unlike Cohen, truly was one of Kravis's personal friends, would show up on Cohen's team. It would be months before the two would patch up their relationship.

After Cohen and Strauss had left for the Plaza, John Gutfreund began to fret that he hadn't been invited. What Strauss and Cohen were saying to Kravis was important, and he, Gutfreund, the chairman of Salomon, had specifically been excluded. Gutfreund knew that Kravis would never have left him out, so it had to have been Cohen, his own partner. One of the Salomon team members ventured that perhaps there had been a misunderstanding: surely Cohen had meant to include both Strauss and Gutfreund but had bollixed the invitation. Another suggested that maybe Kravis had asked Cohen not to bring Gutfreund because he knew how much Gutfreund disliked Drexel. Gutfreund remained unappeased.

But Gutfreund did want to know what was going on behind his back. He couldn't march over to the Plaza himself, of course; "great men don't do that," as one Salomon official puts it, and it didn't seem right to send a junior representative to such a high-level summit.

Finally, Michael Zimmerman had an idea: Gutfreund could send his lawyer. Cohen and Johnson had brought their lawyers along. Gutfreund liked that, and Zimmerman dialed Peter Darrow.

Darrow had been up late every night for the past week, sitting in on the long sessions at the Cookie Palace. He was exhausted, and when Higgins, Salomon's investment banking chief, had assured him that nothing was likely to happen this night, he had left the office early and gone to bed. Now he got up again, dressed, and flagged a cab to Nabisco. Gutfreund was fuming. He gave Darrow a slip of paper with a fifth-floor suite number written on it and told him to find out what was going on.

Darrow marched across the street and took the elevator to the fifth floor. He walked up and down the corridor. The suite didn't exist. Darrow contemplated the situation. He *couldn't* call Gutfreund and say that Cohen had given him the wrong suite number. Then Darrow noticed a man standing outside one of the doors, apparently standing guard. Darrow strode up to him, and gestured casually at the door. "That's Henry's suite, isn't it," he said.

The man nodded. "Are you here for the meeting?" he asked.

Darrow said he was, and without further ado, the man opened the door.

C H A P T E R 13

Gone About As Far As We Can Go

November 2 to November 3

The second Plaza meeting had begun well enough, but by the time Peter Darrow had arrived, it had slipped distinctly off track. With the lawyers along—Ross Johnson wasn't at this meeting although Jim Robinson was—Henry Kravis and Peter Cohen had again confirmed that there would be the fifty–fifty split for a third time, and Beattie began asking for the management contract. Cohen wouldn't let him see it, not until everything else was settled.

So they talked about how the transaction would be financed.

"The way we're planning to structure the deal, it will be all rated securities," said Tom Strauss. "There won't be any junk." With no junk, there was surely no role for Drexel.

"You can't do it that way," said George Roberts. "A deal like this has to have some junk."

Strauss insisted it didn't, and he began debating that with Roberts. As they talked, it became clear that Strauss regarded RJR as a Salomon financing, but Roberts corrected him. "Drexel is going to be the lead," he said.

"No," said Strauss, launching into an impassioned speech as to why it had to be a Salomon deal. "I had sixty-five guys working on this over the weekend."

Roberts couldn't quite imagine what sixty-five guys had been doing—they had been calling accounts—but he knew better than to ask.

Clearly who would lead the financing was a touchy point, and Cohen changed the subject. By ten-thirty, they had agreed on all the other key questions: how the board would be structured, who got how many votes, even who the sixteen directors would be (under a complicated system, some of the directors got only a fraction of a vote).

As they were getting up to leave, Cohen turned to Steve Goldstone. "You can give them the contract now," he said.

Goldstone didn't have it. His briefcase was at the Cookie Palace. Fortunately, Jack Nusbaum, Cohen's lawyer, had both his briefcase and a contract. He gave the document to Goldstone, who flipped it open before handing it to Beattie. "I wanted you to see this," he said, pointing at one of the sections.

Beattie read. Goldstone's paragraph said that Johnson's lawyers and bankers would run the deal. Well, thought Beattie, he didn't care who ran the deal, although he wasn't sure that it should be Goldstone, who wasn't a takeover lawyer. But Beattie didn't say that. Instead, he walked into the bedroom to read through the document.

A few minutes later, Beattie came back into the living room and motioned to Kravis and Roberts that he needed to talk. In the other room, he showed them the management contract. "This is unbelievable," he said. In addition to the equity stake that Cohen had told Kravis about earlier, management was guaranteed a salary of $19 million a year with a $20 million bonus pool if they hit 80 percent of their target earnings. Johnson had veto power over certain corporate actions. Worse, there was to be a management company running RJR. It looked to Kravis as if Johnson planned "to call in four years to tell the investors how they did."

There was no way that Kravis and Roberts were going to agree to that, and while they were discussing just how impossible it was, Darrow walked into the room.

"What is this?" Beattie asked, holding up the contract. "You can't be serious about this. Are you on board?"

Darrow had thought that that question might be coming and he had talked to Gutfreund during one of the breaks about the possibility. They had agreed that, if asked, Salomon should make it clear that it had problems with the management arrangement. That would tell Kravis that he didn't have to agree to the terms to join the Shearson team. It would also put Salomon at risk if the KKR deal fell apart, that KKR would tell the world that Salomon and Shearson didn't agree. "We've agreed conceptually to a management contract," said Darrow. "But we're concerned about governance and the levels of compensation. John Gutfreund and Warren Buffett are particularly sensitive to that."

That was interesting, thought Beattie. Salomon apparently hadn't signed off on this contract. Well, neither would KKR. Goldstone was still lingering in the living room when the group walked back from the bedroom. "We have a lot of problems with this agreement," said Beattie. "The equity will come out of your half. The rest we'll deal with later."

"No," said Goldstone. "If we're going to team up, we have to work that out today. It's only ten-thirty. We've got all night." Goldstone suggested that they reconvene at the Cookie Palace in fifteen minutes, and Beattie agreed.

After Goldstone and the other Shearson people had left, Beattie sat down with a yellow legal pad to draft a term-sheet listing what they had agreed to so far. He was confident that they would have all the wrinkles ironed out by morning.

Johnson had gone home after the first Plaza meeting. He changed out of his suit into more comfortable slacks and a sports coat, and, after a quiet dinner with Laurie, walked back down Fifth Avenue to his office to find out how the negotiations were coming. No one knew just then, but at about eleven, Cohen arrived back from the Plaza to say that Shearson and KKR were close to a deal. A few minutes after that, Kravis, Roberts, and Beattie were ushered into Johnson's office for a final round of negotiations.

Beattie had expected to focus on the management contract, but when Cohen came in, it was to say that Salomon didn't want Drexel in the deal. Kravis brushed that aside. "Drexel has to be in the deal," he said. A few minutes later, Cohen reappeared with Strauss to repeat that Drexel wouldn't be involved.

"We want the best people," said Roberts. "You have your group; we have our group. Drexel is part of our group."

Strauss insisted that Drexel couldn't be involved.

Roberts knew that Drexel and Salomon didn't get along, but he nonetheless regarded who would lead the financing as a minor issue. Surely the problem was just money. "Drexel has to lead the financing," he volunteered, "but we can tell them to split the fee with you."

That didn't do it either.

Cohen and Strauss disappeared. Horrigan wandered in, and Johnson introduced him to the KKR team. Then Johnson and Horrigan talked about the tobacco business. Kravis and Roberts were impressed, but they wanted to clear up one point. "You know if we can work something out, it's going to be different than the kind of deal Shearson was talking about," said Kravis, meaning that Johnson wasn't going to have veto power over board decisions, or a guaranteed salary and bonus. "And our lawyers and accountants are going to have to have a role. They're more experienced."

By this time it was clear to Johnson that Shearson didn't know the first thing about leveraged buyouts. "We want the most experienced people," he agreed.

Since nothing seemed to be happening, the KKR people decided to take a walk around. Kravis said hello to Linda Robinson. Dick Beattie bumped into one of the Davis Polk lawyers, who told him that there shouldn't be a KKR lawyer in Johnson's office if there wasn't a Shearson lawyer there too. Beattie laughed, but when he came back, neither Goldstone nor Nusbaum joined them. By that time Jim Robinson and Horrigan had left for the night—Linda had stayed to draft a press release—so the four, Johnson, Kravis, Roberts, and Beattie, moved to the small conference room next to Johnson's office. The fishbowl was right next door and they could hear the Shearson and Salomon people arguing, although they couldn't quite make out what was being said.

Cohen came in again and again, but he never changed his tune: Salomon wanted Drexel out.

"This is crazy," said Johnson. "Why can't you get together?"

"We've got to do this right," said Roberts. "We need the lowest rate and we need to know that the financing is going to get done. Shearson has never done a deal like this before, so we don't know if they can do it. The last two deals Salomon did are bankrupt."

* * *

In the fishbowl, meanwhile, Cohen was doing his best to convince Salomon to soften its stance on Drexel, but he wasn't having much luck. Gutfreund was hanging tough. The Shearson team would lead the financing, not Drexel. It didn't have to be Salomon per se. Shearson would be okay. But not Drexel.

At first, Cohen was sympathetic. He too wanted control over the refinancing of his bridge loan. He too had had trouble working with Drexel bond syndicates, although given Shearson's limited bond underwriting activities, the problem didn't loom large. But as time wore on, he had more and more trouble figuring out what the problem was. Gutfreund's initial argument, that letting Drexel lead the financing would destroy Salomon's hopes of ever becoming a junk bond powerhouse, was clearly not the whole story. When Cohen suggested that the four banks in question, Drexel, Merrill, Shearson, and Salomon, share the job of lead manager, Gutfreund refused on the grounds that Drexel was impossible to work with.

Then Cohen suggested that each firm take out its own bridge. Gutfreund snapped that that was impossible because it meant coordinating with Drexel. How were they going to decide who refinanced first? he wanted to know. Something like that had to be coordinated, and Gutfreund didn't trust Drexel to play fair. Cohen had bounced the four co-lead idea off Roberts despite Gutfreund's skepticism, and Roberts had rejected it too, on the grounds that it would raise the interest cost; in Roberts's view only Drexel could get the best rate. Gutfreund got huffy when he heard that and insisted that Salomon, a premier bond house, could get just as good a price as Drexel; in any case, he added, this issue was so large it would be priced by the market, not the underwriter. Neither Roberts nor Gutfreund were keen on Cohen's suggestion that Shearson would pay the difference in interest cost of using Salomon over using Drexel. That was deemed both stupid and insulting.

Indeed, Gutfreund's position seemed to get more entrenched as the evening wore on, and the explanations for why a Drexel deal wouldn't work got increasingly inconsistent, even surreal. At one point, Gutfreund conceded that Salomon could not hope to sell the volume of junk bonds Drexel did, and that it didn't want to agree to an issue larger than it knew it could sell. Later, Gutfreund worried that if Drexel were RICOed in the middle of a joint deal with Salomon, Salomon's assets would also be seized.

And where was Drexel anyway? As far as Gutfreund could tell, none of the key Drexel players were there. He had not seen Leon Black, the merger chief, or Peter Ackerman, who was now filling Mike Milken's shoes as junk bond point man, but he was sure that Roberts was talking to them regularly. Indeed, Gutfreund believed that Drexel was making the decisions, since a KKR offer, unlike a Shearson offer, turned entirely on Drexel's ability to sell junk.

"You obstructionist," Cohen yelled at Lee Kimmell, when he was still standing fast for a Salomon-led issue at three in the morning.

Time inched on. While the Salomon and Shearson people argued, Johnson introduced Kravis to Andy Sage. Sage seemed utterly baffled that the question of who led the syndicate had become such a stumbling block and shook his head in amazement when Cohen told him that none of Sage's suggestions for overcoming it had been well received either. "We've got to hurry up," Johnson said again and again. "We've got to get this agreement signed."

By two o'clock, it was clear to Roberts that Cohen didn't agree with Salomon, although he remained the spokesman for Salomon's position. Perhaps that was the problem: Cohen, not himself a syndicate man or even a bond man, was confusing the issue. Perhaps if Roberts discussed the matter with whomever it was at Salomon who was voicing the objections, things would start to make sense. "Is there someone here from Salomon we can talk to?" Roberts asked, thinking Strauss might still be around. "We need someone who can make a decision."

"Gutfreund," suggested Cohen.

Gutfreund? Roberts was startled. He had wasted hours negotiating with Cohen while Gutfreund sat in the fishbowl next door? What was going on here?

Cohen disappeared and came back a few minutes later to say that Gutfreund wasn't available. He had just left the building.

Johnson shook his head in disbelief; then he suddenly stood up and walked out of the office. If Roberts wanted to talk to Gutfreund, Johnson was determined that he would, even if it meant he had to find Gutfreund himself. He didn't have to go far. Gutfreund had left only to walk around the block, and Johnson bumped into him almost as soon as he stepped out of the lobby onto West 57th Street.

Unfortunately, Roberts and Gutfreund didn't make any more progress than Roberts and Cohen had. Gutfreund said flatly that he wasn't going to do a deal with Drexel. Period. That sounded like the end of that, but Cohen came back alone a few minutes later to say that there was still some flexibility. After another round of talks, Johnson finally decided to go home. Although everyone insisted that who led the finance was not a deal-breaker, Johnson realized that it would take many more hours before it got resolved, and he didn't have anything to add. Before Johnson left, he signed the partnership agreement that Goldstone had drafted from Beattie's yellow page outline. He fully expected that Kravis and Cohen would sign before he arrived in the office the next day.

By four o'clock, though, the situation still hadn't changed. Roberts signaled the KKR group to caucus. "We're not going to do a deal tonight," he said. "We need to talk to Peter Ackerman. Maybe Drexel has an idea for getting around this problem."

"Given the difficulty we're having with the underwriting, I don't know how we're going to renegotiate the management contract," said Beattie.

So Roberts announced that KKR was going home.

Cohen, who was so tired and frustrated that he was having trouble seeing straight, thought that that made sense. They would all get some sleep and meet again in the morning. He volunteered that he would stay home until Kravis called to say he was ready to resume talks.

Salomon didn't see it that way; Gutfreund was sure that the only reason that KKR was leaving was that Roberts, who had flown in on the red-eye the night before, was tired, just as they all were tired. "You can't leave now," Michael Zimmerman yelled at Beattie. "We've got to get this worked out tonight."

"We're not making any progress," said Beattie. "We have to talk to Drexel."

"Talk to Drexel?" asked Zimmerman. "Why are you talking to Drexel? You run your deals by yourself. You don't need Drexel to make this decision for you."

"Drexel is our partner," said Beattie. "Peter just spent the evening defending you and your ability to sell bonds. We need to talk to Drexel."

Finally, the KKR team left. Although it was four-thirty by the time he got back to the Carlyle, Roberts dialed Ackerman at his hotel—Ackerman is based in Los Angeles, but he happened to be in New York on another deal—and invited him to breakfast at KKR at eight o'clock. Then he lay down for a few hours of sleep.

Cohen stayed at RJR Nabisco for another two hours, trying to budge Gutfreund, without success. Finally, at about six he went home to bed. About nine o'clock, Kravis called to say that Peter Ackerman had two proposals. Cohen called Strauss and the two met at Kravis's office at ten o'clock. By this time Cohen was beginning to get cold feet about teaming up with KKR. Although he wanted to win, he didn't want a second-tier role, and behind the talk about being equal partners, Cohen had a nagging suspicion that that was what Kravis had in mind.

Neither of Ackerman's two proposals seemed to make much sense to Cohen. One, that the four investment banks work together as co-underwriters, had already been vetoed the night before. The other, a convoluted suggestion for dividing the junk issues between Drexel and the others by type of security, was just a complicated form of each firm taking out its own bridge system that Gutfreund had already deemed unworkable.

So Cohen was disappointed when he went upstairs to the Cookie Palace to report to the troops. Indeed, as Cohen started to explain the two proposals, he decided that what he was describing was so obviously unacceptable that he must have gotten something wrong. He stopped and left the room to call Jeff Lane, Shearson's president. Having had just two hours of sleep, Cohen thought it was possible that he had missed the point. Surely, Lane, who had had a good night's sleep, would glom onto what the Ackerman proposals really were.

Lane called Beattie to say that he was coming down with questions about the Ackerman proposals, but when he arrived with Nusbaum a few minutes later, what he wanted to know about was not the junk issue but how KKR planned to structure the finance. Nusbaum said that he didn't understand where the money for the tender offer was coming from. He didn't think that it would be possible to find that much cash quickly.

Beattie was puzzled as to what that had to do with Ackerman's proposals. Lane didn't explain, although he has said subsequently that what he was really after was why Drexel was so critical to KKR's deal. Lane was convinced that the problem was not underwriting the junk itself, which Lane believed Salomon could handle just as well as Drexel. Perhaps Drexel was making a large bridge loan, something the firm hadn't traditionally done. In that case, Drexel might be offering KKR a package Shearson and Salomon weren't willing to match.

Indeed, Drexel was providing a large bridge, $3.5 billion of the $5 billion total bridge (Merrill was taking care of the other $1.5 billion). After a discussion about why KKR was raising money by selling its particular mix of securities, Lane finally asked some questions about the Ackerman proposals and disappeared upstairs.

The $5 billion of junk was more than even Cohen could take. Shearson and Salomon couldn't hope to sell that much, and if Drexel was RICOed out in the middle of the money-raising, they would be unable to complete the job. This wasn't to be Shearson's deal or even a marriage of equals. KKR was proposing that Shearson be a lowly investor in the KKR deal. Neither of the Ackerman proposals got around that.

Before he told Kravis he was breaking off discussions, Cohen had to decide what Shearson was going to do next, so the strategists sat down to talk things through. Tom Hill had flown to Minneapolis at five that morning for the Pillsbury board meeting, but he left the session to listen in on the Shearson meeting over the speaker phone.

Gutfreund was adamant that it was high time to launch a formal bid. All that was currently on the table from Shearson was an indication at $75. Gutfreund's number, of course, was $92.

Hill didn't want to do anything. "If you make an offer, you cut off any hope of negotiations," he said. "It's a mistake. We want to keep the door open."

Gutfreund insisted that they should bid, and since Shearson couldn't make any offer without Gutfreund's money, Gutfreund was the decision-maker. Shearson would bid, and bid $92 a share.

Neither Johnson nor Goldstone had been involved in that discussion, but since Goldstone was the group's contact with the Special Committee, Gutfreund now told him to call Peter Atkins with the number.

"Bidding ninety-two dollars a share is a mistake," said Goldstone.

"Call Atkins," said Gutfreund.

"There's still a chance that you can get a merger agreement," said Goldstone. After all, he reminded Gutfreund, the last time he had talked to Atkins, he had been pushing the idea of a preemptive bid and Atkins had seemed receptive. In that context, Goldstone insisted, $92 a share was ludicrous.

Gutfreund repeated his order to call Atkins, and Goldstone called. Atkins was in a Special Committee meeting, but he came out to talk to Goldstone. "We're about to bid," said Goldstone.

"Oh?" said Atkins. Finally he was going to hear the much-discussed preemptive offer. "What's the price?"

"Ninety-two," said Goldstone.

Atkins didn't say anything, but Goldstone could guess what he was thinking: Huh?

Kravis hadn't realized that Lane had come down with questions until after he had left, and although he didn't doubt that Beattie had explained Ackerman's proposals correctly, he was slightly worried that Shearson would interpret his unintended absence as a sign that KKR wasn't serious about a compromise. In any event, he was somewhat surprised when Jim Robinson appeared at noon, poker-faced, to say that Shearson had decided that a deal wasn't possible and it was even now calling Dow Jones with an offer of $92 a share.

"But what about our proposals?" asked Roberts.

Robinson didn't answer directly. "We got about as far as we could go," he said.

That didn't make sense. As far as Kravis could tell, Shearson had refused to cut a deal and indeed upped the ante by $500 million simply because sharing RJR didn't fit with Cohen's dream of becoming a Wall Street titan. He was sure that the Salomon–Drexel explanation had little to do with the problem.

Kravis repeated that theory to his investment bankers at a meeting later that afternoon in the KKR conference room. In the course of briefing the team on what had happened the night before, Kravis outlined the terms of the management contract with the caveat that they were to be kept strictly confidential. Kravis knew that the group didn't have a good record on keeping secrets and he no longer trusted them with his own bidding strategy, but he didn't think he could give them a fair account of the past eighteen hours without mentioning Johnson's contract. Actually, he still had trouble believing that Shearson had agreed to it.

Thursday afternoon, Kravis got his first look at the advance copy of the next week's *BusinessWeek*. He was featured on the cover under a blockbuster "King Henry" headline. The article inside not only repeated the Shearson myths about his friendship with Cohen and his goal of protecting his "franchise," it also said that he was personally putting the entire economic system at peril. "The battle for RJR that Henry Kravis started in October 1988 may well turn out [to] have a far bigger impact on Corporate America than the Crash of October 1987."

"This is rough," Kravis complained to Steve Waters after reading the article.

"It's just Tom's style," said Waters, who had worked with Hill and Shearson for years. "It will stop."

Kravis hoped so, and soon. But at least he was getting a break. He was taking the day off Friday to look at prep schools with his fourteen-year-old son Robbie. He wasn't going to think about RJR until Monday.

CHAPTER 14

Jumping Up and Down on a Stick

November 3 to November 7

Al Butler, of course, didn't have a clue that Cohen and Kravis were talking when he boarded his flight from Greensboro to New York on Thursday morning for the ten o'clock meeting of the Special Committee. Felix Rohatyn had said at the Tuesday meeting that Kravis and Cohen's getting back together was inevitable since it made economic sense, but thus far there had been no public indication that a compromise was in the works. Certainly it wasn't mentioned in that day's *Wall Street Journal*. Butler had read the paper on the airplane, and the article on RJR simply repeated the persistent rumors that Shearson was talking to Robert Bass and PepsiCo. According to the report, Forstmann Little was considering forming a third bidding group, a fact that had not yet been communicated to Butler, or, as far as he knew, the Special Committee. Kravis wasn't mentioned in the article at all.

Butler had long since finished reading the newspaper when the plane began to approach New Jersey. By then it was raining so hard that the flight was diverted around Philadelphia. By the time he finally got to Skadden Arps, the ten-thirty meeting of the Special Committee was well underway. Butler had been late for the Tuesday meeting too, because a tractor trailer had turned over in the Holland Tunnel, blocking traffic almost all the way to the airport. He had decided then and there that he was coming in the night before for future meetings. Bill Anderson, who was flying in from Dayton, Ohio, had come to the same conclusion, and they agreed that they would have dinner together at the Regency the night before each Special Committee meeting.

Because he was late, Butler didn't hear the meeting's opening spat. By this time the committee was badly divided. Marty Davis and John Macomber were pushing for a restructuring. Anderson was worried about employees. Charlie Hugel was trying to toe some middle line, which came out looking suspiciously like tipping the auction to Johnson. This particular morning, Davis had arrived steaming because Hugel was talking to Johnson. Why had Hugel ignored Peter Atkins's and Davis's clear instructions not to return Johnson's phone calls? Why had Hugel talked to the Reuters wire, which quoted him as saying "cash is king," which happened not to be true; the committee hadn't discussed the point, much less decided. Davis was disgusted by Hugel's explanation that Reuters had talked only to his secretary.

Butler did arrive in time for the news. Atkins reported that Steve Goldstone had been pushing the idea of a preemptive bid, although he hadn't yet produced a preemptive price. There had been several calls from Geoff Boisi to say that Forstmann Little wanted to put together a bidding group with Proctor & Gamble and Castle & Cooke. The consortium clearly involved presales and hence didn't comply with the bidding rules. Through Boisi, Forstmann had made it clear that he wouldn't bid unless invited; thus far, he hadn't been invited.

Luis Rinaldini, the junior Lazard partner, had just finished a presentation comparing the $75- and $90-a-share offers and Fritz Hobbs was beginning to talk about how hard it was to value the tobacco company, when Goldstone called with the $92-a-share number. That was more interesting than Hobbs's complaint that he couldn't get a handle on the tobacco litigation because the RJR lawyers had refused to discuss it with him—they had produced a twenty-five-page litigation summary—and the talk quickly turned to Shearson.

By this time Ira Harris and Felix Rohatyn had picked up the word that Shearson and KKR had spent the previous night trying to negotiate a partnership, and they were startled that the partnership hadn't panned out. They were also startled by the price:

surely Shearson didn't regard $92 a share as preemptive, as Gold-
stone had promised earlier. Although the fact of the Shearson
bid made it less likely that the two would get back together again,
Rohatyn was still worried: the economic pressure was overpower-
ing. The only hope was that Cohen and Kravis were now so mad
at each other that they would fight to victory.

There was nothing that the committee could do to stop KKR
and Shearson from getting back together, of course, but they
might be able to discourage future negotiations by getting the
bidding process rolling. That meant choosing an auction date and
drafting bidding rules.

One way to drive a wedge between them was getting Ted Forstmann into the loop. Given the rivalry between Forstmann and
Kravis, a Forstmann bid might be the best way to spur competition.

Another option was biting the bullet on a restructuring as a
threatened and possibly real alternative. Davis, Macomber, and
the investment bankers and lawyers all insisted that a restructuring
might even be the best alternative available. Davis was so keen
on it that he had had his corporate finance team look at breakup
values, although he made it clear that the Gulf + Western people
were not going to implement a breakup if that was what the
committee decided to do. It seemed obvious that Johnson and
his team would leave the company if the board didn't do the
leveraged buyout, and Hugel was leery of trying to run or restructure the company alone. However, he knew that Davis and
Macomber were going to keep pushing; he knew he was going to
be hassled about that till kingdom come. So, as the meeting was
breaking up at twelve-thirty he asked Macomber to stay behind
to talk about that. It had suddenly occurred to Hugel that Macomber, who had been a Reynolds director since 1975 and was
currently unemployed—he had stepped down as chairman of Celanese after the sale to West German Hoechst AG—knew tobacco, and Hugel, who was already chairman of RJR, knew food.
Perhaps, if push came to shove, the two of them could run the
company together.

Macomber agreed to think about it, and Hugel heaved a sigh
of relief. Given the testy relationship between Hugel and Macomber, a joint CEO-ship would surely be difficult. It also had a

certain irony: for the past three years, Macomber had been John-son's most vocal critic.

The Forstmann consortium hadn't suddenly appeared from no-where on Thursday morning. Ted Forstmann had been mulling the idea for four days, ever since the final meeting with Peter Cohen at Shearson headquarters, Sunday, October 30. Indeed, although Forstmann had told Cohen when he left the meeting that he was going back to his office to think, that had not been true. Where he had really been headed was the Plaza Athenée, the elegant hotel on East Sixty-fifth Street, for dinner with Castle & Cooke chairman David Murdock, and John Pepper, president of Proctor & Gamble. With the possibility of a Shearson deal crumbling, Forstmann had decided to investigate Boisi's original idea: forming a blue chip consortium.

The meal had gone well. The three had hit it off, and they had generally agreed on how a consortium could work. After strug-gling for two days with the question of whether he wanted to own a tobacco company, given that plenty of people including the Surgeon General and Ted Forstmann thought that cigarettes caused cancer, Forstmann had finally decided to go ahead.

To his surprise, the Special Committee had given him the cold shoulder. When Boisi called Hobbs, Hobbs had insisted that the Forstmann group didn't conform to a key bidding rule: no pre-selling. Boisi had tried to argue that preselling was necessary to line up bank financing and hence to make the highest bid, but Hobbs wouldn't budge. He told Boisi to come back with a bid that involved no preselling, or give up.

Boisi had no choice but to try to reconfigure the consortium with no preselling, and on Thursday afternoon he called Hobbs back to say that the Forstmann group would bid as a partnership and would promise to jointly own the tobacco unit for two years. The arrangement was unwieldy and clearly less than ideal, but it did seem to have some arcane tax benefits, not the least of which was that the food bust-up would be tax free.

Hobbs surprised Boisi again by doing a complete about-face and effusively welcoming Forstmann. The only problem with the new scheme, Hobbs said, was how many companies would be involved.

"What do you mean by a 'few' partners?" asked Fritz Hobbs

at a meeting at Skadden Thursday afternoon. "We understand a 'couple,' but how many is a few?"

Forstmann didn't know, but it was likely more than two, because he had that many already: Proctor & Gamble and Castle & Cooke. But he got the idea. "Three," he ventured.

Three apparently was few enough, which meant that Forstmann had to decide whether he wanted to bring in a third partner, and, if so, who that should be. Forstmann didn't care, but Murdock and Pepper did, and after a fierce internal debate over whether a fourth partner was necessary—adding a partner would make reaching an agreement yet more difficult—they chose Ralston Purina. Other companies had called about buying various RJR's units, but Ralston, the St. Louis–based blue chip, which wanted Milk Bones and Shredded Wheat, seemed the most serious.

Forstmann doesn't usually make a public announcement when he decides to look at a company, but this was a special case. He wasn't hostile, he would never be hostile, and he didn't want to be labeled hostile. So putting out a release saying that the board had invited his bid was critical. Atkins thought it was critical too: he wanted everyone to know that there was another entity looking to bid.

So, on Friday morning the two teams met at Lazard to work out what their joint press release would say. Forstmann had thought that that would take half an hour, leaving his press man plenty of time to get the word out before noon. Instead, the bankers and lawyers spent the whole day arguing over language. First, Atkins rewrote the release from start to finish. Then he suggested that Forstmann include a price. Forstmann said he didn't have a price and wasn't sure he was going to bid; he just wanted to say that he was considering making a bid. Atkins insisted that Forstmann give some kind of price indication, and finally Forstmann agreed to say that if he made a bid it would be for more than $90 a share, which should have been obvious given that KKR's $90-a-share bid was already on the table.

But Atkins did have one constructive suggestion. Where Forstmann had proposed that the Special Committee say that it had invited him to bid, Atkins said he could do one better. "We'll welcome your offer."

Late in the afternoon, while he was still at Lazard working on the language, Forstmann got a note from his secretary that Jim

Robinson had called him at the office. He dialed American Express.

"My guys are jumping up and down on a stick," said Robinson. "They hear that you are doing something."

"I can't confirm or deny that," said Forstmann. "But I can tell you that Geoff told Peter from the start that we had three options, and we've only eliminated one: doing a deal with you."

"I thought you said that if you didn't do a deal with us, you were going to cheer from the sidelines," said Robinson.

Forstmann had had that phrase thrown back at him before, by Peter Cohen. He was beginning to wish he had not chosen those particular words that late night at Johnson's office. "Remember the context of that remark," said Forstmann. "You had just told me that you were talking to Kravis down the hall and I was trying to say that we would not have come out with a hostile offer like he did. I never suggested that if the board invited me to an auction, I wouldn't bid."

"Well, I don't want to get in a beef with you," said Robinson. "I have high regard for you."

Forstmann called back half an hour later to say that he had put out a press release; he read it.

Robinson laughed. "My phone calls sure have impact," he said.

"I'm calling you instead of Ross because I don't want to look like I'm interfering with management," said Forstmann. "This is an auction and I'm making a bid, but I'm friendly to management."

That was a surprise. "You mean to say that we could get into your deal?" Robinson asked.

"On the right terms," said Forstmann.

"I think you should call Ross," said Robinson.

Forstmann tried the RJR Nabisco office, but Johnson wasn't there. He left a message and called Robinson again.

"I know Ross is going to be in Atlanta tomorrow," said Robinson. "Why don't you call him there." He read off the number.

Forstmann wrote it down, but he wasn't sure that his calling Johnson at home was a good idea. Surely, after his son's tragic accident Johnson he didn't need to spend his weekend on the phone with Ted Forstmann. And besides, Forstmann didn't want to be accused of interfering with management's deal. "Look,"

Forstmann said, "if Johnson wants to talk to me, you have him call."

Robinson said he would, but Johnson hadn't called back by six, when Forstmann left for dinner with some of the Goldman Sachs bankers and his new partners to talk about how the bid would work. They all agreed that they were in this together. They would bid together or drop out together; no one would break away to make a separate offer.

The discussion of financing was fairly general. One of the Goldman bankers warned Forstmann that if the price got into the high nineties, the only way to raise the money would be by selling junk. Forstmann certainly heard that, but it didn't set off an alarm bell; he wasn't sure that that was true, and besides, his price probably wasn't going to be much above $92 a share.

Unlike Forstmann, Robinson did talk to Johnson Friday night, and he had more on his mind than the Forstmann consortium. Forstmann hadn't actually made a bid, and Robinson and the other members of the Shearson team agreed that he wasn't likely to make one. Forstmann's partners were, after all, a handful of tightfisted food giants with different interests and different ideas about price, and different, perhaps insurmountable, antitrust problems. Consortium bids usually collapsed; look how much trouble that they had had trying to team up with KKR.

Kravis was another matter. Robinson had been pushing for a partnership with Kravis from the start, and now Johnson was firmly in the do-a-deal-with-KKR camp too. After watching Shearson in action Johnson couldn't "see how a deal of this size can get done without KKR." He had told Frank Benevento precisely that, when Benevento had asked Friday morning about the propriety of billing the company $20 million for his work on the LBO transaction (Benevento's contract said that he would be paid a "standard investment banking fee" for any deal that was consummated). Johnson didn't have a problem with the number per se; Benevento had done good work for the company, unlike some investment bankers he knew. But Johnson warned Benevento that all of the bankers would likely have to take a haircut; by the time KKR and Shearson teamed up there would be nine investment banks involved.

The talks with KKR had broken down so acrimoniously that it would clearly not be easy to get them started again. The fact that Salomon had "gotten hotheaded" and insisted on launching a bid only made the situation even more difficult, but Johnson and Robinson agreed that something might be possible. The problem had nominally been Drexel, so Johnson said that he would start by calling his friend Jeff Beck, the Drexel banker who had pitched an MLP to RJR back in 1986.

And there was another matter that Robinson wanted to discuss: *The New York Times*. James Sterngold, the paper's ace business reporter, had gotten wind of the management contract. Linda Robinson knew from talking to him that the story wasn't going to be favorable. Unlike other reporters who had called with questions about the management agreement, Sterngold did seem to understand how the contract worked, even though his numbers were slightly wrong: he thought that Johnson got 20 percent of the equity if the return to investors was 40 percent, rather than the correct 50 percent. Even using those numbers and a $2.5 billion of equity Shearson planned to commit at its $92-a-share price, Sterngold concluded that Johnson and his group would make $2.7 billion in five years (using the 50 percent number, the total would have been even higher).

That was a correct computation, but it wasn't quite fair. Johnson wasn't personally going to make that much money; it was slated to be shared among a group of almost two hundred managers. Now that the price had jumped almost $20 a share, a 40 percent return on equity was all but impossible, much less a return of 50 percent.

It seemed obvious to both Jim and Linda Robinson what would happen if Johnson didn't do something: he would be transformed by the press into a symbol of Greed. The newspapers were already full of that idea, mostly in connection with Kravis and his unfortunate remark about "protecting the franchise." Jim and Linda thought that one way to deflect criticism was to make it clear that the stock was going to be shared by a lot of people, the more people the better. Jim Robinson suggested that perhaps the best thing that Johnson could do would be to announce that the management stock would be shared by all employees through an Employee Stock Ownership Plan (ESOP).

Johnson was willing to consider the idea, but then Goldstone

and Gar Basin, the Davis Polk partner who had actually negotiated the contract, flatly vetoed saying that or anything else to
Sterngold, or to anyone else. To Linda Robinson's frustration,
the lawyers took the firm position that since the contract was not
fully negotiated, its terms could not be disclosed.

Robinson's frustration was nothing compared to Cohen's rage.
Although Sterngold had refused to tell Linda Robinson where he
had gotten the story, Cohen was convinced that it had been leaked
by his friend Dick Beattie. Beattie was the only person outside
the Shearson group who had a copy of the contract. Surely he
had given it to Sterngold after the talks collapsed Thursday.

Late Friday night, Cohen called Beattie at home to accuse him
of leaking the contract. Between expletives, he told Beattie just
what he thought about his ethics, and even threatened to pull
Shearson's business from Simpson Thatcher.

Back in September Hugel had heard Johnson boast about how
much money he was going to make in a buyout; nonetheless,
Hugel was shocked speechless by *The New York Times* article
Saturday morning. The 20 percent stake was outrageous, particularly when coupled with the original lowball price of $75 a share.
After several irate calls from other directors, Hugel decided to
find out what was going on. Given the hassle he always got for
calling Johnson, Hugel decided to call Davis first. "Have you seen
the *Times*?" Hugel asked when Davis got on the line. "It's
atrocious."

Davis had been out late the night before and hadn't looked at
the paper. He opened it now, responded with several expletives,
and added that although the deal was "cockeyed, it doesn't have
anything to do with the price."

Hugel called Johnson. "Why wasn't the board told about this?"
he demanded.

"It isn't finished," said Johnson. "We're still negotiating."

"Are the terms correct?" asked Hugel.

"No," said Johnson. "The paper got it wrong."

"What's wrong?" asked Hugel. "How does the contract work?"

Johnson wouldn't say. He mumbled about the money being
spread around to more than seven executives.

Hugel knew Johnson well enough to recognize the mumbling
for truth-stretching. But try as he might, he couldn't pin Johnson

down. "Send me a letter explaining the terms," Hugel finally said in frustration.

Johnson said that he would.

But the damage had been done. Whether the terms were right or wrong the *Times* article had "shaken the directors out of their complacency," as one of them put it. "It was a hell of a mess," remembers Special Committee member Al Butler. "We knew it didn't affect the price, but it cast a pall over the whole deal. Suddenly everyone was asking, 'What kind of a guy did you have running your company all this time?' *We* didn't agree to that contract."

To anyone else, Hugel's call might have seemed a prelude to disaster, but Johnson didn't take it that way. Hugel hadn't seemed that upset. Indeed, the article itself hadn't been so bad, just a simple factual story with no banner headline. It had none of the pizzazz of the stories that had gotten Kravis into so much trouble: the *Journal* articles about protecting the franchise and objecting to cigar smoke. Ironically, most of the calls Johnson got that weekend were from the 156 unnamed second-tier management partners who were upset that the contract as reported in the *Times* didn't include them.

Nor did Johnson understand why the numbers would be controversial. As general partner, KKR got a 20 percent carry in every deal, plus fees for negotiating each purchase and running each company. If KKR won RJR, compensation would be much more generous than what Johnson had negotiated for himself.

Whatever Jim and Linda Robinson said about publicity and the need to do something dramatic, no one in Johnson's group was inclined to believe that. Andy Sage was disgusted with the idea of an ESOP and caustically remarked that he didn't think it was necessary for motivational purposes to give stock to the janitor. Goldstone said that there was no reason to renegotiate. The management contract was, after all, a contract between Shearson and Johnson, not between the bidding group and the shareholders. Anything Johnson gave up simply went into Peter Cohen's pocket. A deal was a deal.

When Ted Forstmann got home late Saturday afternoon from a strategy meeting with Goldman Sachs, the housekeeper gave him a message that Johnson had called. Forstmann dialed the number. "I'm sorry we didn't have a chance to talk earlier," Forstmann began.

"My line was open," said Johnson.

Forstmann wasn't sure that that was true—likely Peter Cohen would have hit the ceiling if he had contacted Johnson on his own—but he didn't comment.

"But it doesn't matter," continued Johnson. "We'll talk during the due diligence."

Forstmann was nonplussed: talk during due diligence? No one had ever suggested that to him before. "You saw our announcement," said Forstmann. "I told you when we were trying to work out a deal earlier that I wasn't a financing source, that I was different from the other guys. Now you see."

"Yeah," said Johnson, "I sure do."

Forstmann went through his sales pitch again, adding that he thought that RJR was a great opportunity. Johnson agreed, and said that it would be critical to have him on board, since running a tobacco company was a difficult matter, requiring special expertise. Then, to underscore how different his approach was from Kravis's, Forstmann asked Johnson how *he* personally felt about investing in junk bonds. Was a note so risky that it couldn't pay cash interest something he himself would buy?

"No," laughed Johnson. "My personal accounts are not exactly filled with junk bonds."

"I think it would be great if we can get together," said Forstmann. "I'm sure Peter explained to you why I pulled out. I'm sure he gave you my four points."

"He did," said Johnson. "I'd like to think about it."

"Listen to Jim," said Forstmann. "He has your best interests at heart." Robinson, unlike Cohen, seemed to be pushing for an accommodation with Forstmann. Forstmann wanted to be sure that Johnson understood who he would be teaming up with under the two options. "Kravis has Milken. I have P&G," major corporate partners, and Johnson's friends.

"You know that *The New York Times* has picked up my arrangements," said Johnson.

By this time Forstmann had seen the article. Indeed, it had been the topic of some discussion at the meeting that afternoon.

"Now how would you think that that could have happened?" asked Johnson, implying that it was Forstmann.

Forstmann was insulted. "I would no more do that than fly to the moon," he said.

"Then who do you think did it?" asked Johnson.

"Who's your opponent?" asked Forstmann. Henry Kravis.

"I was told you did it," said Johnson.

"I give you my word," said Forstmann. "I didn't do it."

By this time, Johnson knew from his calls to Beck that teaming up with Kravis was a nonstarter no matter how much sense it made economically. "If Kravis did it," said Johnson, "I can play that game too."

Forstmann was sure that he had talked Johnson into joining his group. He called Boisi. "This is going to work out," he said. "Ross is just learning, but I think I made some headway. We're going to get together."

Boisi was very skeptical. It wasn't clear why Robinson and Johnson were suddenly being so friendly, but he suspected that the purpose was not to come on board but to stall Forstmann from ever making his bid. "I hope you're right," he said. "And if you're right, I hope it's the right thing."

Forstmann called Fraidin with the good news.

Fraidin was skeptical too. "How is Shearson going to fit into this?" he asked.

"That won't be a problem," said Forstmann, who seemed oblivious to the fact that Shearson would want an equity stake in any deal that Johnson was involved in. "They're just an adviser."

"I don't think they see themselves that way," said Fraidin.

Forstmann had hired a pr man, Davis Weinstock, just before announcing his consortium, and he had invited Weinstock to breakfast at his apartment on Sunday morning. It was their first meeting, and Forstmann wanted to keep things straight. "I don't lie," he said. "And that means that you don't lie. I don't expect people to lie about me, but if they do"—"they" being Kravis—"we're going to hit them with the truth."

Weinstock had more on his mind than Forstmann's perception of how to tell the truth. "Something is wrong," he said. "I can't get the guy at the *Times* to focus on the story. He doesn't want to hear about a solidly financed consortium. It's like he hates you."

"Me?" said Forstmann. "That's surrealistic. He doesn't know me. He's never talked to me."

"I can't get him to focus on what you're doing with this consortium," said Weinstock. "He keeps asking all these negative questions."

"Well, call him again," said Forstmann.

Weinstock called Forstmann late in the afternoon. He had talked to the *Times* reporter, James Sterngold, again, but without success. "It's worse," he said. "I've been at this twenty years, and I just know something is going on. Who did you do something to?"

Forstmann kept trying to figure out what Kravis was pulling, and suddenly it dawned on him. Ross Johnson was going to accuse him of leaking the management contract. Well, he'd take care of that. Jim Robinson had given him the number, indeed, even urged him to call. He dialed Atlanta. Laurie Johnson answered. "Oh, hi, Ted," she said. They talked for fifteen minutes, first about Bruce Johnson's accident—by this time he had slipped into an irreversible coma—then about golf.

"Is Ross there?" Forstmann finally asked.

"He's on a conference call," said Laurie, "hold on."

"Don't bother," said Forstmann, "it's not a big deal, just ask him to call me back."

"No, wait," said Laurie. "I'm sure he wants to talk to you." A few minutes later she was back on the line. "Sorry," she said. "He'll have to call you back."

Fifteen minutes later, Forstmann's phone rang. Forstmann had just laid down for a back massage, but he had to ask the masseur to step out of the room. Surely it was Johnson calling back and it wouldn't do to have someone listening in, perhaps hearing inside information, even if it was a masseur whose English wasn't too good.

"Is this Theodore Forstmann of Forstmann Little?" asked a serious voice.

What the hell? thought Forstmann. "This is Ted Forstmann," he said.

"This is Gar Basin of Davis Polk & Wardwell," said the voice. "And I have been authorized by Mr. and Mrs. Johnson to say that you are bothering them at home. Any conversations between you and Mr. Johnson will be initiated by him."

"What did you say your name was?" asked Forstmann, fumbling around for a pencil and paper.

"Basin."

"Well, listen here," said Forstmann, writing that down. "First, I wasn't bothering anyone. I'm a personal friend of Laurie Johnson and a friend of Ross Johnson; I'm a governor of the club where he plays golf. I talked to Laurie Johnson for fifteen minutes, and she did eighty percent of the talking, mainly about personal matters and golf. In no way did I say anything that was insulting to anyone. Second, Ross Johnson's investment banker spent a long time Friday night *telling* me to call; he gave me the phone number; I didn't initiate anything. Third, I know that neither Laurie nor Ross would have told you to tell me that I was harassing them. That's some bad advice they got from one of you dopes. Fourth, after this is over, I'm going to tell Ross about your call."

Forstmann slammed down the phone. By this time he was so steamed up that he called Steve Fraidin, his lawyer, who was spending the weekend with his son and daughter-in-law in Ohio. "You know I believe in families and all that," began Forstmann, but Fraidin could have saved him a lot of grief if only he had stayed home.

Forstmann had been right about one thing. Johnson hadn't asked Basin to call, and he was shocked when he learned much later what Basin had said. Johnson had simply mentioned on the Shearson conference call that Forstmann was on the other line, and Cohen had told Goldstone to make sure that any further communication stopped.

After all, Forstmann was currently at the top of Cohen's hate list. Having vented his anger at Dick Beattie for leaking the management contract, Cohen had shifted his focus to Forstmann's traitorous decision to put together his own bidding group. Cohen was outraged that, after sitting in on Shearson meetings and listening to Shearson strategy, Forstmann and, more particularly, Geoff Boisi thought that they could drop out and form their own bidding group. Cohen was sure that Boisi had been putting together the bidding group even before Forstmann had made his first call to Jim Robinson, and had simply used the meetings with Shearson to pump information for his competing offer. That he had been duped was particularly galling, since both Forstmann and Goldman boasted that their ethical standards were well above the rest of Wall Street.

Cohen was so angry, in fact, that he was determined to expose Boisi for the traitor that he was, even if doing so didn't seem likely to help Shearson win RJR. So Sunday afternoon, Cohen asked Jack Nusbaum to draft two letters, one to Forstmann saying that Boisi's behavior had tainted Forstmann's bid and a second to Goldman Sachs chairman John Weinberg, accusing Boisi of brazenly violating the confidentiality agreement, perhaps without informing his Goldman superiors. "Dear John," the Weinberg letter began. "You may be unaware of the role Goldman Sachs has played in our discussions with Forstmann Little & Co. Briefly stated, Geoff Boisi accompanied Ted Forstmann to all of our meetings and in that capacity he received all of the data referred to in the annexed letter. We believe it is inappropriate, unethical and, since Goldman was acting as an agent of Forstmann Little a violation of the express contract for Goldman Sachs to use that data for unauthorized purposes." Whatever else the letter accomplished, it would not endear Cohen to Weinberg; Boisi was not only a highly respected partner, he was also one of a handful in line for Weinberg's job.

Nusbaum brought the letters with him to the working dinner that night at Cohen's apartment at 1120 Fifth Avenue just up the street from the Metropolitan Museum. Cohen passed them around for comment. No one, not John Gutfreund or Tom Strauss, not Jim or Linda Robinson, raised an objection. Robinson, despite his public relations orientation, didn't really focus on it: he thought that the letter was simply a question of one big ego "kicking gorilla dust" at a second. Jay Higgins, Salomon's investment banking chief, told Gutfreund privately to "stay out of this" and to refuse to sign the letter if asked, but Higgins didn't say anything to Cohen: given Cohen's past behavior, Higgins knew that he wasn't going to take kindly to criticism in front of a group.

Actually, with Cohen in the lead, the team got pretty worked up about Boisi and even talked about suing, although the lawyers insisted that they had no conceivable legal basis for a case.

When tempers had cooled, they also talked strategy.

Nick Forstmann called Ted before breakfast Monday morning. He had just opened his *New York Times*, and he was flabbergasted by what it said. Cohen hadn't done what they had expected—accuse Ted of leaking the management contract—he had done something far worse: Cohen had charged that Ted had broken his "promise" to "cheer from the sidelines" if a deal with Shearson didn't work out. According to the article, Forstmann had violated the RJR confidentiality agreement when he had formed his bidding group, and Shearson was considering a lawsuit to keep Forstmann from misusing secret material that he had obtained under false pretenses. "The information Forstmann Little eventually received," the article quoted "a member of Mr. Johnson's group" as saying, "included detailed financial figures on RJR Nabisco's operations, financial projections, as well as the bidding strategy of the Johnson group, its financing arrangement and its plans to sell most of the company's food businesses."

Ted was so startled that he made Nick read him the whole article over the telephone, and even then he didn't quite believe it. He had never said that he wouldn't bid in an auction. He had never signed a confidentiality agreement with Shearson or even been asked to. His agreement was with the company and he had been scrupulous about observing the terms. What Cohen thought Forstmann could have stolen from Shearson was something of a mystery. As far as Forstmann was concerned, Cohen's ideas about finance were laughable; he didn't seem to have a bidding strategy, if such a thing existed beyond "bid your best"; there hadn't been any discussion about how the food companies should be sold. Rather than share information, Cohen had quickly changed the subject whenever Boisi brought up the idea of presales. As far as Forstmann was concerned, *he* had been giving Shearson ideas, not the other way around.

If the article was a little fuzzy as to just what sins Forstmann had committed, the two-page letter Cohen sent by messenger that afternoon left no doubts. There, in black and white, Cohen explicitly accused Boisi of unfairly inducing Castle & Cooke, Proctor & Gamble, and Ralston to join Forstmann's group. The letter struck a weirdly moral note. "I might finally point out to you that American Express, RJR Nabisco, and presumably all of the other investors for whom you are a fiduciary, entrusted their funds to you expecting that you would observe the highest standards of business ethics when investing their assets. I urge you not to engage in behavior inconsistent with those expectations." This

from a man who had secretly shuttled back and forth between
Forstmann in one conference room and Kravis in another, trying
to get them to bid against each other for a spot on the Shearson
team.

Almost before Forstmann had finished reading, the phone began to ring. Cohen had leaked the letter to the press. He had
also sent copies to David Murdock, Bill Stiritz at Ralston Purina
and P&G CEO John Smale, and to Charlie Hugel. Forstmann
passed the reporters' messages to Davis Weinstock, the new pr
man (that gave Weinstock something to do), but he did return a
call to Geoff Boisi who was even more outraged than Forstmann.

The two wasted much of the day Tuesday drafting a response
to Cohen instead of working on the bid. "The firm of Forstmann
Little & Co. has been built carefully with the highest possible
business standards and total integrity," read Forstmann's letter.
"We have acted in all respects consistent with those standards
throughout this transaction. We need no advice from you in this
regard." Weinberg's response was even stronger, saying that as
a result of the accusations, Goldman's relationship with Shearson
would never be the same. Cohen was so shaken by that that he
called Weinberg as soon as it arrived. "Why are you so worked
up?" he asked. "It was just a letter. I'm young. I'm new to this.
I'm looking to you for guidance. What would you have done in
my place if you were me?"

"I wouldn't have sent that letter," said Weinberg.

CHAPTER 15

Refereeing from Moscow

November 7 to November 12

The last thing Peter Cohen had had in mind when he sent his letter to Ted Forstmann was further upsetting Charlie Hugel, but coming hot on the heels of *The New York Times* article about the management contract, Cohen's letter was the rough equivalent of lighting a match in a kerosene factory. Hugel had initially been inclined to give Johnson the benefit of the doubt, but he had finally come to the sad conclusion that Marty Davis was right. Now Hugel had seen everything: a low initial bid, a sweetheart deal for management, and a blatant effort to bludgeon a competitor out of the bidding. It seemed clear that Johnson and Cohen believed that the friendly committee would turn a blind eye on any abuse, ignoring their fiduciary duty to shareholders as well as a basic sense of ethical play. And Hugel couldn't let that go unanswered.

So even before the Special Committee meeting at Skadden Arps at ten-thirty, Monday, November 7, he had Peter Atkins draft a letter demanding that Cohen back off. "Please be advised that this committee is flatly opposed to your group taking any [legal action again Forstmann Little]," it read. "Whatever your grievances may be, this committee considers the Forstmann Little group to be a credible bidder for RJR Nabisco. The interests of RJR Nabisco shareholders will be best served by the active participation of that group in our process, free from interference by your group.''

That wasn't a big debating point at the meeting, though. The directors—Macomber was in London on vacation but Hugel had invited all the outside board members to join Butler, Davis, and Anderson this one time—were much more interested in the management contract. By this time Johnson's letter to Hugel had arrived explaining how the contract "really" worked. The numbers were apparently the same as the ones in the *Times* article, but to Hugel's astonishment, the letter said that the management group didn't include just seven people but 15,007. Although Johnson hadn't mentioned any ESOP when Hugel had grilled him over the telephone Saturday, he now claimed that he planned to distribute stock to all the remaining tobacco company employees. This was clearly an idea that had come up after the furor over how small the management group was, and Hugel had to laugh. Only Ross Johnson with his fondness for grand gestures would have expanded his group by 15,000 over a weekend; apparently even the janitor *was* included.

After the directors had vented steam about the contract, they turned to the real business at hand: responding to the KKR tender offer. Under the Securities and Exchange Commission regulations, a company had to advise holders with respect to a tender offer 10 business days after it was made.

It had been clear at the first meeting that the directors wanted to hold the company together if that could be done, and the investment bankers had devised several schemes for avoiding a bust-up, none of which were compelling. Under one scheme, not unlike Benevento's Project GM, RJR would split its stock into two pieces, a food stock and a tobacco stock. There was talk of selling or leveraging the food companies. The question of who would run the company if Johnson left raised its ugly head once again; by this time Macomber had told Hugel that he wasn't interested in a joint Hugel-Macomber CEO-ship, although Hugel remained confident that something could be worked out.

Whatever the alternatives were, though, RJR still had to hold an auction. Under Delaware law—RJR was a Delaware corporation even though its headquarters were in Atlanta—a company was obligated to solicit bids once it had been put in play, to guarantee that shareholders got the best price for their stock. The committee had more or less agreed to formally release bidding rules to spur competition, so Hugel turned the discussion to what those rules should say.

The first part of the meeting had been relatively civil, but now it got heated. Hugel and Davis couldn't agree on a key matter: whether the auction would have one round or many. Hugel wanted it to be quick and clean, a one-round affair held as soon as possible. Davis thought that was ludicrous: having sold literally dozens of Gulf + Western units in various kinds of auctions, Davis insisted that the only way to guarantee that the shareholders got the best price was to keep asking for new bids until no one would bid any more. He wanted the rules vague, leaving the board as many options as possible.

Hugel's desire for simplicity notwithstanding, it was virtually foreordained that there would be many rounds. Under the Delaware court's curious concept of "fiduciary responsibility," a board could no longer make an agreement to sell the company in good faith. If a higher offer came along before the check cleared, the board was legally obligated to consider it. Possibly this benefited shareholders in the short term, but it surely undermined corporate ethics.

Another hot point was how the committee would look at cash as opposed to paper. Although Hugel had told Johnson and Reuters that cash was king, it seemed clear that that wasn't true. Most of the directors agreed that they wanted shareholders to get a stub, a residual stock interest in what remained on RJR after whoever bought it had busted it up. A stub protected shareholders against the risk that the company was worth substantially more than anyone thought, either because food company prices continued to go through the roof or because the legal and social status of smoking changed. By forcing the winner to share the wealth with the shareholders, the board further distanced itself from the Greed issue.

After a debate, the directors also agreed with Davis's argument that cram-down paper was valuable too, as long as it traded at par.

The next day, Tuesday, November 8, was Election Day. Hugel voted at seven o'clock—George Bush defeated Michael Dukakis in a landslide—and hurried to the airport for his eight o'clock flight to Moscow. Combustion Engineering has a joint venture with the Soviet government to make instrumentation and calibration equipment at a factory outside Moscow, and Hugel needed to talk to officials about several key issues.

No sooner did he arrive in Moscow than Ross Johnson called to complain about Forstmann Little. Johnson ranted that Hugel had been wrong to let Forstmann into the bidding since there was no way that a Forstmann consortium bid could possibly get through the Justice Department. Then Johnson said that Forstmann's partner Dole had been given all kinds of confidential information about Del Monte and he wanted it stopped. Hugel slowed Johnson down, and eventually Johnson explained that Robert Carbonnell, the head of Del Monte and a long-time personal friend, had walked out of the due diligence session when Dole executives started to ask him about shipping routes and planting schedules.

"I don't know anything about it," said Hugel. But he would find out. To his great annoyance, Hugel spent most of the Russian trip not touring sites and talking to officials, but sitting in ABC's television studio on the telephone to New York.

When Hugel got back to New York on Saturday, there was another nasty surprise: a feature article on the committee in the *Wall Street Journal.*

Up until this time, the committee hadn't gotten much focus in the press. The action was clearly in the Shearson and KKR camps. Now that the rules were out, apparently putting Hugel and the committee in control of who bought RJR, reporters suddenly swarmed. Davis and Atkins had been adamant that no one talk, and although Hugel specifically excepted himself from that rule since he was the committee's chairman and spokesman, Hugel had reminded the board members at the Monday meeting not to take press calls.

The *Journal* article wasn't negative, but it was distressingly accurate. The reporter even knew that Bill Anderson had passed out "stakeholder" literature at one meeting and that Al Butler had been noticeably silent throughout the debate. "We feel used and abused" by Johnson's tactics, it quoted an unnamed director as saying. Clearly someone had talked. Hugel was sure it hadn't been a committee member but an investment banker, but nonetheless he called each of the members to remind them that he would be the sole spokesman.

CHAPTER 16

The Chicago Missile

November 10 to November 18

First Boston managing director Brian Finn hadn't initially been assigned to Jim Maher's RJR team. Although he works in the merger department, he doesn't generally get involved in ordinary deals, not even $20 billion ones. Instead, he focuses on finding tax loopholes and accounting gimmicks that make deals work, things like Robert Campeau's installment notes. So although he had read the many newspaper and magazine articles on the Shearson bid, the KKR bid, the Forstmann bid, and the attempts of various parties to get together, he had done so with no more than his usual interest in business news. What he was more interested in was tax laws. The Campeau loophole had been closed September 21, and since then, Finn had been spending a lot of time with the tax lawyers getting a handle on what might work in 1990. In the course of that, one of the lawyers had pointed out that the installment note wasn't really dead. The prohibition didn't go into effect until December 31.

There was no sense letting a perfectly good tax loophole go to waste, so Finn began to call his colleagues to find out whether anyone was working on a deal that could be reworked to include an installment sale. The answer was disappointing: there was just one, General Cinema's sale of a bottling plant to Pepsi-Cola. Surely there was a way to do something more, and Finn began to ponder whether it was possible for a deal that closed in 1989 to qualify for 1988 tax treatment. Then it hit him: First Boston could act as a bridge.

Say company A wanted to buy subsidiary X from company B. If the two companies did the sale direct, they couldn't hope to close this year because of the long regulatory and antitrust approvals, but if First Boston Acquisition Corp., a newly formed subsidiary with no assets and hence no regulatory or other problems, bought sub X from company B with an installment note, the transaction could close overnight. First Boston would agree to pass through any price adjustment that came out of later negotiations, and company A would preserve the tax treatment of the original sale. Indeed, there didn't have to be a company A at all. First Boston could simply buy something and find a final buyer later.

Or so Finn thought; he needed to run it past a lawyer. Matt Rosen of Skadden Arps opined that as a legal proposition, the bridge installment system worked; he didn't know whether it could be done as a practical matter, but Finn's boss, Jim Maher, was not worried about such technicalities. Maher had still not found a bidder for RJR and he was getting desperate. Perhaps the allure of a tax trick that could save $4 billion if it worked would be enough to convince the Special Committee to hire First Boston. No such luck. "We might be interested," said Peter Atkins, "if you have a client who wants to bid."

So Maher had spent the next week trying to find one. No one seemed to think that the bridge was remotely doable, and by Thursday, November 10, Maher had all but given up. Then Jerry Seslowe unexpectedly said he wanted to take a look.

Seslowe was a somewhat controversial fellow. The former head of the mergers and acquisitions department of Peat Marwick Mitchell, a Big Eight accounting firm, he had decided to plunge into deal-making on his own, and in 1983 formed Resource Holdings with the backing of Jay Pritzker, the Chicago billionaire who later backed Mel Klein and Harry Gray in their leveraged buyout venture. For the first three years, Seslowe did deals quietly, assembling equity partnerships for small buyouts. Then in 1985, Seslowe made headlines when he tried to buy ITT, the $14 billion telephone-insurance-and-hotels conglomerate. Or at least that was what ITT chairman Rand Araskog said Seslowe was doing.

Seslowe himself claimed that he had simply floated a leveraged buyout proposal and been rebuffed. Pritzker had been involved only by association; one ITTer said that Seslowe's role at been as a cat's paw, issuing threats so that Pritzker could keep his friendly-only image pristine. Later, Seslowe made an unsuccessful run at Western Union, the near-bankrupt telegraph company.

Maher had met Seslowe in 1985 when both Seslowe and Resource had worked on Pritzker's purchase of Conwood chewing tobacco. Maher wasn't sure that Seslowe was up to a deal as big as RJR, but he did have an inside line to Pritzker, and clearly Pritzker had the money. So Maher sent Leon Kalvaria, a First Boston vice-president, to Resource Holdings' offices Friday afternoon to make a presentation. Seslowe had seemed impressed, and didn't flinch when Kalvaria told him that the deal would take $750 million of equity, of which First Boston could offer only $150 million. If Seslowe went ahead, he would be on the hook for $600 million.

Seslowe called back that night to say he was on board.

Maher had thought that his troubles would be over as soon as he found a client, but that wasn't the case. When he called Atkins over the weekend to offer to sign a confidentiality agreement giving his group access to information, Atkins told him that wasn't possible. First Boston didn't meet the board's minimum criteria for bidders, and hence wasn't invited. Maher wasn't quite sure what to make of that, so he drafted a letter to the Special Committee formally stating First Boston's intention of making a bid and messengered it to Skadden Monday morning, along with a similar letter from Resource Holdings.

By Monday afternoon, things were progressing well. After a weekend of number crunching, Maher had concluded that the group would need $1 billion in equity, not $750 million. First Boston would kick in an extra $50 million of that, the other $200 million would have to come from Seslowe. Seslowe was sure he could raise that money too.

Although Charlie Hugel had sent a reply on behalf of the Special Committee Monday afternoon, reiterating that First Boston wasn't invited to bid, Luis Rinaldini, the junior Lazard partner on the team, had called Tuesday morning to set up a meeting at Lazard in the afternoon.

That was downbeat. "This board isn't going to do anything controversial," Rinaldini told Finn. "The directors aren't interested in a complex deal or a risky deal." And they certainly didn't want to raise tempers in Washington, which a plan to avoid $4 billion in capital gains taxes seemed sure to do.

Still, there did seem to be a ray of hope. Rinaldini apparently thought that the scheme was workable. Late Wednesday afternoon, one of Finn's associates had gotten a call from a company interested in bidding for the New York Times Company cable unit, which First Boston was in the process of auctioning off. The would-be bidder explained that his banker, Luis Rinaldini of Lazard Frères, had come up with a clever tax strategy he wanted to run past First Boston. The terms were precisely those of the bridge installment note that Finn had outlined to Rinaldini the day before.

Even if the tax strategy did work, there were other problems with the First Boston approach, like getting bank money. Clearly the proposal would make no sense to the Special Committee unless First Boston was able to line up a commitment from a commercial bank to "monetize" the $14 billion installment note. That would have been difficult in any case, since it was fourteen times as large as the only other installment note ever monetized, and the controversy surrounding the bid and the tax strategy seemed sure to make it even more difficult.

Unfortunately, from that perspective, the situation suddenly took a turn for the worse. Seslowe had gotten wind of a problem at the beginning of the week. Ever since he had set up Resource Holdings in 1983, he had shared an office in the Harper & Row building on East 53rd Street with Howard, Darby & Levin, a small law firm run by his friend Phillip Howard. Resource Holdings was Howard, Darby & Levin's largest client, and when Seslowe had decided to go ahead with the First Boston deal, he had naturally asked Howard to represent him.

"We can't," said Howard. "We have a conflict."

A conflict? thought Seslowe. The only people involved in the deal so far were Shearson, Forstmann, KKR, RJR, and the board—and Seslowe knew that Howard wasn't working for any of them. What conflict could there possibly be?

Seslowe got his answer Thursday, November 17, when Howard

walked into his office and tossed a complaint on his desk. Metropolitan Life Insurance Company had just sued RJR Nabisco and Ross Johnson, charging that the two had defrauded investors, including Met Life, by selling bonds even as a buyout was in the works. According to Met Life, RJR owed its bondholders a duty of good faith.

"You know if we win and you win, you'll bankrupt us," said Seslowe.

Howard just shrugged, but the next day a Japanese screen appeared in the hallway, separating the Howard, Darby part of the office from the Resource Holdings part. It turned out that the general counsel of Met Life had noticed that the two firms were in the same office and he panicked that critical information might leak from his lawyers to a bidding group. The screen was the closest Howard could get, on short notice, to a Chinese Wall.

The Met Life suit wasn't exactly a surprise. Ever since the battle had broken out, bondholders had been complaining that they were bearing the brunt of the increased risk, while Johnson enriched himself in the buyout. Certainly, the buyout had been expensive for bondholders. Now that Johnson was talking about piling $14 billion of new debt on their existing $5 billion of old bonds, it was clear that the bonds weren't as safe as everyone thought. Bond prices had tumbled as soon as word of the buyout appeared on the wire; on October 20 alone, Met Life's $340 million of bonds had fallen by $40 million.

Nonetheless, the suit was a long shot. Bondholder rights are laid out in a "covenant" with the company that protects them against certain actions. A buyout wasn't covered by the covenant, nor was a friendly takeover. So the only theory that Met Life had to go on was that Johnson had already begun planning a buyout in April 1988, when RJR sold $300 million worth of bonds to help fund the stock buyback. There wasn't any immediate evidence that that was the case, but Met Life hoped to find some, or at least to convince a judge to block a buyout long enough for the board to sweeten the terms for its bondholders.

After the suit was filed, Felix Rohatyn did ask Atkins if he could take the bondholders' interests into consideration when comparing the bids, and Atkins told him that he couldn't; bondholders could be considered only to the extent that the bid was covered by the covenant, no more. Still, many watchers believe that the suit tipped the board toward KKR. The Met Life charges were meaningless if the company ended up in anyone's hands besides Johnson's: if Johnson lost, his attempt to defraud bondholders, such as it was, had failed.

Finally, Teddy Forstmann was doing his kind of deal. He was putting together what he regarded as a workable financial plan; his team was meeting with the company officials to learn what making cookies and cigarettes was all about, and just how profitable it could be. Usually all the Forstmann Little partners, including Ted, were personally involved in the due diligence, but this time there was so much to do that he and Brian Little had agreed that Forstmann would take care of finance and Little of fact-finding. There was, however, one session that Forstmann wanted to attend: the meeting with von Arx, the U.S. tobacco chief. Johnson had told him on the telephone that there was something special about running a tobacco company, and Forstmann wanted to know what that could be. Nothing in von Arx's presentation made Forstmann think that the job involved any special wizardry, and indeed von Arx denied that it did when Forstmann asked. Forstmann laughed. "Ross told me how tough your job was," he said. "So I wanted to see what you were like."

"Well, I was a little worried too," said von Arx. "I thought you'd be a monster."

"And what was I like?" asked Forstmann. "I wasn't so bad, was I?"

"No," confessed von Arx. "You seemed like an ordinary guy."

Forstmann was spending most of his time putting together a workable capital structure and making sure that the pieces fit. As part of the agreement to get into the bidding in the first place, the Forstmann consortium members had pledged that their system would include no presales; that meant that Forstmann wasn't required to raise cash by selling units within the family if he could get a higher bid from someone else; what his partners were willing to pay gave him a floor on breakup prices. For example, Forstmann thought that he could sell Del Monte for $3 billion, substantially more than the $2 billion plus that David Murdock of

Castle & Cooke wanted to pay. Forstmann was sure that he could sell Milk Bones and Shredded Wheat for well over Ralston Purina's price.

A more serious problem was how to structure the joint ownership of the company. Although Murdock, with his deal-making outlook, was impressed by Reynolds Tobacco's strong cash flow and profits and was eager to own a piece, Bill Stiritz and John Smale of Ralston and P&G, respectively, were queasy. Smale, in fact, said that an equity stake in a cigarette company was totally out of the question. After some back and forth, Smale finally agreed to take convertible debt, which was almost equity but not quite.

That was where things stood on Friday, November 11. Forstmann worked all weekend, and by Sunday night, he had begun to realize that they didn't quite fit. He'd come to the conclusion that he needed to bid in the high nineties to win, all cash, and the cash wasn't there. If he was going to bid, he had to find more cash. It couldn't come from Forstmann Little; under the current plan, the entire $3 billion fund was already committed. It couldn't come from the banks; however enthusiastic Manufacturers Hanover and the others were, there was a finite amount of bank money available, and it was already committed. Forstmann had called each of the corporate partners to ask if it wanted to make an additional commitment; none did. That left the stub as the only possible source of value, and Forstmann didn't think that was going to do it. Under the terms of his stub, modeled after his mezzanine partnership, shareholders got a guaranteed modest interest rate plus a 20 percent stake in the private company's equity; although Forstmann believed that was valuable, he didn't think that the committee's bankers would put a high number on it, since the interest rate was low and the equity speculative.

Geoff Boisi had a final suggestion: a junk bond issue. Boisi talked to the Goldman corporate finance people and they had put together a debt package. There would be a $2 billion bridge loan replaced with junk. To be sure it was relatively clean junk, the interest rate would be just 13 percent, a full five percentage points less than what Shearson had been talking about, and there would be no restrictive covenants. In fact, Boisi insisted that however low the rating, the paper wasn't really junk since Goldman could place it with the sort of top-tier pension funds that were already investors in the Forstmann mezzanine partnership. Forstmann wouldn't have to deal with scrappy Drexel-type investors. Or at least Boisi was pretty sure he wouldn't.

"How sure?" asked Forstmann.

Well, Boisi confessed, he couldn't give an ironclad promise.

"Will you write a $2 billion check for the bridge?" asked Forstmann.

"Goldman can't do that," said Boisi. "We can't put that much of our capital on the line."

"Forstmann Little is putting $3 billion on the line," said Forstmann. "And that's all we've got."

That was not the end of that. Boisi came up to Forstmann's office with David Murdock on Monday afternoon to make a personal appeal. "Are you a chicken?" Murdock demanded.

"I'm not chicken," said Forstmann, "but I promised my investors certain standards. This doesn't meet those standards." It didn't come close and Forstmann was not interested in doing the biggest deal on record if it meant a lousy return for his investors, and unfortunately RJR seemed to (curiously, return to investors was a concept that thus far hadn't come up for Cohen or Kravis). The problem was that junk money had pushed the price so high that if you planned to buy with real money, the return just wasn't that attractive. Even if everything went right, Forstmann's mezzanine investors were only going to make 18 percent. That was better than T-bill rates, to be sure, but it was not what GE or 3M had had in mind when they put their money into a buyout fund. Junk on top of lousy returns was more than Forstmann could swallow. At a caucus in Forstmann's office, Little and Nick agreed. Murdock had left by now, so Forstmann called Boisi back into his office alone, to break the news. "Do you have some kind of religious conviction about this?" asked Boisi.

"No," said Forstmann. "Look. Compared to what Kravis and Shearson are talking about, your junk isn't that bad. Compared to that it's almost sensible. But am I going to do it? No."

Then Forstmann called Fritz Hobbs to say that he was dropping out and that he would be putting out a release first thing the next morning. Although Forstmann didn't say why, Hobbs assumed that the reason was Ralston: Bill Stiritz, a notorious cheapskate, simply hadn't been willing to pay up.

"Why don't you make a bid for tobacco on your own?" asked

Hobbs. Clearly that was what Forstmann himself was interested in. His bid would give the board more options.

Forstmann declined. It wasn't that he couldn't, but after looking at the numbers for a week and a half, he didn't want to. If teaming up with three food giants hadn't been enough to make an all-cash offer, surely Forstmann couldn't do it alone; the returns on the tobacco company alone weren't going to be that much better than the returns on the company as a whole. "Fritz," he said. "We promised each other when we formed the group that we would bid together or not at all."

"Do you have to put out a press release?" asked Hobbs. That would clearly dampen the bidding by telling Shearson and KKR that Forstmann didn't think that the company was worth $90-plus a share. Hobbs tried to convince him not to issue a release. Why didn't Forstmann simply not bid?

"I have to put out a release," said Forstmann. "I have a responsibility to my investors."

Atkins was even more upset about the press release than Hobbs had been, partly because the only reason that Forstmann was able to issue it was that Atkins had forgotten to include a clause barring press releases in the confidentiality agreement. Charlie Hugel was so livid that he called Forstmann from the InterContinental Hotel, where he was having dinner with the Combustion Engineering board before the formal board meeting the next day, to say that the committee would call Forstmann "hostile" if he made an announcement.

"Calm down," said Forstmann. "I'm not trying to hurt you. I have to make an announcement, but I can work with you on what it's going to say."

What Hugel didn't want it to say was that the transaction didn't meet Forstmann's investment criteria, that Gresham's law had forced the price to unrealistic levels, and that junk bonds were destroying America. At midnight, after two more calls from Hugel at the InterContinental, Forstmann agreed to take all those things out and issue a one-sentence release saying simply that he was withdrawing from the fray.

Ironically, hours after that statement crossed the Dow, Bill Stiritz of Ralston called to ask if Ted minded if Ralston made a bid on its own. The consortium members had all promised to bid together–drop together, and although Forstmann was disappointed that Stiritz wasn't holding to his word, he gave him the okay. It seemed unlikely that he was going to win anyway.

Henry Kravis's November 10 meeting with Paul Sticht, the former RJR chairman, had gone well. After Wilson, Sticht was refreshingly up-front. He began by saying that he had an ax to grind. He didn't like Johnson. He didn't like Horrigan. He thought that they were destroying RJR. It wasn't just that Johnson had moved out of Winston-Salem, donated the RJR building to Wake Forest University, and replaced the Reynolds team with freewheelers from Nabisco, he had also demoted Sticht's son Mark, a Del Monte fresh fruit executive. Mark had quit and then teamed up with Sammy Gordon, the deposed fresh fruit chief and arguably the world's best banana man, to form their own fruit exporting company, West Indies Fruit Co.

Sticht was much more interested in talking about Del Monte than Reynolds Tobacco, and despite Kravis's and Raether's reminders that they understood food and grocery but not tobacco, he kept meandering from tobacco production to pineapple importing, and had to be led back to the subject at hand.

Still, Sticht did know a lot about tobacco and was even relatively up to date, having left the board only six months earlier. By this time, Kravis had checked out Sticht's reputation with several mutual friends, including Safeway chairman Robert Magowan and Robert Lanigan of Owens-Illinois, both of whom sat with Sticht on the Chrysler board. As the meeting was winding down, Kravis asked Sticht if he would be willing to serve as interim chief executive for KKR.

"Why don't you talk to Ty Wilson?" asked Sticht.

"We have," said Kravis.

"Well," said Sticht. "I don't want a full-time job." He was already a member of the Chrysler and McKesson boards and was active in running the Bowman Gray Medical Center in Winston-Salem and the U.S. Chamber of Commerce research foundation. However, Kravis had convinced him that a KKR buyout would be less disruptive to employees than a Johnson buyout. He would think about the RJR assignment, and call Kravis back.

He did, to say that he would take the job on a temporary basis. Kravis had a CEO. Although still not a management team. Indeed, the lack of cooperation from operating executives continued to rile Kravis and he had even begun to grumble loudly, if vaguely, to Dillon and Lazard about the poor information. As far as the committee bankers could tell, what Kravis seemed to want were Shearson's working models developed from the numbers that RJR had given to everyone. RJR didn't have those models, nor would they have been the committee's to give if they did; Shearson's models belonged to Shearson. One observer theorized that the real function of complaining about information was not getting better numbers but better treatment: "They were like an unhappy sibling who discovers that if he complains that he didn't get what his brother got, his parents will bend over backward to give him more."

That left the press as Kravis's biggest headache. Since the *Times* article on the management contract, Ross Johnson had replaced Kravis as the most greedy man in America, but the stories about hostile deals and disgruntled KKR investors continued. Worst of all, the press reports that an RJR deal would cost Uncle Sam $5 billion in lost tax revenues had gotten Congress interested in leveraged buyouts. It wasn't clear that anyone in Washington understood how buyouts worked, but several Senate and House leaders announced that they were incensed at the idea of taxpayers and employees being hurt and they were determined to do something about it. Bob Dole, Senate Majority leader, had come out against buyouts early on. On Thursday, November 10, J. J. Pickle, the Texas democrat who chaired the House Ways and Means Committee, announced that he would hold public hearings in early 1989 on leveraged buyouts, featuring testimony from the executives who had been involved in the battle for RJR.

That afternoon, Kravis spent two hours on the phone with a reporter from *Manhattan inc.* magazine. Kravis hadn't given an interview in five years; he had refused to talk to *Fortune* when the magazine profiled KKR in July 1988. *Manhattan inc.*, a hard-hitting monthly, was the last place to expect a sympathetic article. Still, Kravis was mad, and talking to the reporter, who had by this time all but finished a December cover story, was the only way to get his view across. Kravis told the reporter that he had not used the word "franchise" in the meeting with Hill and Cohen on October 21 and that at the meeting the following Tuesday they had "threatened to call us hostile, hurt us with our investors and bring in Jesse Helms. They have tried to do two of those," he said. "We haven't yet heard from Jesse Helms."

When he finally got off the line, he had to hurry. He was going to a Literary Lions dinner at the New York Public Library. Christopher Plummer read a short story by Stephen Leacock. *Daily News* reporter Billy Norwich, who wrote one of the more scurrilous gossip columns in the city, was also in the audience. Kravis pulled Norwich aside, called him an "asshole" and threatened to "break both your kneecaps."

In the end, Brooke Astor intervened, but the episode showed up in *Womens Wear Daily* the next morning. For the first time in weeks, Kravis couldn't blame the bad press on Shearson.

Any lingering doubts that Kravis had that he wasn't getting equal treatment were erased when one of the junior Dillon corporate finance people called Monday afternoon, November 14, to say that John Greeniaus, the president of Nabisco Brands, wanted to have a second meeting. Although the Dillon man didn't say precisely why, he hinted that Greeniaus thought that his first presentation to KKR hadn't been as full as it should have been. By this time, Kravis had picked up the word that Greeniaus and the food people were furious that Johnson was selling them down the river, and he quickly agreed to a second meeting the next morning, Tuesday. Due diligence wasn't really Kravis's job, so he didn't personally attend the meeting, but Raether did, and he was somewhat startled at how it began. "You're not talking to management?" demanded Greeniaus, standing.

"No," said Raether.

"You aren't working with them in any way?"

"No."

"You don't plan to be?"

"No."

"Good," said Greeniaus. He sat down. "I can talk to you."

Greeniaus explained that although the numbers he had given Kravis were correct, they didn't tell the whole story. As a public company, he explained, Nabisco had been run to produce steadily increasing market share and consistent earnings. Lots of money had been spent to hike sales, not profits. Team Nabisco and the Dinah Shore Invitational golf tournament, for example, had been

great for Johnson's ego, "but do they sell another Oreo? No way."
And Greeniaus thought they should be dropped. He also rec-
ommended killing the $2.8 billion bakery overhaul. "I wouldn't
ever do that," he said.

"Then why did you approve it?" asked Raether.

"I didn't," said Greeniaus. "Andy Sage did." According to
Greeniaus, the plant Sage had in mind would be virtually gold-
plated, using technology that hadn't yet been invented. The projected payout was fifteen years, unthinkable for a greenfield site
in the 1980s. (Sage insists that Greeniaus, not he, made the presentation to the board, and that the payout was seven years.)
Greeniaus thought that a more modest $600 million retrofit would
be sufficient.

Greeniaus also thought that marketing expenses, which account
for 40 cents of every dollar of biscuit cost, could be cut dramatically. Cutting advertising might stunt future sales and profit
growth, but it certainly would help current earnings; Greeniaus
was sure that there was a happy medium. Putting all the cuts
together, Greeniaus estimated that he could increase earnings for
Nabisco's U.S. operations by more than 40 percent in the first
year, to more than $600 million.

While Kravis was still pondering that on Wednesday morning,
Fritz Hobbs called with some revised numbers on liabilities. This
time he had a new category, "other," and although it was never
clear to Kravis or, apparently, Hobbs, what was included, the
total had swollen to $1 billion by Friday, the day the bids were
due. If that number was correct, and Kravis was sure that it wasn't,
the value of the company had suddenly dropped by $4 a share.
The timing of the bad news was so suspicious that Kravis considered complaining formally that the number made no sense, but
after talking to Beattie he decided to wait. Clearly the time to
complain was after they had lost, if they lost, when they could
claim self-righteously that the shareholders had lost billions because KKR had been duped.

By this time, of course, Kravis and Roberts were settling in on
a bid, and they were leaning toward a number not much higher
than the $92 a share that Shearson had put on the table. As
Forstmann had already concluded, a buyout in the nineties wasn't
going to be that profitable for equity investors. The return to
investors under Kravis's structure looked slightly better than it

had under Forstmann's because he wasn't going to be paying all cash, and it didn't bother him as much because his standards were lower. More importantly, the money just wasn't there. The banks weren't sure that they could syndicate even $14.5 billion and they wanted a $380-million-plus fee to do it, even at a rate of 3¾ percentage points over prime. Drexel seemed totally unconcerned about raising the $5-billion bridge or the junk to replace it, at a whopping five percentage points over Treasury, but whatever Ackerman said about Drexel's ability to raise money, Kravis was still worried that the deal might collapse if Drexel were hit with a RICO indictment. The rumors that an indictment was coming got louder every day.

Kravis and Roberts didn't discuss any of that with the investment bankers at the meeting early in the afternoon, although they did communicate how they planned to use a lot of shareholder paper. At a meeting just after the bidding rules came out, the Lazard bankers had told Steve Waters that KKR's stub had to include a 20 percent equity stake, and Kravis and Roberts had decided to be even more generous than that when it came to cramming securities down the throats of shareholders. In addition to a 25 percent stub, shareholders would get a large slug of junk paper.

Eric Gleacher and Bruce Wasserstein were pushing hard for a high bid, and so was Steve Waters. "We're in deep trouble if we bid below one hundred dollars a share," said Waters. Before he left, Waters gave Paul Raether a piece of paper saying that they should bid at least $101 and that the winning bid would be $102 to $105. Leon Black of Drexel was cooler—after all, his team was responsible for the bridge- and junk-money. He thought that KKR should bid somewhere in the mid-nineties. On the way out, Gleacher and Waters bet $1 on what the bid would be: Gleacher chose $96 to $98 a share; Waters put his money on $100.

Waters was way off. While the investment bankers waited in a conference room, Kravis and Roberts and their partners and associates gathered in Kravis's office to pick a number. No one thought that Shearson would be bidding close to Waters's $102 to $105 a share; quite the contrary, Kravis had had the impression at the meeting on November 3 that Shearson was having great difficulty raising money and would be bidding low. As he always did when choosing a bidding number, Kravis polled his associates from youngest to oldest for views on the company and the bid. Although the number started in the high nineties, it quickly fell as the team threw out one reason after another why the deal wasn't that good.

Finally, at four o'clock, Dick Beattie banged on the door and told them that if they didn't give him a number soon, they'd miss the five o'clock bidding deadline.

That was that: $94 a share.

Kravis signed the documents and walked into the conference room where the bankers were waiting. When he gave them the number, Waters pulled out his wallet and handed Gleacher a dollar. "What was that?" asked Kravis.

"I just lost a bet," said Waters.

Meanwhile, Casey Cogut of Simpson Thatcher had rushed to Skadden with the final documents. Although security at Skadden was supposed to be tight, no one questioned Cogut as he strolled into Atkins's office to hand over the papers. He noticed on the way out, though, that the security guard was barring a Skadden partner; apparently he didn't have proper identification.

By Friday morning, Johnson's management contract had been substantially renegotiated. Over the weekend of November 12 and 13, Goldstone had agreed to a markup by Peter Darrow, the Salomon Brothers lawyer, and Wednesday afternoon, Johnson, Cohen, and Gutfreund had met at Cohen's office to work out the final details of the "Darrow treaty," including a cut from 8.5 percent to 6 percent in the stake management got to start with. At that meeting Gutfreund had seemed concerned that he didn't know Johnson very well, so he invited him, along with Cohen and Robinson, to his apartment for a drink that evening. Unfortunately, Robinson hadn't been able to make it. He had to be in Washington for Ronald Reagan's last state dinner, and he viewed sitting in a room with British prime minister Margaret Thatcher as more important than a drink with Johnson and his Shearson and Salomon partners.

Preliminaries aside, the only question left on Friday was price, but Cohen was off to a late start when it came to choosing it. Instead of spending the day in his office strategizing, he took a two-hour break to drive out to Kennedy Airport and back. His daughter Lauren was leaving that day for ten days in Moscow and Estonia to play basketball with her high-school team, and Cohen wanted to say goodbye before her flight took off. When Cohen got back at two, he decided to have lunch. Johnson, who had been waiting at Shearson for three hours by now, thought that meant a tête-à-tête for the senior team. When they got to the boardroom, though, he discovered that it was "a real de Mille" affair, with at least fifty investment bankers squeezed around the boardroom table and several satellite tables.

The kitchen was slow, and the lunch didn't arrive until three. When the platters of lobster tail came in, Chas Phillips looked across the table at Gutfreund. The Salomon strategists had had their first lunch in the Salomon Brothers boardroom before they arrived: styrofoam cups of vegetable soup and limp cold cuts on a cardboard platter. "Peter Cohen certainly understands how to run a public company," quipped Phillips to the banker next to him, "but maybe John will learn." Gutfreund, who had overheard, scowled and told Phillips to keep his mouth shut.

Mostly, though, the conversation focused on the bid. The structure would be very different from the KKR structure. Early on, Hugel had told Johnson that cash was king and nothing that had been said since the bidding rules came out made anyone on the Shearson team think differently. Jay Higgins of Salomon Brothers had pushed for a big stub—he had also wanted to give shareholders "the ups" early on—but he had been overruled. Cash was logically the preferred form of payment, and it happened to be how Johnson wanted to pay.

Although he had consistently dragged his heels in the early meetings, Gutfreund was now pushing for a high number. He startled Cohen by suggesting a face value of $100 a share, with $90 a share of that in cash. Cohen had been expected to have to push to get to $100 a share, and he had been so sure that $88 a share in cash was the most that Gutfreund would swallow, that he had had Jim Stern clear the paperwork with Citibank and Bankers Trust up to that level. Although Cohen was happy to raise, he therefore had to go back to the banks with an updated capital structure for the go-ahead.

Unfortunately, the computer broke down, and the Shearson people couldn't immediately generate a spreadsheet to give to the banks. When they finally did, and at four-fifteen, the banks agreed—although the LBO chief at Citibank insisted to Stern that he had better not cut back the PIK paper any further, because the leveraged company needed the tax write-off—Goldstone literally ran to his office at Chase Manhattan Plaza to finish the bidding documents. Johnson and Sage walked the ten blocks at a more gracious pace, and after a half-hour wait, Johnson signed the bid letter. The changes had been written in by hand; there wasn't time to print out a clean copy.

At twelve minutes to five, Richard Truesdell, a Davis Polk associate, and Peter Darrow, the Salomon lawyer, left for Skadden Arps with the bid and a portable phone.

Goldstone called Atkins to say that the papers were on the way. Then he called Truesdell in the car to find out how far he had gotten. The traffic was bad; the cab still hadn't reached midtown.

At a few minutes after five, Hugel called Johnson to ask where the bid was. Johnson didn't know, so Goldstone called the car again. It was caught in a traffic jam five blocks from Skadden. "Get out and walk," barked Goldstone.

Truesdell and Darrow did. They dodged the television cameras in the lobby—Cohen told Darrow later that he had watched him on the evening news—and as the elevator doors closed, Darrow noticed that Ira Harris of Lazard was in the same cab. "You're late," said Darrow.

"I know," said Harris grinning, "but it doesn't matter what time I arrive."

Jim Maher had never had a hope of meeting the deadline. Having started so much later than Shearson and KKR, the group was far from organized Friday afternoon. At five o'clock, terms remained unset, documents undrafted, letters unsigned.

But the pieces of the bid were there: a letter explaining that the First Boston bid was really two bids, a buyout offer for the tobacco company plus an installment note offer for food, a letter from First Boston's junk bond chief saying he was highly confident that he could raise the necessary $1 billion in junk bonds, and a letter from Crédit Suisse's London office—at this time First Boston was 40 percent owned by Crédit Suisse and later became a Crédit Suisse subsidiary—agreeing to lead the $8.8 billion syndicate to buy tobacco. Although he hadn't actually talked to a bank about monetizing the food note, Maher guessed that it could support a loan of 90 percent of its $12 billion face value.

Just before five, Maher called Peter Atkins to say that First Boston did intend to bid, but that the offer would be late. Atkins said that that was okay, and when the document was finally ready at nine-thirty, Finn walked it over himself. He thought that Atkins might have some questions, and as the man who had designed the tax structure, he, Finn, would be able to answer them.

Atkins took the proposal, but he clearly wasn't interested in talking to anyone, so Finn went on home.

By that time most of the other bidders had gone home too. After waiting several hours at his office, Kravis had had a call saying that the committee wanted to talk about the nuts and bolts of his bid at a meeting at Skadden the next morning. Cohen, Gutfreund, and Strauss, playing poker in Jack Nusbaum's office— Gutfreund won $300—got the same message.

Johnson, at the Vivian Beaumont Theatre at Lincoln Center watching Patty LuPone in *Anything Goes*, had had a message from Hugel, but it was somewhat cryptic. Late in the afternoon, Hugel's secretary had called Penny Jordan, Johnson's New York secretary, to find out if she could get Broadway tickets for Hugel for Saturday night. Hugel would be happy with anything, his secretary explained, except *The Phantom of the Opera*. He had already seen that.

CHAPTER 17

The Fix Was In?

November 18 to November 20

As far as Charlie Hugel was concerned, the call to Penny Jordan hadn't had any significance at all. He was going to be spending Saturday night in New York City so that he would be on time for the Special Committee meeting at eight o'clock Sunday morning, and he thought it would be nice to take his wife Nina to the theater in between. But for once, Penny Jordan didn't call back with tickets, and when Hugel mentioned to John Macomber that he and Nina were going to be footloose in Manhattan on Saturday night, Macomber invited them to dinner at his apartment with Special Committee members Al Butler and Bill Anderson. Only Marty Davis wouldn't be there: he already had dinner plans.

At a meeting in New York after the bids came in on Friday afternoon, Hugel and Peter Atkins had made some preliminary decisions. Of the three bids that had arrived on time, full bids from KKR and Shearson, and a complex $12 billion bid for the food company from Ralston Purina, the Shearson proposal was clearly the highest. Not only was its face value $6 a share over KKR's, but it also included more cash, a full $90 a share. KKR, by contrast, had come up with only $75 a share of cash, less than the $78 a share of cash in the original tender offer, plus $19 of paper. The only question was whether the paper was worth what Shearson said it was, or, for good measure, what KKR said it was. So about nine o'clock, the bankers and lawyers decided to meet with both groups on Saturday morning to talk over the nuts and bolts of their bids.

The First Boston bid, which arrived after the meetings had been set up, didn't seem relevant. Although First Boston claimed it was worth as much as $118 a share, the bid was not financed and perhaps not even legally workable. Hobbs and Harris were so unimpressed that, after giving Finn's papers a quick once-over, they went home. It seemed clear that the bid wasn't going to fly. Before the committee rejected it completely though, Atkins wanted to be sure that it couldn't work. So, at about eleven o'clock, he called Matt Rosen, the senior tax partner, and asked him to take a look. Rosen, of course, had helped Finn develop the structure in the first place, and to Atkins's surprise, he quickly announced that although there were a dozen or so unresolved details, the First Boston plan would work, at least from a tax point of view.

That still didn't mean that it was in the running. There was no bank financing behind it, and it was far from clear that there was a hope of lining up the money in 1988. Given how much higher the number was than Shearson's $100 a share, though, it might be worth investigating further—or dangling as a carrot to get the other bidders up. Atkins would talk to the bankers after their meetings with KKR and Shearson Saturday morning.

Although Henry Kravis had been told to bring just a small team to the meeting Saturday, he had decided to make his presentation a tour de force. He had invited all of the key commercial and investment bankers, everyone from Dick Beattie and Steve Waters to Drexel chairman Fred Joseph and Mark Solow, the head of the Manufacturers Hanover LBO department. Just before the call Peter Ackerman, the Drexel junk bond man, had left for Los Angeles; Kravis set up the meeting, started to make arrangements to charter a plane to bring him back as soon as he touched ground, but at the last minute, he changed his mind. Ackerman would just be plugged in by telephone.

After a preliminary meeting at KKR at seven o'clock, the group walked over to Skadden for the presentation. Although he had hoped that the fact of the meeting meant that KKR still had a chance, Steve Waters knew that it was hopeless as soon as the representatives of the Special Committee arrived. It was John Mullin and Bob Lovejoy, nice bright guys, but clearly not the A M&A team.

The investment bankers went over the terms of the securities. That didn't take long. The various pieces of KKR paper, the stub and the PIK preferred, both contained a reset mechanism to change the interest rate to guarantee that they traded at par. The KKR stub was particularly clever. Convertible securities, that is, notes that combined debt, the safest kind of paper, with equity, the most risky, are generally valued at a premium to the value of the debt base because of the equity upside. So KKR called the most risky piece of paper "debt," slapped an interest rate and "conversion feature" on it, and announced that the stub they had created was worth $2 a share more than its $8-a-share face value.

Most of KKR's presentation focused on bigger issues. Joseph said that the Milken investigation had not seriously affected Drexel's ability to sell junk bonds; even if the rumored RICO indictments were handed on Monday, Drexel would be able to place a $5 billion issue. Manny Hanny's Solow said that the commercial bankers were hot on the loan; surely it was the best credit that had come down the LBO pipeline in years. Despite rampant press speculation that such a big loan could not be put together, Solow anticipated no trouble syndicating the $14.5 billion credit. Waters emphasized that, unlike Shearson, KKR had a track record with large LBO deals, whereas Shearson had never done one and might not be able to complete the financing at all. Yes, Waters concluded, doing a deal with Shearson would put the committee at a definite risk.

One of the KKR staffers asked Mullin and Lovejoy to explain the unidentified "other liabilities." They tried, and as they did, it became apparent that the committee had different numbers than KKR did—and that both "other liability" numbers were wrong.

In the elevator on the way down, Kravis, Roberts, and Beattie talked about what to do next. It was clear that they had lost. The committee bankers had in effect conceded that they had been sabotaged. "Let's send that letter," said Kravis, formally complaining that the numbers they had been given were wrong.

So when they got to the lobby, Beattie went to his office a

couple of blocks downtown at 425 Lexington to start drafting. Kravis and Roberts headed uptown to KKR.

While Kravis was meeting with Mullin and Lovejoy, Peter Cohen was in a nearby conference room going over the terms of Shearson's bid with Ira Harris and Fritz Hobbs. Cohen had followed instructions and kept the team small, just Cohen, Tom Strauss, and their respective capital markets and M&A advisers: Jim Stern, Tom Hill, Chas Phillips and Jay Higgins. To Cohen's disappointment, the purpose of the session was not negotiating a contract. Hobbs and Harris only asked questions about how the Shearson securities worked. Unlike the fancy KKR convertible stub, Shearson's stub was simply a junior preferred PIK. As such, it wasn't subject to any premium, and Harris and Hobbs announced that it was worth $2 a share, not $4 a share as Shearson claimed. Hobbs later explained that one reason for the low valuation was that the Shearson stub did not have call protection, that is, there was nothing to prevent Shearson from recalling it at face value at any time. Stern insists that that point was never raised at the meeting; certainly it doesn't make much sense: recalling a note at $4 that Lazard estimated would trade at $2 meant a 100 percent premium for holders, four times the return that anyone was contemplating for the equity. Stern offered to drop the stub altogether and increase the PIK by $4 a share, but that wasn't what Harris and Hobbs wanted either. Stern shrugged. If Hobbs didn't like Shearson's stub, surely he wouldn't like Kravis's stub either, if Kravis even had one, which Stern doubted.

What Hobbs thought about the stub was a minor concern in any case, since it was clear from the questions that Shearson had submitted the highest bid. Indeed, given that, Cohen was slightly puzzled by the repeated request for a copy of all of the computer runs that Shearson had done; Hobbs said that he needed that to properly value the Shearson securities, but the only use Stern could think of for the documents was to give them to KKR.

The meeting ended on a positive note. Harris asked the team to be on call in case there were additional questions before the Special Committee meeting on Sunday morning. That seemed like an open hint that he would be starting contract negotiations soon. The Shearson and Salomon men walked back to Jack Nusbaum's office at Citicorp Center, where the rest of the team was waiting.

After the briefing, Steve Goldstone called Atkins to see how the land lay. "You know, Peter," he said, "we'd really like to get something signed up today. We're willing to include a shop provision." That is, for a limited time, Shearson would allow the committee to use its bid as a stalking horse for a higher one.

"No," said Atkins. "We're not going to sign something up until *we're* ready."

Cohen called Jim Robinson at his farm in Connecticut, but Robinson seemed relatively unconcerned. Today was his birthday. Ross and Laurie Johnson had just arrived for a surprise birthday party. Robinson would worry about RJR only when the formal news came in.

Hobbs left the Shearson meeting convinced that RJR would later sign a merger agreement with Shearson. Whatever he thought of the Shearson stub, the bid was still $1 billion above KKR's. That might be less than he had hoped for, but it was the highest on the table. According to the rules, Shearson had won.

Atkins didn't see it that way. He had spent the morning on the phone with Jim Maher of First Boston and now he said that he thought that the board's clear legal obligation was to give First Boston more time to flesh out the details of its proposal, extending the bidding by at least a couple of days.

Harris exploded. Earlier in the week, after the very first meeting with First Boston, he had argued vociferously for getting the lawyers cracking on the tax structure as a prelude to throwing the bid out as unworkable. Now Atkins was talking about throwing out two legitimate bids when it was crystal clear that First Boston could never get financed, whatever the legal validity of its structure. That was ludicrous.

Atkins held fast, and it would be several hours before the bankers reluctantly agreed to toe the Skadden line.

In the course of the discussions about the morning meetings, Mullin and Lovejoy mentioned that Kravis had complained about some of the numbers, and that they had suggested a Sunday meeting to clear the problem up. That didn't make much sense now. So Atkins called Kravis's office to cancel.

* * *

It seemed clear to Kravis what the cancellation meant: the fix was in. Having sabotaged his bid by feeding him bad numbers, Johnson and Cohen had now locked up the deal. Surely the board would announce a merger momentarily. Even as Kravis was pondering that, Beattie called to say that the letter about the bad numbers was ready.

"Send it," said Kravis.

Beattie called the messenger. Then he headed to Kravis's apartment for a meeting with Kravis, Roberts, and Gershon Kekst, Kravis's top public relations advisor, to talk about an unrelated matter. Half an hour into the meeting, Atkins called to say that he had received the letter. Beattie thought he sounded worried. "We're going to take it to heart," Atkins said.

An hour after that, Atkins called again. "We're not going to need you any further," he said. "You can go home."

"Are you meeting with the other side?" asked Beattie. That would signal that Shearson had won.

"No," said Atkins. "We're not having more meetings with anyone."

Meanwhile, at Jack Nusbaum's office, Peter Cohen was beginning to worry that he had still heard nothing more from Atkins. If the Special Committee was going to approve a merger with Shearson Sunday morning, surely they should be hammering out the terms of the contract now.

It got later and later. Finally, at five o'clock, Atkins called, but not to invite them over. "You can go home," he told Goldstone. "We aren't going to need you any more."

Goldstone didn't ask if they were talking to KKR, but the message was clear. Whatever was going on, it wasn't a Shearson deal.

It was pouring rain Saturday evening when Charlie and Nina Hugel walked up from the Regency Hotel on Park and Sixtieth to the Macombers' apartment at 770 Park Avenue, and they were plenty wet by the time they arrived. Hugel was troubled by the turn that the auction had taken. He definitely wanted to do the right thing, but it wasn't entirely clear what was right. Atkins was insisting that he extend the deadline to give First Boston time to flesh out its proposal, and although Hugel was impressed by the

$118-a-share top value, he didn't think postponing was fair to Shearson. The rules had set a deadline of five o'clock Friday. First Boston had clearly missed that.

Butler and Anderson seemed to agree. Macomber was in Atkins's camp. After spending most of the meal discussing the matter, however, Hugel still wasn't sure what was right. He had begun to worry about something else: if the bidding were extended KKR might drop out. Why this loomed large isn't entirely clear. KKR had not been the high bidder and its presence certainly wasn't necessary to maintain the $100-a-share floor. Cohen was not likely to take away money he had already put on the table.

At Skadden Sunday morning, Atkins was, if anything, more adamant than he had been on Saturday, and Hugel wasn't one to argue with that. "You got lucky," Hugel told Davis when he arrived late for the meeting. "We have to extend the bidding for the First Boston bid."

Davis looked at the First Boston documents, but he wasn't much impressed. He didn't understand how the scheme worked and it didn't look like it could be completed in time. He was, however, distinctly worried about the letter from KKR complaining about bad information. Although it wasn't clear from the text what was wrong with the numbers that KKR had been given, or whether those problems had been enough to push KKR from first to second place, the fact that Lovejoy and Mullin had told Kravis that something was wrong was a big problem. After everything else, the board didn't want to get dragged into a slugfest over whether Johnson had sabotaged the auction. And Davis was leaning toward a second round anyhow. By now Kravis and Cohen had each made it clear—Kravis in the letter, Cohen through Goldstone's call to try to sign up a contract—that they were willing to raise their bids substantially to win, even if that meant throwing caution to the wind. Whatever First Boston was or wasn't able to do in a second round, Shearson and KKR would.

So it was agreed. There would be a second round. The only question was when the new bids would be due. Atkins left the meeting to call Jim Maher. Maher suggested a deadline of December 5, three weeks away, but Atkins said that the latest it could be was November 29, the Tuesday after Thanksgiving. Maher would have three days before Thanksgiving weekend and two days after to find a bank willing to monetize the installment note.

That settled, there was just one more order of business: the confidentiality agreement. Atkins wanted First Boston and Resource Holdings to sign immediately. Maher called Jerry Seslowe at home in Connecticut and told him to get to Skadden as soon as possible. It was pouring rain, but Seslowe drove in. So did Brian Finn, from his house on Long Island. Atkins met them, clean and pressed although he hadn't slept for three days. "I can't sign this," Seslowe said when he saw the confidentiality agreement. "There are all kinds of obligations involved. I don't have a lawyer with me."

"Sign it or go home," said Atkins. "You have fifteen minutes."

Seslowe said he had to talk to the Pritzker people and Atkins agreed to send the document to Chicago by facsimile. After settling Seslowe in a conference room, Atkins turned to Finn. Finn didn't like the confidentiality agreement either, since the presale clause barred First Boston from talking to potential buyers, but he realized that Atkins wasn't in a negotiating mood, so he signed. He also signed a separate piece of paper saying that First Boston wouldn't "Forstmann" the committee by announcing that it had dropped out.

In Seslowe's conference room, meanwhile, Hank Handlesman, the Pritzker lawyer, wanted to "go through this" as if he had all day.

"We're not going through it," said Seslowe. "There's no time. Peter says we have to sign in five minutes."

"Well," said Handlesman. "Maybe we can limit it to my major points. We can skip the little things I wouldn't normally let by."

As they were talking, Atkins had walked into the room. He tapped his watch. Seslowe's time was almost up. "Hank . . ." he said.

Fortunately, Atkins got more reasonable when he heard what Handlesman wanted. He marked the changes on the copy and Seslowe signed.

By Sunday morning, Beattie had had enough of RJR, so while the other members of the KKR team gathered at KKR's West 57th Street office to wait for the Special Committee announcement, Beattie stayed home. He was reading Edith Wharton's *The Age of Innocence* when Atkins called at one o'clock. "We've made a decision," said Atkins. "I'll have a press release to read to you in half an hour."

"Have you sold the company?" asked Beattie.

"No," said Atkins.

A few minutes later, Bryan Burrough from the *Wall Street Journal* called. He told Beattie that the board had voted to delay the bidding until November 29 to give First Boston time to flesh out its proposal.

"How do you know?" asked Beattie.

"Jim Sterngold," said Burrough, referring to *The New York Times* reporter.

Atkins called again at about two.

"Let me tell you what you decided, Peter," said Beattie. "You've postponed the bidding until November 29 to give First Boston time to flesh out its proposal."

"Goddammit," said Atkins. "How did you know that?"

"Can't say," said Beattie.

Atkins read Beattie the press release. Although the rules had said specifically that the committee would not disclose terms of bids it received, Atkins had decided that he had to under SEC regulations, since the numbers affected investors' buy-sell decisions. So the release listed the terms of all three offers, and how the face value was broken among cash, stub, and other securities.

Beattie called KKR. Kravis had gotten so frustrated with waiting that he had already put on his coat to go back home. "I'm on my way," said Beattie. Among other things, they needed to draft a press release of their own.

About the time that Beattie got his call from Bryan Burrough, Linda Robinson got one too. Or at least her caretaker did. Because of the rain, the Robinsons and the Johnsons had left Connecticut early Sunday afternoon and were headed toward New York in separate cars, when Linda's beeper went off, signaling her to call the farm. She did; then she called Burrough. As soon as she had heard what the committee had done, she tried to call Johnson in his car, but his car phone wasn't working very well and it was several minutes before she made contact. Through the static she repeated the news and suggested that they pull over and talk. Through the static Johnson replied that they would meet in New York.

By the time they crossed the Triboro Bridge, Linda and Jim had both talked to Cohen and Nusbaum and they had agreed to head straight to Nusbaum's office at Citicorp Center where the rest of the team was waiting. They were mad.

The only person who was madder than Robinson and Johnson was Peter Cohen. Cohen was seething. He had won fair and square and the committee had snatched away his prize with a cockamamie story about First Boston. There was no way that First Boston's plan was ever going to work. Cohen's people had looked, the Salomon people had looked; the financing could never be completed by the end of the year—it *couldn't* fly. Cohen was sure that the board had concocted the story simply to give KKR a second chance. And apparently the committee had tipped Kravis off that a second round was in the offing. Cohen was sure that Kravis would not have bid $94 a share if he had thought that that was his only chance; $94 a share was not a winning number.

Hugel had tried to smooth the matter over in the press release by suggesting that the KKR and Shearson bids were close, which they weren't; Shearson had offered $1.5 billion more, entirely in cash. Adding insult to injury, the release listed the terms of the Shearson offer, despite Atkins's written promise that he wouldn't. That told Kravis how much money the banks were willing to commit, and how high he had to go to win.

In fact, everyone on the Shearson team was so angry that much of what they said at the meeting at Nusbaum's office didn't make a lot of sense. The Salomon people, for example, were ranting that Ira Harris had put his friend Jay Pritzker up to making the First Boston offer to get back at Salomon for whatever unspecified wrongs had made him leave in the first place. That Harris's job as adviser to the Special Committee was to round up bids apparently didn't enter into the picture. Cohen himself was talking about suing the board. Goldstone said that that was a losing case. No judge was going to be sympathetic to a management charging that the board had been too independent.

C H A P T E R 18

Thanksgiving Maneuvers

November 20 to November 28

Even as the Johnsons and the Robinsons were speeding toward Manhattan on Sunday afternoon, Jay Pritzker was mobilizing his team. He called Mel Klein at home in Corpus Christi to say that "but for us, Shearson would have won," and that he needed Klein and Dan Lufkin, the banker who had suggested RJR in the first place, in New York on Monday morning. Klein and Lufkin shared a plane, and by the time they arrived at First Boston headquarters for a working lunch, Jim Maher had already done what he could to get the ball rolling. He had called Tylee Wilson, the former RJR ceo, to set up a meeting Tuesday morning. He had contacted Citi, Chase, and Bankers Trust about monetizing the installment note. To Maher's surprise, no one seemed particularly eager to investigate the idea. Citi even demanded a $15 million take-a-look fee. Maher flatly refused to pay any fees, and, fortunately, Chase, which had originally wanted a fee as well, rethought its position and said that it would look for free, apparently in hopes of firming up its relationship with First Boston.

At the strategy lunch, everyone agreed that making a second offer was a long long shot and that they might not be able to line up the equity, much less the bank debt, to make the proposal fly. Klein thought that he might have the answer. His friend Henry

Kravis had put out an announcement Sunday afternoon suggesting that he might not bid. Kravis had plenty of money; perhaps he would be interested in the deal if he had First Boston's tax structure. So, early in the afternoon, Klein called Kravis. Kravis was cool, whether because he didn't plan to bid or he didn't like the idea of teaming up wasn't clear. "It can't hurt to talk," said Klein.

True. Kravis agreed to lunch at one o'clock the next day.

After the meeting at Skadden on Saturday morning, Steve Waters had been so sure that KKR was out of the running that he had called Eric Gleacher in Georgia where he was playing golf with Texaco chief executive James Kinnear to tell him, "We're dead." Now, Kravis had gotten an unexpected reprieve, courtesy of First Boston, and Waters was puzzled as to what Kravis thought he was doing. In addition to putting out a statement saying he might not bid, Kravis was bending over backward to tell people that he wasn't serious. He had let slip that Roberts wasn't planning to be in New York any time soon. He had specifically told everyone on the team to go away for Thanksgiving, adding that he was headed for Vail and his associate Ted Ammon for the Caribbean. Waters knew that Kravis was determined to win the RJR fight; presumably the talk was designed to throw Shearson off the scent.

For what it was worth, the number problems seemed to be getting sorted out. At a meeting at KKR on Monday night, the Dillon and Lazard bankers gave Kravis the correct number on "other" liabilities, which was roughly what Kravis had guessed it was in the first place. That left tobacco as the only outstanding problem. Roberts had been so skeptical about the future of the business that he had slashed estimated future earnings increases in half, from $120 million a year to $60 million. That wasn't enough to change the overall value of the company by much—tobacco earnings already totaled $2 billion a year—but it was enough to force a meeting with Ed Horrigan, the vice-chairman and tobacco chief at Nabisco, at 10:30 Tuesday morning. Horrigan hadn't been at KKR's first tobacco meeting; that had been with Dolph von Arx, the U.S. tobacco chief.

The Horrigan session didn't begin well. Horrigan "resented greatly" having been accused of giving KKR bad numbers and being ordered to do "a second tiptoe through the tulips" and he let it show. "I don't need to introduce myself," Horrigan began, oozing hostility. "We all know why I'm here. What do you want to know?"

Just before he walked into the meeting, Horrigan had read a facsimile copy of an article in that day's *Greensboro News & Record* that said flatly that KKR would fire Horrigan and hire Paul Sticht if it won the bidding. So Horrigan launched into a diatribe as to just how inept Sticht was. "The last time he set foot in tobacco land was 1982," said Horrigan, "when we broke ground on the Tobaccoville plant. He never did know anything about cigarettes. You're making a big mistake."

Kravis just listened in silence—what could he say? Finally, Horrigan ran out of steam and the fact-finding part of the session began. Kravis needed two kinds of information: how much could tobacco be cut back in a leveraged environment? how realistic were the predicted price increases in the management scenario?

As far as cutbacks, Horrigan stonewalled. There was no way to operate on a smaller budget, he insisted. None at all.

Steve Waters cut in. He had gotten to know Horrigan several years back when he had negotiated the sale of Piedmont Airlines, of which Horrigan was a director, to U.S. Air, and he thought that Horrigan was perfectly capable of lying if that served his interests. "Come on, Ed," he said. "Take out the frills. There's got to be something in there that could go."

"There's not," said Horrigan.

"You've got a $1 billion marketing budget," noted one of the junior bankers. "Can't you get something out of that?"

Well, Horrigan conceded, maybe if pressed, he could save $50 million.

"We think you could cut two hundred fifty million dollars," said the banker.

"Maybe you could, but I can't," said Horrigan.

"How much does Dinah Shore cost you?" asked Raether.

"Not one cent," said Horrigan. "It's a corporate expense, not a tobacco expense."

Waters kept pushing Horrigan to talk about cuts and scale-backs, but Horrigan wasn't bending.

"What other numbers did you give Shearson?" Raether finally asked.

"I didn't give them any other numbers," said Horrigan. "I just sat and talked to them the way I'm talking to you."

"What's the worst-case model?" asked Waters.

"This is the only model," said Horrigan.

"Ed," said Waters, "remember, I used to work at Shearson. I know how they look at deals. There has to be a worst-case model."

Horrigan insisted that there was no other case. At least he hadn't prepared one.

Clearly that was a dead end. Kravis turned to the other key matter, whether the tobacco price increases and the very slow volume declines that he had been given were realistic.

On this issue, Horrigan was more forthcoming. He was, after all, defending his business. Horrigan talked about demographics and tobacco consumption and price history. He even let von Arx and Jerry Gunzenhausen, the tobacco unit's chief financial officer, answer some technical questions. The bottom line was that it seemed impossible that sales and profits would be much lower than the numbers Horrigan had given them. If Congress barred all tobacco advertising, for example, the company made more money because marketing costs were lower.

"We haven't looked at any numbers lower than these," said Horrigan. "It couldn't happen." Indeed, he continued, even in the worst case, "I'm going to do better than these numbers."

"So you're telling me that I should bid one hundred dollars a share for tobacco alone?" asked Kravis.

"That's right," said Horrigan.

Kravis leaned forward in his chair. "It's been reported in the press that you will leave if we win," he said. "I'd like you to respond to that personally."

"Ed hired me," said von Arx. "I'd have to think about that seriously."

Gunzenhausen also hedged.

Kravis waited for Horrigan to say something, but he didn't. "Ed, you haven't answered," said Kravis.

"Why should I?" asked Horrigan. "You just fired me this morning."

After that, the lunch with Klein was something of a comedown. Kravis had agreed partly out of courtesy and partly because he wanted to meet Lufkin, whom he didn't know. Kravis teased Klein about being so far behind that he was only meeting Ty Wilson that morning, and then Seslowe explained the details of the bridge installment note system. Kravis had met Seslowe before, several years earlier, when Seslowe had tried to sell KKR a bankrupt shipping company, and Kravis knew that Seslowe was a fantastic salesman, but this scheme just didn't seem to work, even as Seslowe was describing it. There was no way to get the financing lined up by the end of the year, and Kravis was sure that the board wouldn't take it unless the money was in place.

"What do you need us for?" Lufkin asked Kravis. "You can just use our idea."

"True," said Kravis. "I could just use your idea. But that's not the way I do business. If I use your idea, I'll take you as a partner."

Klein wanted to talk numbers, and after some back and forth Kravis said that he might be willing to give the First Boston group a 20 percent stake.

"We need half," said Pritzker.

Kravis said he would have to think about that. "We'll call you back," he said when the lunch broke up at two-thirty, but when he did call, late in the afternoon, it was to say that splitting the deal fifty–fifty didn't make sense. If he made a bid, and he wasn't sure he would, he would go it alone.

The message that KKR wasn't "serious" was getting through to Shearson loud and clear. When Peter Cohen called Dick Beattie Monday night, just before leaving for Brussels for a Société Générale board meeting, Beattie had agreed that the First Boston scheme was flatly unworkable and had volunteered: "George is in California. Henry is going skiing."

Given what had happened thus far, Cohen thought that the chances that Kravis wouldn't bid again were remote, and Linda Robinson was equally unimpressed when Kravis tried the same story on her. When Robinson called Wednesday morning to ask whether she should make an offer on the show horse that they were considering buying together, Kravis responded with a non sequitur. "We're right where we want to be," he said. "Third place. I love being in third place. We're taking the weekend off. George is in California. Paul has left for Florida. A couple of the young guys are going to the Caribbean. In an hour and a half, I'm leaving for Vail. We're not going to think about RJR again until Monday. We might not even make a bid."

"What about the horse?" asked Robinson.

Kravis thought for a minute. Yes, he said, suggesting a price. On the horse he did want to bid.

Robinson didn't waste any time trying to figure out what Kravis was up to. She had other things on her mind. *Time* magazine had been calling Robinson about an article ever since the battle began, and Robinson had consistently refused a Johnson interview. No major article had yet appeared. Then, on Tuesday, someone from the *Time* advertising department in New York called someone in the Reynolds Tobacco advertising department in Winston-Salem to say that Ross Johnson was going to be on the cover, and the company might want to pull advertising, including a Winston cigarette ad on the back cover, from the single issue.

Robinson quickly learned that the article was built around the thesis: "Seldom since the age of the nineteenth-century robber barons has corporate behavior been so open to question. The battle for RJR Nabisco seems to have crossed an invisible line that separates reasonable conduct from anarchy." The cover line read, "A Game of Greed: This man could pocket $100 million from the largest corporate takeover in history. Have buyouts gone too far?"

She still hadn't decided what to do when, on Wednesday morning, Bill Liss, RJR's pr chief, got a call from Joseph Kane, *Time*'s Atlanta bureau chief, asking for a "cover quality" picture of Johnson. Although Liss was technically representing the company and the board, he was a personal friend of Johnson's; Liss's boss John Martin was a member of the management group. So Liss rationalized that an article about Johnson might also say something about the company and the board and was therefore his concern. Wednesday afternoon, Liss told Kane he could set up an interview with Johnson as long as *Time* took the story off the cover.

Kane hadn't really expected to get an interview, but now he played hardball. He said he wasn't bargaining; *Time* was doing a story, period. If Johnson wanted to give an interview there would be no strings attached.

Liss suggested a gallery of raiders on the cover.

Kane refused that offer too.

Liss called twice more with other suggestions for a "quid pro quo." He even woke Kane up at one-thirty in the morning.

Meanwhile, Johnson, in West Palm Beach for the long week-end, called his golfing buddy John Meyers, a former publisher of *Time*. Meyers thought that Johnson should do an interview, and by this time Robinson had decided that she did too. Although there was nothing she could do about the already written negative story, she had been told that the interview would run as a box on the buyout in general and the management contract in particular, and she thought that that made it an opportunity to jump past the Greed label that Johnson had picked up with the *New York Times* article. Late in the afternoon on Thanksgiving Day, Liss called Kane again to offer to fly him to Florida on the RJR corporate jet for an interview with Johnson at the Jupiter Hilton. *Time* refused the jet, but sent business reporter Frederick Ungeheuer down from New York on a commercial flight.

Robinson wasn't at the interview—Liss and Martin were—but she had coached Johnson over the phone beforehand. He was to focus on the benefits to shareholders of the buyout and his intention of giving a large block of stock to the employees through an ESOP. Johnson thought he did that.

"What about the management contract?" Ungeheuer had begun.

"This is the question on which I'm just getting murdered," said Johnson.

"That's why I'm asking it," said Ungeheuer.

"My job is to negotiate the best deal that I can for my people, so I negotiated a deal where we'd get eight and one-half percent and then have incentives that went to twelve percent and then to eighteen and one-half percent if we hit certain targets along the way."

"The proposal bankers were looking at only had seven people in it."

"This is absolutely wrong," said Johnson. He had planned to set up an ESOP.

So what was Johnson actually going to get?

A hundred million dollars.

"Does any chief executive deserve that kind of reward?"

"If he is an owner, he does. It's hard to answer. Actually, it's kind of Monopoly money. But we're putting in twenty million dollars which we had to borrow on a recourse loan. So if I fail, I'm on the hook. But making one hundred million dollars was not my motive by any stretch of the imagination."

"What can a middle manager, or, say, a secretary expect?"

Three to twenty-five thousand in five years.

Did he consider himself an "inside raider"?

"The obvious response is no, but why no? I haven't been the most orthodox CEO because I figure if you always run by tradition, I would probably still be an accountant for General Electric." The bid, like his other actions, had been in the best interests of shareholders.

Given his insider understanding of the company, why had he bid a low $75 and then raised to $100?

"Times change. We looked at seventy-five dollars and, remember, I had no financing. It was about a thirty percent premium. And we would not have disposed of as many companies as we will have to dispose of right now."

"Shearson and Salomon, the investment firms, would have to put up eighteen billion to twenty billion dollars and trust you with that for five years?"

"Exactly."

"With fifty percent of the vote?"

"They could throw me out too. I figured that was a good test." Actually that statement was disingenuous; under the terms of the management contract, Johnson effectively couldn't be fired: it would cost Shearson too much.

"What about the employees?" Johnson had said that he would have to lay off at least eight hundred.

True, said Johnson, "but the people that I have, particularly the Atlanta people, have very portable types of professions: accountants, lawyers, secretaries. It isn't that I would be putting them on the bread line. We have excellent severance arrangements."

However well Johnson thought that the interview had gone, the article that appeared in the magazine on Monday, November 28, was so awful that Charlie Hugel had trouble believing that Johnson had said the things that he was quoted as saying. "Monopoly money"? "Portable professions"? Johnson sounded about as sensitive to employees as Attila the Hun. As one of the directors later put it: "Employees are assets, and any manager who doesn't see that is a fool. We could see that Johnson didn't."

It wasn't just the quotes, of course, but also the fact of the cover and the thrust of the article. After six weeks of being in the spotlight, the last thing that the directors wanted was an article in America's largest news magazine criticizing buyouts and Johnson and, implicitly, RJR. The deal had taken on such a pall that it was hard to open a newspaper without being confronted with a scathing analysis. Even on Thanksgiving Day, *The New York Times* had reported that House Speaker Jim Wright was so determined to stop buyouts that he had talked to Representative John Dingell, whose Consumer Protection Committee oversaw the SEC, about the matter. According to the article, Wright didn't have a specific proposal, but he had reminded Dingell of a law designed by Sam Rayburn during the Depression that gave the SEC the power to break up the big utilities, and had even given Dingell a copy of Rayburn's biography for inspiration.

However much Hugel and the other Special Committee members wished that the buyout would go away, the bidding date was set for November 29, and the board certainly wanted the best price. From that standpoint, the *Time* article and KKR's blatant hints that it might drop out were bad news. Indeed, at a meeting with the Lazard bankers Monday afternoon, Jim Stern had said flatly that he didn't think that KKR would rebid, apparently signaling that Shearson saw no reason to raise its bid above $100 a share.

After he heard that, Felix Rohatyn decided to see if he could stir up some competition, by calling both Shearson and KKR. First he called Jim Robinson. It might have been more logical for Rohatyn to call Cohen, since Cohen, not Robinson, was head of the Shearson bidding group, but Rohatyn didn't know Cohen and he and Robinson were long-time friends. Rohatyn knew that Robinson was working on the deal because when he had called Robinson one Sunday afternoon with a question about the Governor's Council on Social and Economic Priorities on which they both sat, Robinson had complained that he was spending all his time on RJR. "You shouldn't be doing that," Rohatyn had remarked. Surely quarterbacking a Shearson deal was Cohen's job. But as long as Jim was on the deal, Rohatyn thought it was simplest to talk to him, so he did. Robinson didn't have any comment on Rohatyn's statement that management was considering a restructuring at $100 a share and that a stub was key to the deal. Then Rohatyn called Kravis with the same message.

"I'm not sure I'm going to bid," said Kravis. "I've been getting an awful lot of bad press."

"Your press isn't going to get worse if you bid," Rohatyn pointed out. "It might get worse if you don't."

"Well, I don't know," said Kravis. "I'm still thinking."

By Monday afternoon, Jim Maher was ready to congratulate himself on having done the impossible. He had lined up $1.2 billion in equity, mostly from Pritzker-controlled entities, and he had made unexpectedly good progress on monetizing the installment note. To his great surprise, Chase apparently was willing to commit to the $12 billion note. Everyone but the chief credit officer had signed off.

Then the phone rang. It was the account officer from Chase. The chief credit officer had vetoed the monetizing line. Maher couldn't believe it. The Chase man said that he thought he could still work something out, but Maher didn't have time for that. He called Harry Gray, Mel Klein's partner and the former chairman of United Technologies. Gray called Willard Butcher, Chase's chairman, to find out what was going on. Butcher didn't know and didn't think he could do anything. He was leaving for Russia at noon on Tuesday, and he was reluctant to overrule the credit officer.

So Gray called John Reed, chairman of Citicorp. For years, Gray had been on the Citicorp board; perhaps that would speed things up. Reed said he'd set up a team to look at the monetization, but he couldn't make any promises about the timing. Twenty-four hours was awfully short notice for a $12 billion loan.

Peter Cohen wasn't having a replay of the lunch mess the afternoon of the last bid. Instead, he had called a meeting of just a handful of top strategists in his office Tuesday morning: Cohen, Jeff Lane, and George Scheinberg—Shearson's president and vice-chairman, respectively—Andy Sage, Frank Benevento, and on a phone hookup, Jack Nusbaum. Cohen had invited Johnson, but he didn't come; the bidding was out of his range.

Cohen had already put his best offer on the table, so there wasn't much he could do in terms of sweetening, at least if economics prevailed. Even if there had been a lot of room to sweeten, Cohen was in a difficult tactical position. Having been the high bidder by $1.5 billion in the first round, Cohen was effectively bidding against himself. One thing Cohen could do was sweeten Shearson's stub so that it approached KKR's stub in value. But although there had been persistent hints that a stub was important—Fritz Hobbs had even called Salomon's Chas Phillips to rhapsodize about 35 percent—Cohen decided against sweetening it. At the meeting to discuss the $100-a-share bid, Hobbs had told Cohen that cash was more important than the stub. Indeed, Cohen's view was that the only way to clinch victory was to increase the cash. The money would come straight out of Shearson's pocket, but he believed that a hike of $1 or $2 a share, a total of $228 million to $456 million, would do it.

Sage wasn't against that, but he suggested that for extra protection, Shearson should make a two-pronged offer, one with a high cash value, and one with a high face value. Whatever Hugel had said about cash being king, Sage didn't think it was true. Certainly the press didn't believe it. Articles on the bidding consistently listed by the face value, not cash value, or even what the Special Committee thought they were worth. Coming up with an offer that had a higher face value and the same expected return to investors was a relative simple matter: Shearson simply cut the amount of cash coming out of its pocket and substituted PIK paper. That made the deal riskier because it increased the leverage, but Cohen wasn't worried about that.

The problem with making a two-pronged offer, however, was that it was likely to turn into a one-pronged cash offer at the higher price. Surely the committee would choose the prong with the high face value and then dangle a contract in front of Cohen until he replaced the paper with greenbacks. Cohen wasn't willing to take that risk.

That settled, Cohen called Hill and Stern into his office. Hill made an impassioned speech that Kravis wasn't real and that the group should not raise its offer. Stern was even more forceful. He wanted to lower the bid, to show the board that it had made a bad mistake by delaying the bidding for First Boston's phony bid.

"No," said Lane. "We're not going to do that." Lane, like

Cohen, knew that Kravis was real. Besides, it was foolish to do something that would irritate the board.

What they were going to do was raise the price, assuming Salomon was on board. Salomon wasn't. When Cohen called Gutfreund and Strauss they announced that they too wanted to lower the bid and that they weren't sure that the $100 that they had offered in the last round should remain on the table.

"Well," said Cohen. "What about this. Shearson will put up your share of the price increase and we'll take your share of the fee."

There was a long silence.

"I sure scared you," laughed Cohen.

After a brief conversation, Gutfreund finally agreed to raise the bid slightly, as long as Salomon kept its fee. Slightly meant $1 a share in paper, although Cohen pushed hard for $2 or $3 a share in cash.

Kravis and Roberts were poker-faced during their last meeting with the investment bankers on Monday afternoon, November 28. Again the bankers told them to bid $102 to $105 a share; again Waters and Gleacher placed bets on what number they thought KKR would choose. There wasn't any particular reason that it should be higher than the $94 a share they had bid in the first round. Certainly the numbers hadn't changed substantially. The $1 billion in "other liabilities" had turned out to be illusory just as Kravis had expected; Roberts had agreed to raise the tobacco earnings estimate by $60 million, to the numbers Ed Horrigan had given them in the first place. That kicked the value up by $2 a share.

Gleacher bet on $98 a share, the same figure he had bet on last time: Kravis and Roberts didn't seem any more interested this time than they had been the first time around. Waters had been spending a lot of time with Kravis and Roberts over the past couple of days, and he knew that they were determined to win, so he put his money on $105 a share.

Waters was nearer the mark. After the bid went over to Skadden by messenger at five, Kravis told his bankers that he had chosen $106 a share. Gleacher gave Waters back his dollar, and the team sat down to wait.

No one called.

Across town at Jack Nusbaum's office the Shearson people were waiting too. And by six-thirty no one had called them either. Tom Hill had one of his people call the Carlyle to see if Roberts was registered; he was, although it wasn't quite clear what that meant. Peter Cohen left to take his wife and kids to dinner to celebrate his twentieth wedding anniversary. At eight, Johnson called from his office to say that he was going too: "There's no point in sticking around. We can't win no matter what we do."

By this time it seemed clear that nothing would happen soon, so Tom Strauss took Higgins, Phillips, and the other Salomon bankers to Christ Cella, the steakhouse on East 46th Street, for dinner (Gutfreund had to go to a client dinner but he joined them for dessert). The worry about RJR didn't keep them from having a grand time. Ron Perelman, the raider who had made a run at Salomon the year before, happened to be sitting at the next table, and they spent the evening teasing him and some of the other nearby diners. On the way out they passed Citicorp chairman John Reed, who was sitting at a table full of commercial bankers. "We're hoping to spend a lot of your money soon," said Strauss.

Jim and Linda Robinson, meanwhile, were having a rubber-chicken dinner at the Marriott hotel—Marriott's version of "Chicken Nancy," to be precise, although the dish fell short of the White House fare—to raise money for the Boys Club of America, a related but different group from the one that had sponsored the October dinner at which Johnson gave Hugel the Harriman Award. Although the night the RJR bidding closed wasn't ideal for a charity function, Linda had long ago bought a table, since the guest of honor was Texaco chief executive Jim Kinnear, one of her biggest clients.

As it happened, Kinnear's investment banker was Eric Gleacher, the Morgan Stanley M&A chief who was also representing Henry Kravis, and he was sitting at Linda's table with his wife Anne. Linda had her portable telephone, antenna up, ready to get the word that the Special Committee wanted to talk. "What did you bid?" Linda asked Gleacher between dinner and dessert.

"Ninety-four," kidded Gleacher, exactly what KKR had bid on the first round.

"And what do you think we bid?" she asked.

"One hundred and one," Gleacher guessed.

"That's about right," said Jim.

Then Gleacher's tone got serious. "When are you guys ever going to figure out that the Special Committee isn't going to give this company to Ross Johnson?" he asked.

The Robinsons looked at each other. That was interesting.

Linda's beeper went off. She looked down at the display: it listed Johnson's office number, so she left the table to call.

"You liar," she snapped at Gleacher when she came back.

She had just been told that Bryan Burrough, the *Wall Street Journal* reporter, had called to say that KKR had bid $103 a share to Shearson's $101. Burrough was usually right, and Robinson assumed that he was right this time too—he wasn't—and his numbers seemed to mean that Kravis had won.

Kravis hadn't won yet, although he was certainly the favored bidder.

When Hugel, Atkins, and Rohatyn opened the second-round bidding packets at five o'clock, it was clear that the numbers weren't even close. Kravis was way out in front with a blockbuster bid of $106 a share, $80 in cash plus $17 in preferred stock, and the $8 stub which KKR said was worth $9 a share because of the "conversion" feature. Shearson was still talking about much more cash, a total of $88 a share, but the face value of the bid was $101 a share and the securities looked the same as when Shearson had tried the first time around, and had been told were lacking. The First Boston bid still wasn't financed, and it was no longer in the running on price either. Although Maher hadn't included the information in his formal offer, he had told Atkins over the telephone that the $115 a share price corresponded to selling the food companies for $17 billion, $3 billion more than Maher thought he could get; the most likely estimate for the value of the bid was $111 a share. Given the lack of financing and the risk that the tax strategy wouldn't fly, Atkins and Rohatyn agreed that the bid could be dropped as too vague.

The $5 a share difference between the Kravis and Cohen bids translated into almost $1.2 billion in total dollars. That was so much that it seemed inconceivable that Shearson could be sweet-talked into topping KKR, and since $106 a share seemed well above what Dillon and Lazard thought that they could get in a restructuring or recapitalization, the next step was obvious.

At about nine o'clock, Atkins dialed Dick Beattie.

CHAPTER 19

Negotiating in the Middle of the Night

November 28

By this time, Henry Kravis and George Roberts had had enough of waiting in the office for the phone to ring, and they had left for dinner with all of the KKR partners at La Campagnola, the Italian restaurant on First Avenue owned by Kravis's friend Ron Rosa. Dick Beattie, Ted Ammon, and the KKR associates and investment bankers remained at 9 West 57th to wait for the call.

Although Beattie had half expected to get the word that KKR had won, he had not anticipated hearing anything until midnight. "Are you talking to the other side?" Beattie asked when Atkins called from Skadden, slightly suspicious that Atkins was warming up to ask him to bid once again.

"No," said Atkins.

That was just what Beattie had wanted to hear: KKR had won. "We're on our way," he said. "Is there any food there?" After all, Beattie hadn't eaten.

"Yes," said Atkins.

On the way out, Beattie called La Campagnola. "We've just ordered," said Kravis, when the maitre d' brought him to the telephone.

Beattie told him to hotfoot it to Skadden. "We'll meet you there," said Beattie. Only Kravis wasn't at Skadden when Beattie arrived, and he didn't show up during the half-hour that Beattie chatted with Ira Harris over the buffet tray. So Beattie called the restaurant again to make sure that Kravis had left.

He hadn't. "We've just started the appetizer," he said. "We'll be there soon."

"Well, you had better hurry," said Beattie. "Felix needs to talk to you, and if you don't get here soon, he's going to leave." Rohatyn hadn't actually mentioned leaving, but Beattie thought that that story might get Kravis moving.

It did. "Felix is going to leave?" said Kravis. "We're on the way." He rushed back to the table, paid the check, and headed to Skadden Arps without his dinner.

It was nine-thirty at night.

By this time, Shearson had finally gotten some news, but it wasn't encouraging. When Steve Goldstone had called Atkins at about ten o'clock to find out what was going on, Atkins had said that "you can go home." Atkins wouldn't elaborate, but Goldstone called Nusbaum who called Bryan Burrough, the *Wall Street Journal* reporter, who said that KKR was even then at Skadden negotiating. According to Burrough, the bids were neck and neck.

Nusbaum dashed off a letter to the Special Committee criticizing it for "negotiating in the middle of the night," and called a messenger to deliver it immediately. Letter notwithstanding, it wasn't quite clear that KKR had won. All Shearson had to go on was a rumor passed by a newspaper reporter; no one from the committee had officially said so. Earlier, Cohen and Gutfreund had agreed that they would keep topping KKR until they won, but that had been premised on knowing *what* KKR had bid, which they didn't. Gutfreund, in particular, didn't want to bid in the dark.

"Well, if they are talking to KKR and didn't even call us, KKR's bid must be so much higher that their lawyers said we're out of the running," said Hill. "They must be up in the $105 to $110 range." Hill also guessed that the bid was mostly paper: the first bid, although apparently fake, had been heavy on paper, and Jim Stern knew from talking to the banks that KKR had lined up only $14.5 billion of bank debt. "Let's go to $108," suggested Hill.

"No," said Gutfreund. Hill's best guess was not good enough. If Gutfreund was putting Salomon's money on the line, he needed to *know*. It wasn't immediately clear how to find out.

At Johnson's office, meanwhile, the focus was on golden parachutes and whether the board was going to take them away as part of accepting the KKR offer; Johnson's chute alone was worth $23 million. About midnight, Johnson called Hugel at the Regency to find out.

"We're not changing the parachutes," Hugel insisted.

"By the way," said Johnson, "what exactly is going on?"

"Remember that conversation we had this morning?" asked Hugel. Johnson had called Hugel to say that he thought that KKR wouldn't bid, and Hugel had responded that either KKR wouldn't bid or it would submit a blockbuster. "Well, that's what happened."

"KKR made a blockbuster?"

"Yes," said Hugel. "You lost by a clean five points." Hugel's other phone rang. It was Peter Atkins, and Hugel said he had to take it.

"I'll call back later," said Johnson, but what Hugel had told him was enough to make one decision. If he had lost by $5 a share, he was dropping out. Johnson told Linda Robinson to call the press to concede, and half an hour later, she called *The New York Times*. "Our best information is that the other side has clearly made the best bid," she said. "We are not currently considering sweetening our bid. It's over."

Hugel's call from Atkins had come in the middle of a conversation that Atkins was having with Goldstone about extending the bidding to a third round. As Goldstone put it to Atkins, Shearson had bid low because the committee had put it in an impossible situation; having been the high bidder in the first round, it was, in effect, bidding against itself. "You've just entered an auction with no rules," he said. "It's your duty as a fiduciary to help both bidders. That is the only way to get the best bid."

Atkins put Goldstone on hold while he talked to Hugel. "We don't agree with your analysis," he said when he got back on the line. "You're grownups. You're big boys. You gauged the competition. You made your bid. You were wrong."

Goldstone kept pushing: at least Atkins could tell him what KKR had bid.

Atkins refused. "I can't tell you what KKR's bid was," he insisted. "Why don't you ask Johnson? He's talked to Charlie Hugel."

Goldstone called Johnson. "What's this all about?" he asked. "Did Hugel tell you what they bid?"

"No," said Johnson. He'd just gotten off his second call to Hugel. "He said we lost by five points. It's over."

"It may not be," said Goldstone.

"It is as far as I'm concerned," said Johnson. "At these prices, bidding any more is absurd."

"That's not your decision to make," said Goldstone. "That's the bankers' judgment." As Gutfreund had pointed out so many times, it was the bankers' money. "Do you want to cut their legs off? If they keep bidding you might get another $1 or $2 for the shareholders."

Johnson shrugged. He was willing to try.

So Goldstone called Nusbaum's office. Clearly that was mayhem. Cohen was talking about suing the Special Committee, an idea that Goldstone had told him again and again was preposterous. Goldstone said that they had to do something to stop the committee in its tracks. Once the contract was fully negotiated, it would be hard to break the momentum to keep it from being signed. Whatever Atkins said, the committee couldn't turn down a new bid. "Bidding is the only way to make this a three-ring circus," he said.

Gutfreund had already made it clear that he wasn't bidding before he knew precisely what KKR had bid, including the terms of the securities, and he was sure Goldstone knew. Hugel had talked to Johnson, hadn't he? "You're withholding information from us," said Gutfreund.

"I know I'm not," said Goldstone. "And I don't think Ross is, but it doesn't matter. Make your best bid. If that's higher than KKR's, you win. If not, you weren't willing to outbid them anyway."

Gutfreund wouldn't budge.

Goldstone was so frustrated that he was literally yelling at Gutfreund to make an offer.

But Gutfreund refused.

At Johnson's office meanwhile, the mood had changed. Although Johnson wasn't interested in making another bid, Ed Horrigan was, and he had found out from the *Times* reporter what KKR's offer was. Frank Benevento quickly cranked those numbers through his LBO model to come up with a grid of possible PIK heavy bids that were nominally higher than $106 a share.

Jim Robinson got excited about that and called Cohen at Nusbaum's office to find out if the Shearson model was the same. In the course of talking about whether any of the bids on the grid made sense, one of the bankers in Nusbaum's office told Cohen that Linda Robinson had conceded. No one had told Cohen that Linda was going to do that, and he was outraged. "That may be Ross's position," he said when she told him that Johnson had told her to throw in the towel, "but it isn't my position." However embarrassing it was, he ordered her to call back and unconcede.

By this time, Goldstone had talked to Atkins a second time, and he reported that Atkins now seemed more inclined to consider a bid if it came across the transom.

Nusbaum drafted a second letter to the full board criticizing it for not responding to the first letter—to be fair to Atkins, it was the middle of the night—and repeating Shearson's desire to make another bid.

Still, when Cohen left at two in the morning, it wasn't quite clear that Shearson would make one. Although Cohen wanted to win, he wanted to know what he was bidding against first. On that point, at least, he agreed with Gutfreund.

Atkins hadn't been lying when he told Goldstone the auction was over. As far as price was concerned, the bidding had stopped at five o'clock. Kravis was at Skadden negotiating the provisions of the securities he would pay the shareholders, and the language of the merger contract, everything, that is, except price.

As far as the securities went, Rohatyn was insisting on two changes. The more important had to do with the preferred PIK stock that counted for $17 a share. Rohatyn was worried that PIK would take a beating when KKR flooded the market with RJR junk bonds to refinance the bridge, and he wanted KKR to agree to a quicker reset to protect the shareholders. After some dickering, Kravis did. Rohatyn also wanted Kravis to stretch the conversion date on the stub by an extra one to three years. Not only would the stub-holder get more interest, he could also make a better judgment about whether or not to go through with the conversion.

Kravis agreed to that too.

The board had put together a list of critical employees' issues called "Schedule II." Most of the items had to do with maintaining current benefits and providing fair severance to employees who were fired as a result of the buyout. Kravis agreed to many of the items. The others had to wait for Hugel.

By one o'clock the key points were finally settled. Rohatyn and Harris had gone home. Only a few highly technical questions remained to be hammered out, and Peter Ackerman was then taking care of them. Although Kravis had told investment banker Bruce Wasserstein when he called at eleven not to come to Skadden until the next morning, Wasserstein hadn't been able to resist, and showed up at about eleven-thirty. As they were getting together their papers to leave for the night, Kravis, Roberts, Raether, and Wasserstein strolled out into the hallway. Someone told them that Joe Perella, Wasserstein's partner, was on the line from Tokyo. Wasserstein took the call on the phone in the corridor.

Perella was frantic. He had just seen a story on the Dow wire that said that KKR had bid $103 and Shearson had bid $101. No further details were given about the KKR bid, but the report said that Shearson's bid was $88 a share in cash and $13 in other securities. The numbers were wrong, at least as far as the KKR bid was concerned, but clearly someone on the committee was talking to Dow Jones, and probably to Shearson too. Indeed, the wire seemed to confirm Kravis's worst fear: that his bid was being shopped.

Perella faxed the article to Skadden, and, document in hand, Beattie marched off to find Atkins. Atkins was in his office on the 46th floor—the negotiations with KKR had been in several conference rooms downstairs—surrounded by litigators. Beattie hovered at the doorway, but he didn't go in. Whatever Atkins was up to looked serious.

One of the junior lawyers motioned to Atkins that Beattie was waiting. "You've got some problems?" asked Beattie when Atkins came out.

"They're going like gangbusters," said Atkins.

Beattie figured Shearson was threatening to sue. "Well, we've got a little problem," he said. He showed Atkins the wire. "And we want you to come down and talk about it."

A few minutes later both teams were assembled in the conference room.

"Someone is leaking to the press," said Beattie, holding up the fax. "We're very angry about this."

Atkins said that they were angry too and that he would talk to his people again.

"Can't we move the board meeting up?" asked Beattie. Atkins had told him that the full board would begin deliberations at eleven. Surely they could start at eight instead.

"No," said Atkins. "It's not possible under the bylaws." The meeting had already been formally convened. With Shearson threatening to sue, Atkins wasn't going to do anything that wasn't by the book.

"What about having the Special Committee meet right now?" suggested Beattie, knowing that that was unlikely, since it was now two in the morning.

Atkins shook his head. Nothing was going to happen, he insisted.

Beattie knew that Atkins didn't entirely control that. If Shearson made a new bid, Atkins had to advise the committee to consider it. So when he finally left at five, after spending three hours negotiating the fine points of the merger contract, Beattie went back to his office to draft a letter putting a time fuse on the KKR bid. The $106 offer was to expire at one o'clock that afternoon.

Even before Hugel had called the Special Committee meeting to order at seven forty-five in a conference room on the 35th floor, many of the board members—Hugel had invited all of the non-management directors to join the committee that day—knew that KKR had won and that Shearson was considering making another bid. That had been in *The New York Times'* late edition that morning. The paper quoted a member of the management team as saying that Shearson had won the first round, KKR the second, and they would see who won the third.

Rinaldini of Lazard stood up to review the terms of the KKR securities. Grierson, the vice-chairman of British General Electric, interrupted: why were they talking about the KKR bid since the Shearson offer contained more cash.

Rohatyn responded that what mattered was not cash but overall value, and by that standard KKR was the winner.

"Is this the result of a negotiation?" asked Robert Schaeberle, the former Nabisco chairman.

"Only on the terms of the securities," said Harris, "not the price."

"We had the same kind of discussions with Shearson after the first round," said Atkins. Actually, they hadn't. Shearson's first round meeting had distinctly not been a negotiating session.

Someone asked if Drexel could really sell the $5 billion of junk bonds that KKR needed to finance its offer. Rohatyn replied that he thought so; he had been impressed with Ackerman at the meeting the night before, and besides, Dick Beattie had said he was "confident" that Drexel could do it.

"What about management?" asked John Medlin of First Wachovia.

Atkins didn't know what KKR planned although it seemed clear that Johnson's team was out.

"What role is Paul Sticht going to have?" asked Juanita Kreps, the former Commerce Secretary.

Atkins wasn't sure, but he thought KKR would be sensitive.

"Schedule II?" asked Macomber. The employee benefit and severance matters.

"Still an open item," said Atkins.

Things were a bit chaotic at Shearson on Wednesday morning. Cohen had talked to Nusbaum and they had agreed on two things. First, Shearson would make another bid. Second, that Goldstone hadn't been aggressive enough the night before, and that Nusbaum should personally go to Skadden and force Atkins to consider the new Shearson offer.

While Nusbaum got together his papers and headed to Skadden, Cohen looked at the numbers. Early that morning, Stern had put together a grid similar to the one Benevento had given Jim Robinson the night before, showing how much different packages of cash and PIK were worth. Cohen chose a package with a face value of $108 a share: $84 a share in cash, $4 less than in the previous offer, plus $20 a share in notes and the $4 stub. That was $2 billion above what he had thought made sense when he made his "best" bid of $100 a share a week and a half earlier, but so what? Cohen had been cheated by the Special Committee twice now, and he wanted to win.

Cohen called Gutfreund, who knew from reading *The New York Times* that KKR had bid $106, $80 a share in cash, and

Gutfreund quickly agreed to Cohen's new price. Just before Cohen called Nusbaum with the new terms, Peter Darrow reminded Gutfreund that Johnson had promised to scale back his contract with every price increase. After a flurry of phone calls, Johnson agreed to cut management's initial stake again, to just 4 percent, less than half the original 8.5 percent. "If I give you any more, I'll be paying you to do this deal," Johnson told Cohen.

Given Atkins's attitude the night before, it wasn't entirely clear that the committee would take the new bid, but Tom Hill thought that he might be able to loosen things up. He dialed Atkins's boss, Joe Flom, the dean of takeover lawyers, who just happened to be in his office that morning.

"I don't understand what's going on," said Hill. "We're trying to make another bid and Peter won't take it. If we can't get him to listen to us, we're going to have to put the bid on the wire."

Flom didn't know what was going on either, but he told Hill he would find out. As far as Flom could see, the board should take the highest offer on the table, regardless of who made it.

Still, when Hill got off the line, he wasn't sure that his call would have any effect. Although he was sure that Flom would call Atkins, he wasn't sure Atkins would listen. Atkins seemed to be very stubborn.

Except for the discussion about cutting back the management contract, Johnson hadn't been involved in the Shearson deliberations at all, and by the time he heard about the revised bid, he was already sitting in a windowless 32nd floor conference room at Skadden Arps waiting for Hugel to invite him to the board meeting, three floors up. It was weirdly reminiscent of the wait on October 19 at the Waverly Hotel; the same group of executives, Johnson, Sage, and the other three management directors, was sitting around a similar table wondering what the board was up to in a distant conference room.

The phone call about the management contract was the last time that Johnson was consulted about what to do. It was clear to everyone, including Johnson, that he didn't matter much any more. As long as he was willing to stay on the team, Cohen was in the driver's seat.

*   *   *

At about eleven o'clock, Hugel invited Kravis and Roberts into the boardroom to make a presentation on their bid. That was short and sweet. There were no questions about the securities or the price, only what KKR intended to do once the deal closed, and Roberts told the directors just what they wanted to hear: KKR would sell as few assets as possible and it would keep as many current employees on the payroll as possible. If that struck anyone as odd, given that KKR was presumably buying the company to make money, he didn't say so.

One of the directors asked Kravis to extend the deadline past one o'clock. "I can't make any promises," said Kravis.

At noon, Hugel recessed the committee meeting so that he and Atkins could work out the few remaining Schedule II guarantees with KKR. Atkins had commandeered an empty office across the hallway from the boardroom. It belonged to a Skadden partner who had taken the week off to be with his wife and newborn baby, and Hugel, Kravis, and Roberts settled down to negotiate. Later, Atkins told Kravis and Roberts that they could stay in the office; it was more comfortable than the conference room where they had started.

While Hugel and Kravis were talking about moving expenses, one of the Skadden partners came in to say that Jack Nusbaum was on the thirty-second floor and wanted to talk, so as soon as the last employee issues were worked out, Atkins went downstairs, leaving several other partners to handle the question of breakup and topping fees, that is, the size of the consolation payment KKR would get if the deal collapsed after it was signed.

By this time Nusbaum had already been waiting for half an hour, and he was irritated that he hadn't received more immediate attention. He had even called Cohen, who told him that if Atkins wouldn't take the offer, "we'll use a stick," and put the terms of the bid on the Dow wire. When Atkins finally arrived, Nusbaum handed him the letter he had written at midnight, complaining that there was no response to the first letter, and said he had something more. "We're making a new offer," of $108 a share. "It's negotiable."

Nusbaum wasn't specific as to what about the offer was negotiable, but Atkins assumed he meant the price. "Is documentation for the increased financing being sent?" he asked. After all, the committee had made it clear that it would consider only bids with firm financing.

"No," said Nusbaum. "The people who are authorized to increase are the same as those making the offer."

Atkins went back upstairs. The Special Committee was cool about the new offer, despite the high face value. "The management group knows how to make their best proposal but they haven't done it," said Rohatyn, when Atkins told the directors about the lack of financing commitment and "negotiability."

The obvious next step was for Atkins to find out how high management would "negotiate" and for the investment bankers to find out what kind of paper was involved, but first they had to talk to KKR. Investigating the new Shearson offer was going to take time, and it was clear that that would push the board's being able to make a decision well past the KKR deadline of one o'clock. So at twelve-forty, Hugel, Atkins, and Rohatyn went back to the KKR office to ask. The lawyers were still arguing over what KKR should get in breakup and topping fees. "There's a new management offer," said Atkins.

Kravis and Roberts had been expecting that all morning, but they were nonetheless angry that it had finally come. Atkins hadn't said what the bid was; presumably it was higher than $106, although perhaps not much higher. So they agreed to extend the deadline by one hour on condition that RJR pick up their out-of-pocket expenses to date, legal fees to Simpson Thatcher, bank fees, and the cost of printing and mailing several tender offer documents to shareholders, a total of $40 million.

At twelve-fifty, five minutes after Hugel had left, Beattie got a call from his office. It was the associate Beattie had assigned to watch the Dow ticker for news about RJR. "There's a new management offer," said the associate.

So Atkins had just said. "How do you know that?" asked Beattie.

"It's on the tape," said the associate.

"You're joking," said Beattie.

"No," said the associate, sounding hurt. "I'm serious. I'm sitting right here in the library like you told me and there's a new management offer on the tape."

"It can't be," said Beattie. "No one is dumb enough to put an offer on the tape. That just tells us what their bid is."

" 'RJR management group boosts bid to $108 a share,' " read the associate. " 'F. Ross Johnson, president of RJR Nabisco Inc., said that a management group has submitted a revised proposal . . .' "

Beattie interrupted. "Send that over," he said.

Atkins had gone straight from Kravis's office to Nusbaum's conference on the thirty-second floor. "Sharpen your pencils and put your best bid on the table," Atkins told Nusbaum; he needed a number by one-fifteen. Nusbaum called Cohen, and Cohen caucused with his team to choose a new number. Someone called Johnson to say that it was $115 a share and then called back again half an hour later to say that Cohen decided to play it safe and had bid only $112 a share now, leaving $3 a share for the final round that was sure to follow.

With the $112 a share in hand—the extra $4 a share was all PIK paper—it was clear to Atkins that there was no hope of meeting Kravis's two o'clock deadline either. Atkins would have to get yet another extension. Given all Kravis's previous complaints, he would surely be suspicious of another request for time, so Ira Harris suggested that they offer to sign a deal at $106 with a $1-a-share topping fee in exchange for a week to think. Just to be sure that KKR didn't later complain that the playing field hadn't been level, it seemed like a good idea to ask for KKR's final bid as well. Atkins never got as far as asking about a better price. As soon as he mentioned a shop-able $106 a share, the KKR people began hassling about whether the process was fair. "There's a wire story that says that they bid $108," said Cliff Robbins, a KKR associate.

"That may be on the wire," said Atkins, "but don't assume it's their bid."

The KKR team caucused. The benefit of signing the $106 deal after they knew they had been topped was clear: $228 million of topping fees guaranteed. However, signing wasn't the way to win. Kravis and Roberts definitely wanted to win; they were in the business of buying companies and they were not going to be beaten at the eleventh hour by an upstart like Shearson. By this time it was clear that the board wanted KKR to win and that KKR would get RJR in a tie. So Kravis matched Shearson, raising to $108 a share, which was what Shearson had put on the wire.

Since Atkins had mentioned it, Kravis also demanded a $1-a-share topping fee plus expenses, in this context $400 million rather than the $40 million Kravis had quoted earlier, since most of the bank and investment bank fees kicked in only after the merger agreement was signed and hence hadn't been included in the earlier expense list. Unlike the last bid, this one had no fuse. Kravis didn't have a clear enough idea of what was going on to include one; a fuse that expired too early would knock KKR out.

For the next five hours, nothing happened in the KKR room. For a while, the KKR people joked and gossiped.

Then Beattie lay down on the floor to take a nap. He hadn't had any sleep in the past thirty-six hours. When he woke up an hour later, nothing had changed. Apparently it was going to be a long time. It was no longer so clear that KKR was in the lead. Several times, Beattie wandered out into the hall to watch the activity outside the boardroom. Bankers and lawyers kept rushing in and out. It was easy to guess that they were headed downstairs to negotiate with Shearson.

Worried that events might slip out of KKR's control, Beattie told his junior partner Robert Spatt to work out the last details of the contract with the Skadden lawyers so that KKR could present the board with a signed contract when the bidding finally ended. Then he suggested to Kravis and Roberts that they take a walk. They were complaining that they had been double-crossed. A walk might calm them down.

At least Kravis had an idea what was happening. Johnson didn't, and he was becoming increasingly agitated. At about two o'clock someone had brought in some sandwiches, but no news. Later still, someone told them to move to a larger conference room with two windows, although it was raining so hard that there was no point in looking out.

Sage lingered in the hall, but didn't catch anyone. The board meeting was three floors up, and neither Hugel nor any of the other directors ever wandered down. He had been told that Jack Nusbaum was on the floor, but he was nowhere to be seen.

Finally one of the Lazard bankers showed up to ask if Johnson would agree to the Schedule II benefits list.

Johnson wouldn't.

* * *

The Special Committee was in a fix. They had been considering the KKR offer for six hours now and they wanted to sign it up. The lawyers insisted that they couldn't. Michael Mitchell, Skadden's chief litigator, was the most outspoken. "The board can't accept the KKR offer," he said flatly, not now. Management claimed that its offer was worth $112 a share and there was no reason to believe that they were acting in bad faith. The KKR offer was not only worth much less, but it was also expensive: the top up and expense provisions would cost the company $650 million if it signed with KKR now and chose Shearson later.

Of course, that might not be how things would look in a couple of hours. "Dillon Read has never agreed with Shearson's evaluation of their stub," noted John Mullin. "All those PIKs they are talking about issuing will probably push the value down even further."

So the committee agreed to further investigate the Shearson proposal. One of the Skadden lawyers would give Nusbaum a copy of the contract that KKR had negotiated—with certain deletions like price—and the investment bankers would try to negotiate up the terms of the securities, to guarantee that they were worth as much as Shearson claimed.

Jim Stern didn't know that Shearson was in the lead when Luis Rinaldini and Fritz Hobbs came down to talk about the paper, so instead of conceding on technical points, Stern played tough. Shearson had proposed a three-year reset on the preferred PIK, and Stern was not keen to adopt Rinaldini's one year. Stern thought that that kind of reset on a PIK security, which the stub was, would be very expensive. Besides, as Stern saw it, a one-year reset didn't make a lot of sense. Under the Shearson plan, all the food assets would be sold and the bank debt paid off within two years. Two years was the time to refinance, and to reset the interest rate on the preferred.

Logical or no, Rinaldini kept insisting.

And Stern—and Cohen—wouldn't budge.

Late in the afternoon, Mike Gizang, one of Atkins's corporate finance partners, came down to tell Nusbaum that he had to agree to sign the KKR contract that had been negotiated the night before.

"Can I see it?" asked Nusbaum.

Gizang gave him a copy, and after reading it through, Nusbaum agreed that Shearson was willing to sign.

Charlie Hugel reconvened the meeting of the Special Committee at six o'clock. Having failed to get sufficient protection from Shearson on its paper, the bankers had concluded that the $112 a share was "substantially equivalent" to KKR's $108. That meant that the directors were free to make their choice on other factors. Or ask for a final, tie-breaking round. Then the committee made its penultimate decision. Both KKR and Shearson would be given a final chance to hike their offers. If they remained tied, KKR had won.

Hugel, Atkins, and Rohatyn walked across the hallway to the KKR office. Kravis and Roberts were very edgy. They had all but left half an hour earlier when it looked like the board wasn't going to take their offer that night, and had agreed to stay only after Beattie insisted that they were fools to leave. Now, at Atkins's request, they walked down the hall to yet another empty office. "We want your final offer," said Atkins.

"Is the other side being asked the same thing?" asked Beattie.

"Yes," said Atkins.

"Before we get to that, I want to know that our bid won't be discussed by the board with Johnson in the room," said Beattie.

Atkins couldn't promise that: he didn't know. But he conceded it was a fair point.

Beattie walked into the hallway with Atkins, Hugel, and Rohatyn to talk about how the problem might be handled. After a brief conversation, Atkins left to talk to the other lawyers. They quickly concluded that there was no legal basis for keeping Johnson and the other management directors out of the board meeting. For lack of a better idea, Atkins suggested that they simply ask if management planned to attend. Perhaps this was a non-issue.

Atkins went downstairs to find Steve Goldstone, who had arrived in the afternoon to represent Johnson. Goldstone thought that what he was being asked was, did Johnson want to make a presentation to the board. "Is Kravis?" he asked.

"No," said Atkins.

Goldstone went into Nusbaum's conference room, and a few minutes later he came back. The consensus of the Shearson and

Salomon bankers was that the last thing they wanted was to have Johnson talk to the board; Johnson couldn't elaborate on the financial structure, and his presence in the boardroom would only remind the directors of *Time*, Greed, and the management contract. "We don't plan to be at the board meeting," said Goldstone. "If KKR is invited to make a presentation, we'd like a similar opportunity."

When Atkins got back to the thirty-fifth floor, Beattie and Rohatyn were talking about the New York City public school system. Beattie, a former member of the city's Board of Education, was just launching the Fund for Public Education, while Rohatyn, the chairman of the Municipal Assistance Corporation, that issued New York City bonds, was trying to block a state bill for a separate school construction authority.

"I can assure you that the management directors won't be at the board meeting," Atkins told Beattie.

"Fine," said Beattie. He went back into the KKR office. By now all of the KKR people were there, and Kravis polled around for their views on increasing the bid. Kravis himself was sure that KKR was already ahead and that bidding again was simply bidding against himself; he thought that at most they should hike the price 50 cents a share in paper. After some discussion, Roberts suggested 50 cents a share in cash. Then they agreed to $1 a share, half in cash, half in paper.

"Look," said James Green, the KKR associate in charge of the bank financing. "If we're going to raise, why don't we go all cash? The money is there."

So it was agreed. They might be kicking themselves tomorrow for having given away $228 million in cash, but they wanted to win.

"We need to put a time limit on this," said Beattie.

"Twenty minutes," said Roberts.

"That's not long enough," said Beattie. "Thirty minutes." Beattie called Atkins, Hugel, and Rohatyn back into the office. "There are two conditions to our bid," said Beattie. "First, I need you to assure the group, as you've assured me, that management won't see our bid."

Atkins did.

"Second, I'm giving you a signed contract. I need it back in half an hour." At 8:40.

"That's not a lot of time," said Atkins.

"That's all you get," said Beattie.

As Atkins left, Roberts noticed that his investment bankers had moved out of the conference room into the hallway, apparently in an attempt to get closer to the action. "Let's give them a scare," he said to Kravis and Beattie. "Let's put our jackets on." He looked at Beattie. "You yell after us that we're making a mistake."

Kravis and Roberts put on their jackets and marched out the door of the conference room toward the elevator.

"You're making a mistake," yelled Beattie. "You should stay. We'll get this worked out."

Meanwhile, Rinaldini had called Stern in the Shearson conference room downstairs. "We need your best offer," he said.

Stern thought that Rinaldini was talking about the terms of the preferred, although the answer would have been the same on price. "You've got it," he said.

"We'll be back to you," said Rinaldini.

Nusbaum assumed that it would be several hours before the committee called for a third round of bidding. Since it was eight o'clock, well past dinner time, Darrow, the Salomon lawyer, suggested that they head around the corner to the Shun Lee Palace on East 55th Street for dinner. Everyone came with him except Nusbaum and Stern. Nusbaum was too nervous to eat. Stern had lost his appetite.

By this time Johnson had given up any lingering hope that he would be invited into the board meeting. Although the cold cuts Skadden had served for lunch hadn't been bad, cold cuts weren't what he wanted for dinner. So at about seven-thirty, even before Rinaldini had made his final call, Johnson, Sage, and the other management directors had left for dinner. They were in the mood for something Italian.

In the boardroom, Rohatyn announced that the bids were still equivalent and the committee—and the board—could choose whichever it wanted. It was no surprise that the committee picked KKR, or that the board approved that unanimously.

But there was one problem: who was going to run the company in the time between now and when the KKR merger went through? Legally, Johnson's management team. Just to make sure that nothing untoward happened in that period, the board voted the five members of the Special Committee onto the Executive Committee, which oversaw all major corporate actions.

KKR's half hour was almost up. Three minutes before the deadline, Rohatyn had gone over to the KKR office to asked for an additional ten minutes. Kravis, making a show of impatience, agreed, and Hugel, Atkins, and Rohatyn showed up again ten minutes later to say that they needed to talk to Kravis and Roberts alone. Kravis, Roberts, and Beattie walked back to the first office with Hugel's team. Rohatyn shut the door.

Atkins was holding a copy of the KKR contract. "There's a problem," he said. He showed Beattie a paragraph with some changes marked; they were highly technical. "We can agree to that," said Beattie.

Then Atkins turned to Kravis. "You've won," he said. "Here's the signed contract."

Ten minutes after that, Nusbaum called Cohen. Atkins had just slunk into the conference room, Nusbaum explained, to say that KKR had won. "You bid the same number," Atkins had said. "You chose the same pinprick on the map. The committee chose on the basis of other considerations." Atkins had refused to say what those other considerations were, or to take his eyes off the floor.

Cohen said something about suing, but Johnson, whom Jim Robinson had called at Capriccio, the Italian restaurant where he had gone for dinner, would have none of that. He had been ready to concede the night before, and he was determined to concede now. Cohen was too tired and disappointed to fuss. It wasn't until Thursday morning that he exploded. When he read the terms of KKR's winning bid in the *Wall Street Journal*, he realized that the bidding hadn't even been close.

EPILOGUE

Greed Really
Turns Me Off

While Peter Cohen was grumbling that he had been cheated and would sue, Henry Kravis was savoring his victory. Although he was so tired from the late-night negotiating sessions that his eyes weren't red-rimmed but totally red, he embarked immediately on a tour of his new territory, flying on his G-3 to Atlanta and Winston-Salem to inspect the facilities. He talked to Johnson, who agreed to stay long enough for Kravis to get a grasp on operations, and Ed Horrigan, who threatened to leave if he weren't named CEO. "We haven't made any decisions," said Kravis.

Most important, Kravis faced the press. For years he had had a firm policy of not talking to financial reporters—he couldn't avoid society reporters—but having done the biggest deal in the world, there seemed to be no choice. So hours after the merger agreement was signed, Kravis's pr man had already set up appointments with both Jim Sterngold of *The New York Times* and Bryan Burrough of the *Wall Street Journal*. Later Kravis also sat down with an editor of *Fortune* for the first of a pair of first-person interviews on the takeover battle deal for the January 2 issue; curiously *Fortune* chose Johnson, not Cohen, for the companion, although it had clearly been Cohen's deal. Naturally, Kravis defended buyouts. "Washington is also concerned about greed," he said. "They should be. Greed really turns me off." Be that as it may, KKR quickly announced that it would pay itself $75 million for negotiating the takeover, plus $40 million a year to "manage" the company.

The victory tour and interviews were, however, slightly premature. Kravis and Roberts still had to raise the money to pay for the RJR prize, and that turned out to be even more difficult than anyone had anticipated. Even with an elaborate road show, the sort of thing KKR never had to do, there was only barely enough bank money, and that only because the Japanese had unexpectedly come on strong. Drexel was able raise $3 billion only by paying a "fee" as high as 2 percent. On February 9, Kravis and Roberts both signed the papers finalizing the loan with matching Mont Blanc pens.

Running the company was unexpectedly difficult as well. Within three months of the auction, Johnson, Horrigan, and most of the other senior RJR executives had pulled the rip cords on their golden parachutes. That triggered a near crisis. Although Kravis had not expected either man to stay, he had not anticipated that they would leave simultaneously—or before KKR had lined up permanent replacements; Paul Sticht, after all, had only agreed to run the company from Winston-Salem part-time. Fortunately, the headhunter that Kravis had hired back in December came through with the winning name in March: Louis Gerstner, Jr., the president of American Express. Gerstner didn't know anything about tobacco, but he was highly respected for his hands-on approach and his financial savvy. Ironically, Gerstner's management contract was almost identical to the contract that had become such a public relations problem for Johnson.

Despite KKR's assurances to the Special Committee that it intended to hold the company together, Kravis immediately began to dismantle. By the end of September he had raised more than $4.5 billion selling the European biscuit operations and the Del Monte fresh and canned fruit units. Negotiating the sales, of course, also provided generous fee income for the investment banks Kravis chose for the job, Morgan Stanley and Goldman Sachs (Lazard Frères was working on the sale of RJR's twenty percent stake in ESPN, the cable sports network). To no one's surprise, Gerstner closed the Atlanta headquarters in July, transferring operations to New York; later that month, James John-ston, the newly hired tobacco chief, announced a ten percent payroll cut; employees blamed that on Ross Johnson. He had, after all, put the company in play.

Johnson, of course, didn't think he had done anything blame-worthy. Putting the company in play had been a bonanza for shareholders. Fewer employees might have been laid off had he won than under the Kravis plan, Johnson insisted, and fewer would have been displaced. No one would ever know whether that was true, but one thing was certain. Johnson had been more gracious in defeat than Kravis had been in victory. In his *Fortune* interview, Johnson had explained that he had lost because he was naive. "It wasn't until we made our final bid that I came to the conclusion that you don't play by the rules."

Although Johnson had usually been described as callous to employees by firing those who failed to perform, he now spent much of his time helping the members of his group find new jobs. For his part, Johnson decided not to get a new job. Having worked so hard for his shareholders and been so publicly condemned for his greed, Johnson decided to take a break. He played golf, trav-eled to London, Istanbul, and Vail, and seemed happy to be unemployed. Six months after the sale closed, he had lost thirty pounds, bought several pieces of real estate from bankrupt Florida thrifts, and sworn off ever working nine to five again. By then he had formed the RJM Group to offer strategic consulting to For-tune 500 companies. Although he refuses to say just who is on his client list, he allows that he is busy—but not so busy he doesn't have ample time for golf.

For Peter Cohen, RJR was the beginning of the end. Shearson careened from one disaster to the next. The Boston Company, a Shearson money management unit, was caught cooking the books to make profits look more rosy; Balcor, the firm's real estate tax shelter subsidiary, all but collapsed when shares of the partner-ships it had sold went sour, and Shearson lost $500 million on a bad bridge load to Prime Computer, $140 million on securities underwritten for MCorp and $115 million on its $400 million portfolio of junk bonds.

When Cohen belatedly began to look for help, it was too late.

Robinson refused to give Shearson a cash infusion in the spring of 1989: although he publicly supported Cohen, Robinson wasn't willing to put more capital into a cyclical brokerage and investment banking behemoth. He had been saying for years that he intended to cut AmEx's sixty percent stake, and he meant it. So when Moody's announced in November that it would cut Shearson's credit rating unless something were done—dramatically increasing Shearson's cost of doing business—Robinson proposed everything but upping his investment. He tried shaking up management. He talked about a public share sale. He even opened negotiations with Ronald Perelman, the hated raider, for a 10 percent share.

When that didn't work, Robinson floated a proposal to pump $1 billion of cash into the ailing unit, partly out of AmEx's pockets. That, however, was not enough. The public offering failed—as did one final effort to sell Shearson off, this time to its one-time chairman Sandy Weill, now chairman of Primerica—and Robinson bit the bullet. He fired Cohen in January, 1990 and poured $1.35 billion of cash into Shearson, raising his ownership to 100 percent. (Cohen isn't hurting financially: he got $10 million in severance in exchange for promising not to sue Robinson or any member of his family, including Linda.)

Howard Clark, Shearson's new chairman and formerly AmEx's chief financial officer, has spent much of his time undoing Cohen's excesses. Gone is the corporate fleet, the corporate art collection, and the ski chalet in Denver. Workers have been laid off, commissions cut, and the junk bond portfolio sold. And in a symbolic move, Clark in mid-1990, split the Shearson and Lehman names. Shearson now handles all of the firm's retail business; Lehman, investment banking—just like they did in the good old days.

Several days after the RJR battle ended, John Gutfreund announced that Salomon would get deeper into merchant banking by teaming up with Don Kelly, the former Esmark chief and merger maven. Deals quickly followed. In March, Salomon bought Envirodine, the Chicago-based maker of sausage casing and plastic cutlery, for $786 million. Three weeks later, the firm announced that it would pay Jimmy Goldsmith $1.2 billion for the Grand Union grocery store chain. By early summer Salomon had launched yet another merchant banking offensive: in conjunction with Blackstone Group, the merchant bank headed by former Lehman Brothers chairman Pete Peterson, Salomon would raise $750 million to invest in bankrupt thrifts, $75 million of it from Salomon's own pocket.

Ironically, Salomon wasn't plagued by the problems that hit the rest of the Street in the fall of 1989. Because the firm had little exposure to junk bonds or bridge loans, the collapse of those markets had no effect on the bottom line. "We're the only firm that didn't lose more on junk than we collected in fees," noted Jay Higgins in July, 1988. Salomon still isn't an M&A powerhouse. But never mind. These days the big money is in trading and arbitrage.

At Christmas, Drexel chairman Fred Joseph announced that the firm would plead guilty to six counts of criminal fraud. A year later, Drexel went bankrupt, caught between the collapsing junk market, and the escalating demands of senior partners for cash payouts. Why the demand for junk bonds died so suddenly in mid-1989 isn't entirely clear. Some say that it was because Mike Milken was no longer around to run the bond selling daisy chain; others that the rules Congress imposed on the thrifts killed pushed billions of dollars of unrated securities onto the market.

One factor was certainly the desperate condition of so many of the companies that junk had financed. Campeau, for one, choked on its debt, and so did Southland and Interco. Those problems were enough to kill the bridge loan and bank finance markets (banks also got a kick from the Comptroller of the Currency who required them to list highly leveraged transactions in a separate category for accounting purposes). And the flow of deals suddenly slowed to a trickle: less than $10 billion of leveraged buyouts were completed in 1990, down from $100 billion in 1989.

Ironically the biggest dealmaker for the year was Ted Forstmann, the lbo artist whom Kravis had once mocked for his "inability"—or unwillingness—to close a transaction. Because Forstmann had subordinated debt in a prepackaged fund, he didn't have to use junk, and when the market collapsed he was the only player still in the running. In January, 1990, Forstmann bought Gulfstream aerospace for $1.6 billion. Six months later, he picked up General Instrument for $1.2 billion. Forstmann insists that both deals show more promise than anything in the KKR portfolio.

Even if the junk market revives, it seems unlikely that KKR will be buying any more companies soon. Although Kravis had noted in his *Fortune* interview, "Sure, there are bad LBOs, but they are only hiccups in the business, the exceptions. Knock on wood, KKR hasn't had any like that," KKR had, and by mid-1990, half a dozen deals were publicly on the rocks. Seaman Furniture and SCI Television missed payments on their debt and were forced to reorganize. Hillsborough Holdings, the remains of the Jim Walter Corp., filed for bankruptcy protection, after admitting to investors that it wasn't possible to reset the interest rate on its bonds high enough that they would trade at par.

Resets were a looming problem for RJR too. A year after the deal closed, one issue of PIK paper was trading at fifty cents on the dollar and the other wasn't far behind. Although Kravis insisted that the price would revive long before the April, 1991 reset deadline, he decided not to wait. In June, 1990, he announced a massive restructuring that would leave RJR with quadruple its original equity base and bonds with no reset provision. Under the terms of the proposal, KKR investors would cough up $1.7 billion of new money and convert a $500 million loan to equity, while banks would put up a new $2.25 billion and outside investors would purchase $1.8 billion of convertible preferred stock.

Even that might not be enough. RJR's most serious problem was not financial. Although the deal had been premised on rising cigarette profits, profits weren't rising. Indeed, just after the deal closed, the public mood turned decisively against smoking. The federal government prohibited smoking on all domestic airline flights while the FTC began investigating the sale of cigarettes to children. One proposed RJR brand, Uptown, was killed when word leaked out that it was targeted at blacks; another died because it was targeted at young women. Indeed, the future of smoking didn't look bright. In the spring of 1990, both California and France announced aggressive advertising campaigns against smoking, funded by stiff taxes on smokes.

Of course, RJR will continue to be a big money maker for Kravis and it could still be a big money maker for his investors as well. Whatever investors do or don't make on their money, Kravis will always be remembered as the man who did the 1980s' biggest deal.

Acknowledgments

The events described in this book occurred only seven months after I was viciously stabbed on the East River Esplanade. That I was able to consider writing a book, much less returning to work at all, was due largely to the the selfless help of my many friends and acquaintances, most especially: the Rev. Gerald G. Alexander, Charles Bailey, Michael and Karen Braziller, Kristin Brown, Katharine Callaghan, Fr. Norman Catir, Bruce and Judi Colville, Nandrea Lynn Courts, Kenneth Dake, Brian Devereaux, the Rev. Stephen Garmey, Theresa Lee, George and Leslie Mims, Lesa Mullikin, Linda Macklem Oehl, Mary Anne Ostrom, Christina Pagano, Elizabeth Pearce, the Rev. Thomas Pike, Brigitte Schnaeggens, Brian and Teresa Schneider, Sarah Sears, Lorana Sullivan, Charles and Lynn Urstadt, and Gertrude Vaughan.

Alexander Cohane, Tim Greer, Phil Thomas, Jeannette Walls, and Julia Willkie helped me track down obscure pieces of information. Larry Armour, Bob Baker, Peggy Cronin, Tom Daly, Linette Dunbar, Barbara Eggen, Leslie Harrison, Michael O'Neil, and Sharon Taylor were patient with my many phone calls and questions. Brian Schneider helped me to think through what I wanted to say. Chuck Bailey, Phyllis Kaplan, Jane Kettlewell, Jennifer Foley, Danny McNevin, and Charlie Urstadt were ever encouraging, as was Kenneth Dake, who late one night when I was feeling most discouraged insisted on taking me and the dusty Cadillac to the car wash.